Deconstructing
Evangelicalism

Deconstructing Evangelicalism

Conservative Protestantism
in the Age of Billy Graham

D. G. Hart

Baker Academic

A Division of Baker Book House Co
Grand Rapids, Michigan 49516

Published by Baker Academic
a division of Baker Book House Company
P.O. Box 6287, Grand Rapids, MI 49516-6287
www.bakeracademic.com

Printed in the United States of America

Library of Congress Cataloging-in-Publication Data
Hart, D. G.
    Deconstructing evangelicalism : conservative Protestantism in the age of Billy Graham / D. G. Hart.
       p.   cm.
    Includes bibliographical references and index.
    ISBN 0-8010-2728-4 (cloth)
    1. Evangelicalism—United States—History—20th century. 2. Evangelicalism—United States—History of doctrines—20th century. I. Title.
BR1642.U5H374 2004
280'.4'097309045—dc21   2003056033

To
Scott Clark, Iain Duguid, Bryan Estelle,
Bob Godfrey, Mike Horton, Dennis Johnson,
Hywel Jones, Peter Jones, Julius Kim, James Lund,
George Scipione, Bob Strimple, and Dave VanDrunen,
with whom it was an honor to work during
my wilderness wanderings in Southland

Contents

Preface

My good friend Leo Ribuffo, who teaches U.S. history at George Washington University, in a chapter for a book on religious advocacy and historical scholarship, referred to me as an "evangelical."[1] Back when that essay appeared, in 1997, I was less bothered by that designation than I am six years later. After all, *evangelical* was one half of the identity of *evangelical historians*, a group of scholars to which I had aspired to belong for a time in my life. To be included on a roster that listed Mark A. Noll, George M. Marsden, Nathan O. Hatch, Harry S. Stout, Grant Wacker, Joel A. Carpenter, and Edith Blumhofer, even if only second string, was indeed a compliment. So Leo's reference passed without damage to our friendship.

But on further reflection, I am not so sure I should have let the designation stand—since I coedited the book I could have changed it. A better description would have been to call me a Presbyterian historian. I am a member of the Orthodox Presbyterian Church and have served as an elder in the Christian Reformed Church and the OPC. For almost two decades, I have belonged to Reformed and Presbyterian communions. Because I am apparently serious about Christianity, meaning I observe certain Protestant practices and hold specific Protestant convictions, I am in the eyes of many scholars an evangelical.

Part of the reason for writing this book is to account for this odd form of pigeonholing. Of course, some Presbyterians do not mind being classified as evangelicals. My reasons for minding would take up too much of the space at the front of a book typically reserved for throat clearing. My objections to evangelicalism are also available elsewhere.[2] Still, it is curious that the evangelical movement in the United States is so oppressive that it can claim even those who do not want to belong to it. Evangelicals would likely be upset if I picked certain Presbyterian and Reformed convictions and practices, such as the deity of Christ and prayer, and using them as a standard concluded that all evangelicals are religious heirs of John Calvin and John Knox. After all, being Presbyterian involves more than prayer and beliefs about Christ, just as being evangelical often includes a number of doctrines and practices to which Presbyterians and Reformed Christians might plausibly object. So why is it, then, that evangelicalism has become so elastic as to include believers whose beliefs and practices are at odds with the low-church, revivalistic form of piety produced and distributed by numerous successful parachurch agencies? In other words, why does church membership not matter when scholars, religious leaders, and journalists discuss and write about religious identity in America, especially the evangelical one? If my denomination is not a member of the National Association of Evangelicals, if I do not give to the Billy Graham Evangelistic Association, if I do not read *Christianity Today* for edification, and if I refuse to put an *ichthys* medallion on my car, why am I considered an evangelical? Do these scholars, parachurch officials, and pundits know something that I don't? Can they actually see into my heart?

These are questions that have informed *Deconstructing Evangelicalism*, which is one part history, one part theological critique. Both parts question how useful the term *evangelical* is as a designation of religious identity in North America. For academics, this book poses a question about accuracy in describing the American Protestant landscape. For religious leaders, it raises the issue of whether evangelicalism is a Christian identity sufficient to sustain serious faith. In neither case, however, is this book intended to be an exposé of either bad faith or poor scholarship. The believers who have championed evangelicalism deserve respect if only for pious intentions, remarkable energy, and an uncanny ability to organize. Likewise, the academics who have supplied the most important works on evangelicalism have produced solid and reliable scholarship. I am particularly indebted, both personally and professionally, to the evangelical historians with whom Leo Ribuffo lumped me six years ago. My only quibble, and it is one sufficiently large to merit a book-length explanation, is that this scholarship could be more precise if it used identities other than evangelical to understand Protestants in North America.

The students who enrolled for my spring semester 2003 class on evangelicalism in the United States at Westminster Theological Seminary in California may have received more than they bargained for when they registered. Part of their assignment was to read this book in manuscript form. And part of why I delight in teaching seminary students came in the form of thoughtful comments and hard questions this group of students asked about this book and my own interpretation of American evangelicalism. I am grateful to those students for the responses that improved this book. Obviously, the question remains for readers whether these improvements are sufficient to render plausible the idea that evangelicalism, as a form of Christian identity, needs to be abandoned.

Introduction

Evangelicalism Deconstructing

The history of evangelicalism in the United States was not supposed to turn out this way. What had been the Horatio Alger story of twentieth-century American religion by the year 2000 turned out to be the equivalent of Humpty Dumpty. To be sure, the evangelical narrative did not put its best foot forward in the twentieth century by splitting the American mainline denominations between fundamentalists and liberals. But after the ignominy of the Scopes Trial in 1925, a bunch of forward-thinking evangelical theologians, sometimes called neo-evangelicals, hatched a scheme to give conservative Protestantism a face-lift. They would accent the positive and avoid the sort of theological mudslinging that had given fundamentalism such a bad reputation. Important pieces, such as the National Association of Evangelicals (1942), Fuller Theological Seminary (1947), and *Christianity Today* (1956), fell into place. Providing important assistance were the herculean efforts of Billy Graham, whose good looks and organizational muscle made at least one evangelical Protestant a household name. By 1976 the renovation was complete. In fact, while inconceivable only a decade earlier, each of the major political parties' candidates for president of the United States in the 1976 election claimed to be a born-again Christian, so attractive was the evangelical identity. *Newsweek* magazine blessed conservative Protestantism's success by baptizing the bicentennial of the United States' founding "the year of the evangelical."

Since 1980, however, when evangelicalism enjoyed even greater success with the election of family-friendly Ronald Reagan, the proverbial wheels have come off this overachieving religious movement. Part of the problem may have been that the spoils of success did just that—they spoiled. Electoral politics proved to be a difficult arena in which to persuade the breadth of the American public that the narrow way of faithfulness was best. Then the downfall of televangelists Jimmy Swaggart and Jim Bakker conjured up older images of charlatan preachers such as Elmer Gantry, men who claimed to know God's will even when such knowledge coincided with activity that suggested men of God thought they knew better.

Still, the crisis among evangelicals went deeper than the hypocrisy of television preachers or the volatile mix of piety and politics. Several theologians wrote books during the 1990s that suggested evangelicalism was suffering as much from bad faith as from damaging publicity. David F. Wells arguably made the biggest splash with the first volume of his series on contemporary evangelical theology, *No Place for Truth* (1993), a book somewhere between social history and theological reflection. In a fairly complicated argument that traced bad doctrine to large social and economic developments in the modern West, Wells blew the whistle on the hollowness of American evangelicalism. His conclusion provided the proverbial rain on evangelicalism's late-twentieth-century parade: "The growth and prosperity of evangelical institutions during the 1970s and 1980s have brought with them much bureaucracy, and bureaucracy invariably smothers vision, creativity, and even theology. Leadership is now substantially in the hands of the managers, and . . . [t]he only semblance of cohesion that now remains is simply tactical, never theological."[1]

A year later, Wheaton College historian Mark A. Noll leavened his critique of evangelical intellectual life with theological insight in *The Scandal of the Evangelical Mind* (1994). To be sure, his concerns were narrower than Wells's—the academic institutions and scholars within evangelicalism rather than the theological vitality of the movement. Still, Noll's opening sentence was not one evangelical leaders could use in fund-raising letters. According to Noll, "The scandal of the evangelical mind is that there is not much of an evangelical mind."[2] If Noll's and Wells's books were not enough, the founding trustee of Scotland's Banner of Truth Trust, Iain H. Murray, piled on with *Evangelicalism Divided* (2000). Although written with developments in Britain in view, the book clearly faulted American evangelicalism for overreacting against the militancy of fundamentalism and, in the process, abandoning central Christian truths. Other books also indicted the evangelical movement, but the cumulative effect of Wells, Noll, and Murray was to raise serious questions about a religious phenomenon that only fifteen years earlier had looked so promising.[3]

Scholars were not the only ones to ask whether evangelicalism had any substance beyond vague and warm affirmations about a personal relationship with Jesus. Religious historians contributed simultaneously to a parallel discussion about their religious identity as evangelicals. This debate was less accessible, confined as it was to scholarly journals. But its implications were equally momentous for a religious category that was becoming increasingly slippery. If the academics paid to study evangelicalism were not sure what they were examining, how could rank-and-file pastors and laypeople have confidence when describing themselves as evangelical? On the surface, this debate among evangelical historians was about whether the evangelical tradition was fundamentally Reformed or Wesleyan in its theological orientation. The principal interlocutors were Donald W. Dayton, arguing for the preponderance of Wesleyan influence, and George M. Marsden, whom Dayton believed had skewed the history of twentieth-century evangelicalism as little more than a footnote on Calvinism. Potentially, this debate had the makings of another theological donnybrook, with Dayton lining up behind the teachings of Jacob Arminius, and Marsden marshaling the anathemas of the Synod of Dort, home to the famous "five points of Calvinism." This dispute also resonated with such clichéd dichotomies as head versus heart, doctrine versus life, ministers versus the laity, and creed versus the free movement of the Spirit.[4]

Douglas A. Sweeney, who summarized and assessed each side in the discussion, recognized that the debate was as much about what had come of the movement spearheaded by the founding editors of *Christianity Today* and Billy Graham and associates as it was about developments in American Protestant history. As Sweeney explained it, the issue was not whether Carl F. H. Henry studied with Benjamin Warfield or whether Harold John Ockenga spoke in tongues during his undergraduate days at Taylor University. Rather, it was whether the men who put together the institutions of the evangelical establishment actually fashioned a core religious identity capable of uniting all Protestants who were outside or uncomfortable with the mainline Protestant denominations. Sweeney's verdict did little to curtail enrollments at evangelical seminaries, cut subscriptions to Christianity Today, Inc.'s many magazines, or stop the sale of Contemporary Christian Music CDs. But it could have; he wrote, "When the fragile unity of the founding neo-evangelicals ended, nothing remained to support the common perception of evangelical unity."[5]

What's Wrong with Evangelicalism?

The theological critiques and historical soul-searching of the 1990s raised important questions about how to fix evangelicalism. For some, like Wells, the solution resides in more and better doctrine. For others, like Noll, evangelicalism needs to abandon restrictive and simplistic theological formulas. Greater zeal and faithfulness, along with greater discernment about evangelicalism's recent past, are also factors some see as crucial to the movement's recovery. The one response that few have considered is perhaps the most radical and the point of this book: Instead of trying to fix evangelicalism, born-again Protestants would be better off if they abandoned the category altogether. The reason is not that evangelicalism is wrong in its theology, ineffective in reaching the lost, or undiscerning in its reflections on society and culture. It may be, but these matters are beside the point. Evangelicalism needs to be relinquished as a religious identity because it does not exist. In fact, it is the wax nose of twentieth-century American Protestantism. Behind this proboscis, which has been nipped and tucked by savvy religious leaders, academics, and pollsters, is a face void of any discernible features. The nonexistence of an evangelical identity may prove to be, to borrow a phrase from Noll, the real scandal of modern evangelicalism, for despite the vast amounts of energy and resources expended on the topic, and notwithstanding the ever growing volume of literature on the movement, evangelicalism is little more than a construction. This book is a work of deconstruction.

Of course, the assertion that evangelicalism is largely a constructed ideal without any real substance is highly debatable. Part of what makes such a point contested is almost sixty years of publications, organizations, and Protestant leaders with an evangelical perspective cheerleading for the cause. How can anyone reasonably state that evangelicalism is the creation of certain beholders' imaginations when magazines such as *Christianity Today* and *Books & Culture,* schools such as Wheaton College, Trinity Evangelical Divinity School, and Fuller Seminary, and organizations such as the National Association of Evangelicals and the Billy Graham Evangelistic Association not only exist but thrive? If evangelicalism is not the best way to describe these institutions, some may ask, then what is? What is more, if these agencies are evangelical, then evangelicalism, ipso facto, must be real; it must stand for a certain strand of Christian faith and practice.

Another factor that makes questioning evangelicalism's reality difficult is the large number of North Americans who regard themselves as evangelicals. In 1976, the so-called year of the evangelical (another indication that something is really there), the Gallup Organization started asking respondents the following question: "Would you describe yourself as a 'born-again' or evangelical Christian?" Of the one thousand Americans surveyed, an impressive 34 percent answered in the affirmative. Since then the annual responses have varied, with 1987 representing the low point (33 percent) and 1998 the high (47 percent). The 2001 survey yielded a still sturdy figure: 40 percent of Americans considered themselves evangelical.[6] Scholars of American religion, never slow to spot a trend, picked up on such statistics and churned out a remarkable range of studies devoted to this sizeable segment of the American population. Religious historians, for instance, have charted the fortunes of evangelicalism since its emergence in the eighteenth-century North American British colonies. Meanwhile, sociologists of American religion have documented recent manifestations of evangelical zeal in electoral politics as well as in everyday domestic life. So again, readers could well ask, before donating this book to the local public library's annual book sale, who would be so foolish as to challenge the many signals indicating the existence and vitality of this religious phenomenon called evangelicalism?

Yet the central object of *Deconstructing Evangelicalism* is precisely to question the statistics and scholarship on evangelicalism. The reason is not simply to be perverse or provocative. Good reasons exist for raising questions about whether something like evangelicalism actually exists. In the case of religious observance, evangelical faith and practice have become increasingly porous, so much so that some born-again Christians have left the fold for more historic expressions of the Christian faith, such as Roman Catholicism, Eastern Orthodoxy, and Anglicanism.[7] At the same time, in the sphere of religious scholarship, evangelicalism has become such a popular category of explanation that it has ceased to be useful.

Better reasons, however, may also be offered for looking behind the evangelical facade to see what is really there. As the following chapters attempt to show, evangelicalism was a religious construction of particular salience during the late twentieth century. The general contractors in building this edifice were the leaders of the 1940s neo-evangelical movement who sought to breathe new life into American Christianity by toning down the cussedness of fundamentalism while also tapping conservative Protestantism's devotion and faith. Yet without the subcontractors in this construction effort, the neo-evangelical movement would have frayed and therefore failed much quicker than it did. The carpenters, plumbers, and painters in the manufacturing of evangelicalism were the historians, sociologists, and pollsters of American religion who applied the religious categories developed by neo-evangelicals to answer the questions their academic peers were asking about Protestantism in the United States. The emergence of evangelicalism as a significant factor in American electoral politics did not hurt these efforts and, in fact, may have functioned as the funding necessary for completing the evangelical edifice. Especially after the election of Ronald Reagan as president in 1980 and the formation of the so-called Religious Right, religious leaders and religion scholars had a much easier time convincing skeptical academics, policy wonks, publishers, and pundits that evangelicalism was a given of American life, a thriving movement, and therefore important.

Consequently, evangelicalism, as the term is used, is a construct developed over the last half of the twentieth century. Prior to 1950 the word had not been used the way religious leaders and academics now use it, and even then it was not a coherent set of convictions or practices. For that reason, its construction is as novel as it is misleading. This book offers an explanation as to why evangelicalism as currently used became a useful category for journalists, scholars, and believing Protestants. But it is more than simply an account of a specific word's usage. It is also an argument about the damage the construction of evangelicalism has done to historic Christianity. As much as the American public thinks of evangelicalism as the "old-time religion," whether positively or negatively, this expression of Christianity has severed most ties to the ways and beliefs of Christians living in previous eras. For that reason, it needs to be deconstructed.

Evangelicalism before Evangelicalism

In 1989, Martin E. Marty, a leading historian of American religion and senior editor at the *Christian Century*, wrote a piece about the prospects of evangelicalism after a decade or so of national exposure. Aside from a variety of astute points about tensions within this ill-defined group of Protestants, Marty clearly recognized that he and the magazine for which he wrote were not evangelical. He could not help but note the irony that hosts to evangelical conferences regularly introduced him as a "nonevangelical" despite his membership in the Evangelical Lutheran Church of America, one of the few denominations that actually had the e-word in its name. From Marty's perspective, evangelicals were moralistic and conservative and debated biblical infallibility and the specifics of Christ's return as part of boundary maintenance. Despite evangelicalism's confused identity, Marty and his readers had no difficulty distinguishing evangelical Protestants from the mainline ones who regularly wrote for and subscribed to the *Century*. In other words, evangelicalism was *different* from regular or mainstream Protestantism.[8]

At the beginning of the twentieth century, this distinction between mainline and evangelical Protestantism did not exist. To be a member or officer in one of the largest and oldest American Protestant denominations was to be an evangelical. One way to illustrate this point is to look at the sort of statements issued in 1908 at the founding of the Federal Council of Churches. This body, of course, is rarely considered one of the institutions or agencies of evangelicalism and for good reason. It is the forerunner of the National Council of Churches, the ecumenical agency of the mainline Protestants whom contemporary evangelicals suspect of having abandoned the Bible, evangelism, or both. The Federal Council is also an interesting case of evangelical identity because it embodied, even if in a moderate manner, the ideals of the social gospel. One of its most notable early items of business was the "social creed of the churches," a ten-point platform designed to ease the tensions between labor and capital produced by a rapidly industrializing economy.[9] The social gospel orientation of the FCC is significant because evangelicals are supposed to be different from mainline Protestants, at least since the early twentieth century, in that the former held on to an individual gospel while the latter put the salvation of society close to if not above evangelism and missions.[10]

Yet the delegates who gathered in early December 1908 at Philadelphia's Academy of Music for the first conference of the Federal Council believed they were engaged in an evangelical enterprise. One reason for thinking this was that the gathering heard J. Wilbur Chapman, a Presbyterian revivalist and a colleague of Dwight L. Moody, speak on the importance of evangelism. Another was that some of those who gave speeches used the e-word interchangeably with the work of the new agency, even if they were not as culturally sensitive as their successors would be.[11] For instance, in speaking on "The Church and the Immigrant," Ozora S. Davis told delegates that one of the purposes of the Federal Council was to "determine how far there may be in modern conditions a unique demand for a federated endeavor on the part of the evangelical churches in attacking the problem presented by immigration."[12] Then there were the various initiatives of the Council that tapped typically evangelical mores, such as opposing divorce, Sabbath breaking, and the consumption of alcohol and "preserving and guarding" the family "from anything that may defile its purity and choke its flow."[13] Even the executive committee could not resist thinking of the new organization as an evangelical endeavor. In its report, it described the joy with which the "spirit . . . is abroad in the Protestant and evangelical churches of our country in connection with the movement represented by the Council."[14]

Of course, the men responsible for the Federal Council were using *evangelical* in an older sense, and that is precisely the point. For Protestants at the turn of the twentieth century, to be part of mainline Protestantism was to be evangelical. This identification of the mainstream with evangelicalism did not, moreover, involve a break with the revivalistic connotations of evangelical history. For instance, in one of the chief reference works of the early twentieth century, James Hastings's *Dictionary of the Bible* (1898), the article on evangelicalism defined it as chiefly a "movement of revival." The article went on to credit evangelicalism with the Christianization of the United States, even adding to American churches "more than one million members" and the "provision of ordinances for the ever-extending population."[15]

The evangelical roots and identity of mainline Protestantism also show up in the way later mainstream Protestants, who wrote after the modernist-fundamentalist controversy and so knew something about a difference between conservative and liberal Protestantism, continued to locate the origins of the mainline denominations' cooperative efforts in the revivals for which evangelicals were famous. In his history of the American Protestant ecumenical movement, Samuel McCrea Cavert conceded that revivalism, "which was the dominant form of religious activity in the nineteenth century," had been an important ingredient in the formation of the Protestant mainstream. To be sure, "conflicting views about revivalistic practices and ideas were sometimes a source of schism," but because "revivals largely ignored denominational differences, emphasizing only what was relevant to conversion and personal holiness," they "fostered a common body of Protestant sentiment."[16] John A. Hutchison, a philosophy professor at the College of Wooster who went on to chair the philosophy department at Columbia University, wrote the first institutional history of the Federal Council and was more direct than Cavert in linking evangelical and mainline Protestantism in the United States. One of the first manifestations of the sort of ecumenism that would characterize twentieth-century mainline churches was, in Hutchison's estimation, the First Great Awakening. Here "strict denominational lines were blurred and a common religious pattern . . . was begun." Hutchison also credited these revivals with stimulating an interest in the kind of "moral and social problems" for which twentieth-century mainline Protestantism was well known and that the Federal Council sought to nurture.[17]

The point here is not about the theological origins of the mainline Protestant churches or the degree to which they were or are conservative or liberal. Instead, it is about the way the word *evangelical* was used before 1950. Whether a church, minister, or member was liberal or conservative, whether the Bible was inerrant or simply inspired, whether Christ's return was imminent or immanent, American Protestants thought of themselves as evangelical, that is, as members of communions that were trinitarian and possessed roots that went back to the Protestant Reformation. This shared use of the term *evangelical* explains why, within five years of each other, one of the greatest defenders of Calvinism and one of the foremost proponents of modernism could both claim the evangelical label for very different ends. In 1920, in one of the last pieces he would write, Benjamin Warfield, the venerable defender of Calvinism at Princeton Seminary, voiced opposition to the ecumenical drift that he believed was ruining American Protestantism. The essay was titled "In Behalf of Evangelical Religion," and the object of Warfield's penetrating intellect was "The Plan of Union for Evangelical Churches," a scheme developed after World War I to bring many of the denominations in the Federal Council into closer relationship. The creedal statement that was supposed to provide the basis of union was lacking, Warfield argued, because it said nothing about the Trinity, the deity of Christ, or the Holy Spirit. He conceded that these were not "distinctively evangelical truths, but the most fundamental truths of common historical Christianity."[18] Warfield suggested that if this plan was to unite *evangelical* churches, it needed to contain *evangelical* beliefs.

However, part of the reason the proposed plan for uniting *evangelical* churches was vague on *evangelical* belief was that liberal Protestant theologians, such as Shailer Mathews, the dean of the University of Chicago Divinity School, could use the word to describe their own theological position. In 1924, he wrote *The Faith of Modernism*, which was designed in part to respond to arguments against liberalism made by the likes of Warfield's colleague J. Gresham Machen. As much as contemporary usage places *evangelical* and *liberal* in different categories, Mathews used the word *evangelical* in an older sense, one that had little of Warfield's confessional precision. "Modernists," Mathews asserted, "as a class are evangelical Christians. That is, they accept Jesus Christ as the revelation of a Savior God." He added that, briefly put, "the use of scientific, historical, social method in understanding and applying evangelical Christianity to the needs of living persons, is modernism."[19] Of course, later evangelical theologians would take issue with Mathews's definition of evangelicalism. And again the point of this exercise is not to decide whether the University of Chicago or Princeton Seminary was a better source of Christian truth. It is simply to show that the word *evangelical* throughout the majority of American history did not have the significance it does today. In fact, if the experts who conduct opinion polls were asking during the 1920s the same questions they do today about Americans who identify themselves as *evangelical*, both Warfield and Mathews would have answered the same way.

Evangelicals Commandeer Evangelicalism

The use of the word *evangelical* began to change in the aftermath of the fundamentalist controversy. In the 1940s, specifically, the word began to be used exclusively by Protestants on the non-liberal side of the 1920s debates. To call them fundamentalists would be accurate since these Protestants shared much in common with the theology and piety of those who had opposed modernism during the 1920s. But this description would also be inaccurate since these non-liberals did not want to carry the baggage of fundamentalism. They wanted to reform conservative Protestantism and smooth its rougher edges. In so doing, they opted for a new label—*evangelical* instead of fundamentalist.

The Protestant leaders responsible for this shift in nomenclature and who gained control of the word *evangelical*, taking it away from the mainline, have often been described as neo-evangelical, a designation that may have accounted for their denominational diversity. Part of what made the mid-twentieth-century construction of evangelicalism impressive was its organizational might. Neo-evangelical leaders established an array of institutions that provided an outlet for born-again Protestants and raised their visibility. The 1940s witnessed the creation of the National Religious Broadcasters (1944), the Evangelical Foreign Missionary Association (1945), the World Relief Commission (1945), the National Sunday School Association (1946), and the National Association of Christian Schools (1947). Fuller Theological Seminary, founded in 1947, functioned as the think tank for the movement. The Evangelical Theological Society (1949) tapped a wider circle of scholars who hoped to develop an evangelical perspective in biblical and theological studies. During the 1950s, evangelicalism's institutional solidification continued with the formation of the World Evangelical Fellowship (1951). Evangelicalism's leaders also started a magazine, *Christianity Today* (1956), that provided a forum for theological reflection and increased the impression of unity among Protestants outside the mainline denominations. The mother of all these endeavors was the National Association of Evangelicals, an organization hatched in 1942 for the express purpose of facilitating unity among conservative Protestants. This unity, as the title of the NAE's magazine—*United Evangelical Action*—aptly put it, was for the sake of accomplishing specific goals, from evangelism and missions to transforming American society. One of the interesting features of this organizational growth was the use of the term *evangelical* to describe these agencies and efforts. Almost by sheer tenacity neo-evangelicals had created a new religious identity, and *evangelical* was its designation.

At the same time, however, the architects of evangelicalism did more than simply stomp their feet and insist on sole rights to the word. They also laid out a case for evangelicalism that was designed to maintain the movement's conservatism while shedding fundamentalist belligerency. This was the point of a piece that Harold John Ockenga, the first president of the NAE and of Fuller Seminary, wrote in 1947 for the mainstream magazine

Christian Life and Times under the title "Can Fundamentalism Win America?" The Boston pastor—he managed (somehow) to be the senior minister of Park Street Congregational Church while also overseeing the NAE and Fuller—answered his own question with a resounding no. Fundamentalism's solutions to the world's problems, Ockenga argued, have "been weighed in the balances and found wanting." The reason for his negative assessment was fundamentalism's divisive spirit. "Fragmentation, segregation, separation, criticism, censoriousness, suspicion, solecism is the order of the day for fundamentalism," he wrote.[20] In Ockenga's estimation, the NAE was perhaps not the only hope but certainly a "ray" of it. "Here has been displayed the spirit of cooperation, of mutual faith, of progressive action, and of ethical responsibility, so conspicuously lacking elsewhere."[21] Ockenga clarified that evangelicals were just as conservative as fundamentalists about doctrine; he even admitted that the evangelical faith was "fundamentalist." But for evangelicals, conservative doctrine did not require isolation from American society and institutions. In effect, Ockenga was offering an improvement on both liberalism and fundamentalism. Evangelicalism would combine the best of both, the social involvement and activism of the former with the theology and evangelistic zeal of the latter.

Carl F. H. Henry, in his capacity as editor of *Christianity Today*, ran with the distinction Ockenga drew between evangelicals and fundamentalists. In a series of revealing articles, the context of which was fundamentalist criticism of Billy Graham's decision to enlist mainline Protestants for his New York City crusade, Henry charged fundamentalism with "inadequate scriptural content."[22] In so doing he put greater distance between evangelicals and fundamentalists, even to the point of insisting that the true inheritors of Christian orthodoxy were the former. For Henry, according to the dictionary, an evangelical was simply a person who believed that the gospel consisted in an acknowledgment of human sin, redemption through Christ, and the need for conversion. As such, evangelicals, not fundamentalists, were the successors to Augustine and the Protestant Reformers.

The conception of evangelicalism as the orthodox party in American Christianity (prior to Vatican II, Roman Catholics were still considered beyond the pale) paid dividends when editors at Westminster Press, a mainline Protestant publisher, asked Henry's and Ockenga's colleague from Fuller Seminary, Edward J. Carnell, to write the volume on orthodox Christianity, *The Case for Orthodox Theology* (1959), for a series on contemporary theology. The other contributors included L. Harold DeWolf, who wrote on liberal Protestant theology, and William Hordern, who argued a version of the neo-orthodox position. In 1960, a summary of Carnell's outlook appeared in the *Christian Century*, further evidence that neo-evangelicals were benefitting from good publicity and that they had succeeded in occupying the conservative stronghold in American Protestantism. Again, the neo-evangelical position pointed out fundamentalist failings. Carnell called fundamentalism "cultic orthodoxy" in contrast to the "classic" orthodoxy of evangelicalism, which faithfully adhered to the authority of the Bible. Whereas fundamentalists added dispensationalism, separatism, and literalism to their understanding of the Bible, evangelicals apparently took the Bible straight.[23] Carnell and the editors of the *Century* apparently missed the irony of an evangelical doing to fundamentalism precisely what Carnell had said was wrong with the "cultic" side, namely, being negative. Even so, Carnell's article and book were evidence of the successful strategy by neo-evangelical leaders to construct a new Protestant identity in which *evangelical* was the equivalent of conservative Christianity—the faith once delivered to the saints.

The neo-evangelical accomplishment of securing the conservative mantle took a while to bear fruit in public discourse. In religious publishing, the two largest magazines, *Christian Century* and *Christianity Today*, by the 1960s had already recognized *evangelicalism* as an identity separate from fundamentalism. But in nonreligious sectors, journalists and observers of the American scene took longer to acknowledge the new presence in religious circles. Several examples indicate that evangelicalism was emerging as a new and large constituency in the United States. One was the decision of editors at J. B. Lippincott to publish a series titled Evangelical Perspectives edited by John Warwick Montgomery. All published between 1970 and 1972, these books provided a forum for evangelicals to engage a range of issues pertinent to non-evangelicals, from race relations to social reform.[24] Another vehicle that alerted observers to evangelicalism's growing presence were the books written by Richard Quebedeaux, a campus minister at the University of California, Santa Barbara. Both published by New York's Harper & Row rather than obvious evangelical presses in Grand Rapids (Zondervan, Eerdmans, and Baker), *The Young Evangelicals* (1974) and *The Worldly Evangelicals* (1978) provided a road map to the Protestant world outside the mainline denominations for journalists and academics. Of course, when the 1976 presidential race heated up, with born-again Christians at the top of the Democratic and Republican national tickets, and after *Newsweek* declared the bicentennial year the year of the evangelical, books such as Quebedeaux's became essential reading. Suddenly, evangelical Protestants were not only a formidable constituency in the United States but were also vying for political power.

Perhaps it was not the most visible article, but *Wilson Quarterly*'s piece by Cullen Murphy in 1981 vindicated the efforts of neo-evangelicals some forty years earlier. Later the managing editor of *Atlantic Monthly*, Murphy began his essay with words that must have delighted Carl Henry and associates. "The most important development within American Protestantism since the early 1970s," Murphy opined, "has been the ascendancy of the evangelicals, a phenomenon that most journalists have described only in political terms." His dating might have been off—way off from a neo-evangelical perspective—but to recognize that evangelicalism was part of a thriving religious reawakening and not simply a grab for power was to bless the efforts of those who had been assembling a Protestant constituency to match a constructed identity. When Murphy added in his opening paragraphs that "[f]undamentalism is merely a subculture within 'mainstream' evangelicalism, a relatively young and extreme movement within an older, moderate one," he was declaring victory in a still much contested competition for the soul of conservative Protestantism.[25]

The irony of Murphy's declaration was that at precisely the same time that the people who comment on and interpret contemporary affairs—journalists, columnists, and academics—were recognizing evangelicalism, the construction effort begun back in the 1940s was beginning to unravel. Murphy acknowledged that he had written his essay in consultation with Timothy L. Smith, a religious historian at Johns Hopkins University who challenged the definition of evangelicalism that the likes of Henry, Ockenga, and Carnell had concocted, which may explain why Murphy ignored pre-1970 developments. Despite the dispute over the meaning of evangelicalism, the term stuck as a remarkably useful construct for religious historians, sociologists of religion, and pollsters. All of a sudden the analysis and interpretation of American religion became more precise, with the evangelical identity a new concept to use in reckoning with those Protestants who were neither liberal nor fundamentalist.

Accordingly, the volume of literature on evangelicalism since 1980 has increased with remarkable speed. Yet as useful as academics found the concept, clergy and laity, along with evangelical leaders and editors, discovered the idea to be incredibly cumbersome and unwieldy. Hence the irony that the people paid to be professional skeptics—academics—have had more faith in the reality of evangelicalism than the allegedly gullible believers who gather for worship on Sundays and are not usually up to the complexities of scholarly analysis. A double irony is that the people in the pew invariably distrust academic discussions of faith. Yet scholars and pundits have done more to keep evangelicalism alive than have church members, for although evangelicalism may have been useful for scholars in search of new perspectives, it has proven remarkably barren in sustaining the faith of believers who need spiritual sustenance more than trendy analysis.

An Overview

This book is about the way neo-evangelicals built the evangelical edifice and how academics have maintained the facade of the building commonly known as conservative Protestantism. It is less about the actual history of neo-evangelicalism during the three decades after World War II than it is about the conflicting images that hounded evangelicalism during the last two decades of the twentieth century. On the one hand, we now have more books, scholarly articles, and patterns of analysis regarding evangelicalism than we once had on Puritanism, revivalism, the social gospel, or neoorthodoxy. At the same time that the field of evangelical studies has proliferated, the wheels have come off the evangelical movement; *evangelicalism* no longer makes sense of the average congregation's ministry or the individual believer's devotion. Over the course of the pages that follow, I hope to offer some insight into the irony of evangelical success in the academy and failure in the pew. But the chief aim is to document the construction of evangelicalism as a scholarly tool of analysis and the concomitant deconstruction of evangelicalism as an expression of Christian faith and practice.

The first part of the book examines the scholarly construction of evangelicalism during the last twenty-five years, with chapters on religious history, social scientific studies of religion, and students of public opinion. In the writings of these academics, evangelicalism sent down deep roots and became a solid tool for understanding religion and public life in the United States. The last half of the book explores the way evangelicalism as a post–World War II religious movement has fragmented. The themes selected to illustrate evangelicalism's deconstruction are church polity, creed, and worship. The point of these chapters is to show how, without a self-conscious notion about ministry, a common theology, and a coherent understanding of worship, evangelicalism has deconstructed.

By way of introduction, a few words need to be said about the selection of the themes in the second part. To some readers they may look arbitrary. Others might regard them as an imposition on a group of believers who instinctively balk at creeds, formal worship, and church order in favor of the free movement of the Holy Spirit. Although I acknowledge the tension between these categories of assessment and the antiformal nature of born-again Protestant devotion, the subjects of creed, liturgy, and polity are not necessarily capricious or unfair. In fact, they are particularly important to the larger argument of *Deconstructing Evangelicalism*.

Throughout the history of Christianity, the faith believers confess, the order and elements they follow in worship, and the organization of the institutional church have been constitutive elements of being a follower of Jesus Christ. Of course, with their roots in the antiformalism of revivalism and pietism, born-again Protestants have stressed the spirit of Christianity as opposed to its letter (read: forms). Although this experiential form of faith has generated much Christian zeal and activity, it has also obscured the degree to which human life is inherently formal in the sense that specific statements and definitions, certain observances, and well-run organizations are crucial to everyday life. As such, evangelicals have been unable to resist formal expressions of Christianity; think of pamphlets such as *The Four Spiritual Laws,* the order of a Billy Graham crusade rally, or the organizational order supplied by the Evangelical Council for Financial Accountability. What is important to see about the formalism of evangelicalism is not simply the inherent tension between its piety and its practice, between the desire to be free from forms and the inevitability of leaders and structures. Also significant is that, because of their antiformalism, those who call themselves evangelicals have substituted their own religious forms for the ones that historically governed Christianity, whether Roman Catholic, confessional Protestant, or Eastern Orthodox. In effect, the evangelical movement of the late twentieth century replaced the church with the parachurch, and it developed forms to match.[26]

By assessing evangelicalism, then, according to its creed, liturgy, and polity, this book uses categories that emerge readily from Christian history and even from within the evangelical movement itself, though in nondenominational as opposed to denominational categories. At the same time, this analysis provides the basis for understanding why evangelicalism has deconstructed. My point put simply is that the movement neo-evangelical leaders patched together ended up splintering because it lacked the discipline and rigor of the church. Of course, the aim of evangelicalism was to find a lowest common denominator faith that would take members from diverse denominations and independent congregations and stitch them together into a recognizable quilt. It was, as Jon R. Stone has rightly observed, a work of coalition-building.[27] The problem, however, was that the effort to establish a flexible and potent union of Protestant conservatives was predicated on a fundamentally liberal maneuver. To defend and propagate the essential truths of the Bible, neo-evangelical leaders pared back denominational (read: churchly) accretions such as a full-blown creed, an order of worship, and a polity to govern ordination and exercise discipline. In effect, the creation of a core set of common beliefs was similar to (if not the same as) the liberal attempt to separate the kernel from the husk of the Bible. The study that follows could lead to the rather disconcerting conclusion, then, that for mere Christianity to survive, wise and constant diligence needs to be directed to as complete a reflection on biblical truth as possible. In other words, to preserve the minimum, you need to defend the maximum. This is logic that those who call themselves evangelical have instinctively avoided.

In some ways, what follows has already been said by others frustrated by evangelicalism's soft center and the attendant fears about the end of Christianity. For instance, almost two decades ago the Reformed ethicist at Fuller Seminary, Lewis B. Smedes, asserted provocatively that "[e]vangelicalism is a fantasy." His explanation went to the very point about the evangelical movement being a coalition instead of a church. Smedes added, "All the cracks in the earthen vessel notwithstanding, it is the Church—and not an ism—which Jesus Christ founded to be the carrier of his great treasure."[28] A decade later, the religious historian Nathan O. Hatch declared before a gathering of neo-evangelicalism's stalwarts, "In truth, there is no such thing as evangelicalism." The point was not directly about the church, though by acknowledging evangelicalism's historic character as a movement and a coalition of decentralized discontent within America's denominations, Hatch was implicitly raising the issue of ecclesiology. His following comments made this interpretation more than plausible. "The evangelical world is extremely dynamic," Hatch asserted, "but there are few church structures to which many of its adherents or leaders are subject." The result is an unstable constellation of personalities and organizations that in his estimation is "problematic for theological integrity," the very opposite of what the coalition builders had in mind. The movement was supposed to yield doctrinal faithfulness, not undermine it.[29]

As much as the following pages build on the insights of Smedes and Hatch, this book fleshes out in greater detail their point about the downside of the evangelical movement by contrasting it with an understanding that begins with the institutional church, or what Richard John Neuhaus has called "ecclesial Christianity."[30] Showing the hollowness of evangelicalism is insufficient without an alternative. For evangelicals to be the sort of faithful Christians they hope to be, they need to consider whether the very convictions and practices that bind them together week in and week out when they gather for worship under the supervision of church officers determine their religious identity more than the occasional rally or conference designed to build fellowship and facilitate effective strategies for social transformation. In other words, they need to consider the very structures and forms that Christ himself instituted in the Great Commission, where word (teach), sacrament (baptize), and ordination (go) constituted the call to his apostles.

Ironically, this consideration could also benefit the academics who study American religion. Just as evangelicalism leaves out important features of Christianity, thus making the coalition something of a parasite on historic Christian communions, so the contemporary use of evangelicalism as a tool for analysis neglects significant elements of what it means to be an observant Christian. If historians, sociologists, and pollsters looked at phenomena such as creeds, worship, and church government, the landscape of American Christianity might look very different. For this reason, this book is an evaluation not simply of those who belong to the evangelical coalition but also of those who use the designation in scholarship. The argument that follows is that in both cases, in the pew and in the study carrel, evangelicalism leaves out important aspects of Christian belief and practice that are remarkably fruitful for understanding the place of Christianity in modern American society. As a result, just as those believers who think of themselves as evangelical might be better off if they relinquished the label, so academics might produce better scholarship on American religion if they ceased relying ironically on categories supplied by the owners of the evangelical construction company.

Part 1

The Making
of Evangelicalism

1

Religious History Born Again

Between 1980 and 2000, a tsunami of studies on evangelicalism in the United States deluged the field of American religious history. One way of measuring this historiographical storm's devastation is by looking at reference works—placid places that seem impervious to surging waters and powerful currents. As irksome as bibliographical guides may be, the ones covering American religion tell a remarkable tale. For instance, in what had been the industry standard when this writer entered graduate school in 1983, Ernest R. Sandeen and Frederick Hale's *American Religion and Philosophy* (1978), an annotated bibliography on American church history, evangelicalism created barely a ripple. In the subject index, *evangelicalism* did not appear (*evangelical* did so only in the name of specific denominations), and in the title index, only four books or articles begin with the e-word. In Sandeen and Hale's table of contents, evangelicalism as we have come to know it appeared only under the headings "fundamentalism" and "neo-evangelicalism." Within the latter section, the compilers could find only thirteen titles.[1] But within fifteen years, the flood of historical literature on evangelicalism had become so large that bibliographers could fill two volumes with books and articles on evangelicalism. The first of these was Joel A. Carpenter and Edith L. Blumhofer's *Twentieth-Century Evangelicalism: A Guide to the Sources* (1990), followed by Norris Magnuson's *American Evangelicalism: An Annotated Bibliography* (1990).[2] And as if to show that the outpouring was not a flash in the pan, Magnuson produced a supplement to his first volume called *American Evangelicalism II: First Bibliographical Supplement, 1990–1996*, a work, as the title indicated, that covered only a seven-year period.[3] The study of evangelicalism, at least within the quiet stacks of the reference room, was atop the charts.

This unprecedented expansion on the shelves of the academic library's reference section received annotation from two of the more formidable members of the American religious history guild. In 1982, Martin E. Marty analyzed developments in his field during the 1970s, partly as one of his editorial duties at the *Journal of Religion* and partly in response to the recent comments of Stanford University historian Carl Degler that the history of religion in the United States had "fallen into disfavor among historians or been forgotten."[4] Marty's rejoinder was designed to show the error of Degler's assertion, namely, that the field of American religious history was not merely extant but thriving. Yet when it came to work on evangelicalism, Marty conceded that Degler may have had a point. "Given the generation-long surge of conservative Protestantism," the University of Chicago scholar wrote, "one would have expected more vitality in historical fields surrounding it." But by the time of Ronald Reagan's election, "There was a paucity of good research."[5] Evidently, the interest in evangelicalism that neo-evangelicals had been generating for almost three decades had yet to take root in the academy.

Ten years later at the annual meeting of the American Society of Church History, Jon Butler rendered a vastly different verdict on the history of evangelicalism. Religious historians had not only made up for the paucity of good research a decade earlier but had mounted what the Yale historian called "the new 'evangelical thesis' in recent American historiography." Butler clarified that what he detected in research and writing on American history was not only that religion was an important component of the nation's past but also that historians had identified evangelicalism as the most important factor in the shaping of American identity. "In fact," he explained, "during the past two decades evangelicalism (and not merely 'religion') has emerged as the *single* most powerful explanatory device adopted by academic historians to account for the distinctive features of American society, culture, and identity."[6] In a long paragraph, Butler cited books by prominent historians that attributed everything from the American family and American bigotry to the American Revolution and African-American culture to the genius or stupidity, depending on the scholar's perspective, of evangelical Protestantism.

Never mind that Butler's and Marty's dates were not entirely synchronized. Butler dated the growth of "born-again history" to 1970, while for Marty it had not made a dent even by 1980. Never mind as well Butler's skeptical conclusion, in which he told historians, in so many words, to put up or shut up. If evangelicalism were the "foundation of American identity," then it demanded "critical scrutiny, not ready, enthusiastic born-again acceptance."[7] The fact that is difficult to overlook in these leading historians' assessments of their field is the one evident on the reference shelves. During the last quarter of the twentieth century, a faith once dismissed as backward and rural had become one of the most important interpretive tools for historians studying the relationship between religion and United States society.

The success of neo-evangelicals in gaining recognition for their understanding of conservative Protestantism may go even deeper than the publication of bibliographies or the remarks of reputable religious historians suggest. Take, for instance, evidence behind Butler's provocative paper and the books listed in Sandeen and Hale's reference work on American religion. What happened in the field of religious history was not simply that scholars began to write books on the Billy Sundays, anti-slavery movements, and Lyman Beechers of American history, which did in fact happen. Just as important was that works already written before 1980 were by 1990 being classified differently. When before a book might have been listed in a section on Congregationalism, Puritanism, or revivalism, now the same work emerged as a book on evangelicalism. In effect, the success of neo-evangelicals, in creating a separate religious identity, tracing its history, and showing its ongoing relevance, generated a scholarly groundswell. Just as evangelical leaders in the 1940s had created a lowest common denominator for different Protestant groups outside the established National Council of Churches, so academics who studied American Christianity began to lump diverse religious movements together as evangelicalism. So successful has evangelical historiography been that James Turner, professor of history at the University of Notre Dame, could write, evangelical historians "are uncovering the buried and ill-understood past of evangelicalism; all, in doing so, are revealing the centrality of evangelicalism in the wider American past."[8]

As accomplished as the literature on evangelicalism has been, students of American religious history have not carefully scrutinized the deficiency of using evangelicalism as a tool of scholarly analysis. If, for instance, evangelicalism is a lowest common denominator form of Christianity, advocated by a specific group of nondenominational Protestants just after World War II, is it the best way to explore the variety of Christian expressions in the United States? Or has it actually contributed to the neglect of important components of Christian faith and practice, even among those believers who might claim to be evangelical? Ironically, the historians best positioned to guide the historical profession in attending to the nuances of the Christian past, the ones known as conservative Protestants and so apparently aware of older pieces of the Christian religion, are the very ones who have led in the construction of evangelical history. This resurgence of evangelical history has yielded the impression that something old has been discovered when it could actually be that scholars have taken something recent and read it selectively into the past. For this reason, noticing what evangelical historiography leaves out in the history of American Christianity may be as important in evaluating evangelicalism as is the recognition of "born-again history." What may be especially worth pondering is the coincidence of evangelical historiography's success and the failure of church history in the field of religious studies. If this coincidence also involves correlation, then the recent historiography of evangelicalism may be more a curse than a blessing.

The Recovery of American Religious History

A watershed of sorts for the field of American religious history was Henry F. May's 1965 essay, "The Recovery of American

Religious History."[9] After presenting his ideas in various conference and seminar settings, the accomplished University of California, Berkeley historian eventually submitted his reflections on the place of religion in the canon of American intellectual and cultural history to the *American Historical Review*, the journal of the largest historical professional organization, the American Historical Association. The reception by editors and readers before publication was mixed. As May recalled, one of the outside readers feared that the article would "stir up the animals."[10] The piece may well have been catalytic but not in the way of provoking the United States' religious rabble. Instead, May's essay became in the minds of many historians a turning point. Religious history was previously the domain of those May referred to as "seminary historians" who sometimes conceived of their craft as "chronicling the work of the Holy Spirit." May's essay helped to bridge the gap between secularist and providentialist accounts of America's religious vitality.[11] From 1965 on, American religious history blossomed and finally gained a hearing in the mainstream academy. May's article served as the benchmark.

Because of its iconic status in the discipline, this essay is useful for gauging the meaning of evangelicalism for an older generation of church historians, May's "seminary historians." After all, May was less pointing toward a bright future for the expansion of American religious history as a field in need of greater study than recognizing a recovery that already existed. The work produced by scholars who taught in seminary and divinity school contexts allowed May to speak with greater confidence about the importance of religion in the development of American culture. Interestingly enough, however, the recovery of American religious history had not explored evangelicalism in a significant way, certainly not as the concept has come to be used by contemporary historians. Part of what the historians of an older generation had recovered, in May's estimation, was how mainstream Protestantism, the tradition beginning with Puritanism and extending toward Jonathan Edwards and the New Divinity, was "revivalistic, emotional, even somewhat pragmatic."[12] In other words, an older group of historians such as Timothy L. Smith, who later taught at Johns Hopkins University, Winthrop S. Hudson of Colgate-Rochester Theological

Seminary, William G. McLoughlin Jr. of Brown University, and Sidney E. Mead of the University of Chicago Divinity School had begun to add revivalism to the narrative of American cultural history. But this did not constitute an evangelical historiography, or what Jon Butler called "born-again history." It was simply a recognition of the prevalence of revivalistic methods and piety in what Butler would later describe as "Christianizing the American people."[13]

Books by Winthrop Hudson and Sidney Mead indicated the way in which an older generation of "seminary" historians regarded evangelicalism before 1976. Hudson, who taught at the University of Chicago, Colgate-Rochester, and in retirement at the University of North Carolina, was prolific in his ability to summarize and synthesize the major developments in American Protestantism, which during his time was synonymous with American religion. His book *Religion in America,* first published in 1965 and kept in print through several revisions, became a standard text for courses in American religious history at colleges and universities and for surveys of American church history in seminaries. It followed in broad outline the periodization and themes that Hudson had worked out in *American Protestantism* (1961), a book that was part of the Chicago History of American Civilization series, edited by Daniel J. Boorstin. With credentials such as these, Hudson was one of the major interpreters of American Christianity; therefore, his grasp of evangelicalism also reflected the views of most American church historians.

What emerges in Hudson's work is a conception of evangelicalism that is largely synonymous with revivalism. In the former of these two books, Hudson noticed that evangelicalism made itself known as early as colonial America but did so in the form of the revival. He described it as a "type of religious vitality and fervor which is most closely associated in the popular mind with the rise of Methodism."[14] Hudson did distinguish between regular evangelicalism and a popular form, regarding the former as the progeny of Puritanism's experimental Calvinism and the latter as more compatible with the Arminianism and spontaneous structures of Methodism.[15] Consequently, for him, evangelicalism could not be reduced simply to revivalism, though someone as observant as the biblical scholar Charles A. Briggs, who dabbled in the history of American Presbyterianism, noticed the affinities between Puritanism and revivalism and essentially labeled the former Methodistic.[16]

Yet when Hudson turned from the narrower topic of Protestantism to the broader one of American religion, his previous nuances of evangelicalism melted in the heat of revival. In his survey of American Christianity, evangelicalism fades from his narrative after the early nineteenth century and appears only to support his claim that the nineteenth century was the Methodist era of American Protestantism. The "triumph of Methodism" meant the defeat of Calvinism, a body of belief that by implication was incompatible with the evangelistic urgency of nineteenth-century itinerants and evangelists.[17] But whatever the merits of Hudson's analysis of the fit between revivalism and Calvinist or Arminian understandings of salvation, evangelicalism, as a later generation of historians would come to describe it, did not make much of a dent in his assessment of American Christianity, especially in *Religion in America*. If neo-evangelicals were hoping to use the freshest findings of the academy to support their contention that evangelicalism was the party of orthodoxy, the only support they would find from a historian such as Hudson was in his interpretation of fundamentalism. He saw Billy Graham and his colleagues in the National Association of Evangelicals as heirs of fundamentalism, even though he also recognized that they had employed the word *evangelical* to overcome fundamentalism's poor image. The neo-evangelicals' effort did not take, however, with Hudson, who put quotation marks around *evangelical* whenever he employed it in connection with the post–World War II revival. From the perspective of this mainline Baptist historian, the neo-evangelicals were basically fundamentalists, which was revivalism's last gasp before the toxic air of modernity overwhelmed mainstream American Protestantism.[18]

Sidney E. Mead offered a similar perspective on revivalism and American Protestantism in his book *The Lively Experiment* (1963). Like Hudson, Mead was clearly speaking from within the fold of the church history establishment, having served as president of the American Society of Church History and having taught for much of his career at the University of Chicago Divinity School. Indeed, he was, as the dust jacket for *The Lively Experiment* announced, the dean of American church historians. Even so, evangelicalism registered only a sidebar in Mead's ledger of American religion. Like Hudson, Mead recognized it as synonymous with revivalism. To be sure, revivalism was one of the main influences on American Protestantism, ranking fourth in Mead's top-six list, which included antitraditionalism, voluntarism, a missionary impulse, anti-intellectualism, and denominational competition. In fact, revivalism could possibly take credit for several of these features. Mead did not balk at recognizing revivalism's influence, although he saw it as largely harmful, yielding superficiality, the cult of personality, and even the commodification of religion. Still, Mead's treatment of revivalism occurred in the context of his assessment of the mainstream Protestant denominations, not as a particular strain of Protestantism distinct from the mainline. Revivalism was the system that the largest denominations used to gain new members and to spread from the eastern states to the West. Only with the fundamentalist controversy did a singular form of Protestantism depart from the mainstream. Yet here Mead argued that fundamentalism was less an attempt to conserve Protestant orthodoxy than a political ploy to take charge of denominational machinery. According to this interpretation of the Protestant churches, then, evangelicalism as an orthodox expression of Christianity did not exist. It was synonymous with revivalism and nineteenth-century mainline Protestantism, thus raising questions about whether neo-evangelicals or liberals were the true heirs of the evangelical heritage.[19]

Although Timothy L. Smith never taught at a seminary, he was a minister in the Church of the Nazarene throughout his distinguished career at the University of Minnesota and Johns Hopkins University. His most important book, published in 1957 and the recipient of the American Society of Church History's Brewer Prize, *Revivalism and Social Reform*, is a fairly accurate reading of the state of evangelical history before Ronald Reagan and the Religious Right. Based on his Harvard University dissertation, the book chronicled the effects of revivalism on nineteenth-century America, not simply within Protestantism but also on the nation. Smith was not concerned with the cycle of awakenings in the United States; in fact, he had very little to say about the so-called Second Great Awakening, even while devoting considerable attention to Charles Grandison Finney, or about the relationship between the revivals of the eighteenth century and those of Finney's era. Revivalism was, for Smith, simply the vital center of church life in the United States, penetrating even New England and the writers that intellectual historians studied. The quest for holiness that revivalism nurtured also accounted for numerous social reforms, from temperance and Sabbath observance to the abolition of slavery. This piece of Smith's argument was his most stunning. Today it has become a truism to say that revivalism was responsible for many of the nineteenth-century reforms that political liberals welcome as part of the United States' march of progress. But at the time of Smith's writing, liberal Protestantism, the supposed opposite of revivalism, received most of the credit for promoting social reform. Revivalism was allegedly otherworldy and strictly geared to saving souls. Smith upended that conception by arguing that movements such as the social gospel, the progeny of liberal Protestantism, may have actually been the Johnny-come-lately in the race for applying Christianity to social welfare.[20]

As positive as Smith was about revivalism, and as much as he would later be recognized as an "evangelical" historian, he had very little to say in his book about evangelical Protestantism per se. If a reader of *Revivalism and Social Reform* went to Smith's index, for example, to find what the author had to say about born-again Christianity, he or she would discover only three entries, all of which used *evangelical* as an adjective, not as an *ism*. These were "Evangelical Alliance" and "Evangelical Association," both of which were institutions, and "Evangelical Arminianism," a variety of doctrine that Smith contrasted with orthodox Calvinism. Of course, he may have simply assumed that the book was about evangelicalism. But the afterword that Smith wrote for the Johns Hopkins University Press 1980 edition of the book also failed to mention evangelicalism or the emerging field of study. Instead, as he explained, his original interest was in revivalism, particularly the Wesleyan strain of it, and its ongoing vitality in mainstream American Protestantism.[21] In effect, Smith's interests were denominational, though as the book made clear, Wesleyan perfectionism influenced the whole of American Protestantism, from frontier revivals to Boston lyceums. Even when he commented on the recovery of American religious history after the original publication of the book, the connection he noted was not the rising interest in evangelicalism or its influence in American public life but the academic study of millennialism and its influence on American exceptionalism. In sum, if Smith had wanted to take credit for generating interest in evangelicalism, he had the opportunity to do so. The fact that he did not demonstrates just how far the category was from the consciousness of religious historians prior to the rise of the Moral Majority.

Another interesting case that shows how little an older generation of religious historians thought of evangelicalism as a separate religious classification is William G. McLoughlin Jr.'s *Modern Revivalism: Charles Grandison Finney to Billy Graham* (1959), published on the heels of Smith's pathbreaking study. In some respects, McLoughlin's book is a more interesting test for evangelicalism than Smith's because it covers the century when the modern movement came to prominence. By the 1930s, for instance, historians recognized a division in American Protestantism between fundamentalists and the mainline denominations. In addition, McLoughlin wrote one of the first scholarly treatments of Billy Graham, *the* evangelist of the neo-evangelical movement and also a power broker within neo-evangelical circles. Consequently, by virtue of his material, McLoughlin could have recognized, and been one of the first to do so, the claims that neo-evangelicals were making about being the orthodox party in American Protestantism, with roots in Puritanism, the First and Second Great Awakenings, and the protests of conservatives who opposed theological liberalism. Yet McLoughlin offered little to support an evangelical version of Protestantism stretching back through the centuries. Instead, for McLoughlin, evangelicalism was essentially synonymous with or a type of revivalism. As he explained in his preface, "This book is concerned with religious revivalism in the United States since 1825. . . . [It seeks] to discover why revivals have constantly recurred, what their effects have been, and what they meant not only to those directly concerned but to all Americans."[22]

In some ways, the narrowness of McLoughlin's self-described scope is unfortunate because his book could have provided valuable insights to neo-evangelicals about their religion. But because *Modern Revivalism* was explicitly about revivalism, it missed Protestants who, while sympathetic and perhaps more dependent than they knew on the ethos of revivalism, were seeking to create an identity as *evangelical*. Toward the end of his narrative, McLoughlin commented on the irony of revivalism contributing to secularization, the very cultural development against which neo-evangelicals such as Graham flexed their institutional muscles. "Revivalists have had to attract the attention of the masses without at the same time losing the support and respect of the clergy," McLoughlin wrote. But in trying to "follow the maxim of the apostle and be all things to all men . . . they inevitably diluted and confused a message which, if it was to have any force, had to be concise, direct, and clear-cut." In other words, they reduced Christianity "to a hard core of universally acknowledged fundamentals," something that could also be said of an organization such as the National Association of Evangelicals or a publication such as *Christianity Today*, and "in the course of explaining these truths they either reduced Christianity to banalities or inflated it to vagaries."[23] Because of criticisms such as this, it was easier to avoid the relevance of McLoughlin's insights for the neo-evangelical movement and simply to chalk up his point to the academy's congenital contempt for revivalist Christianity.

Still, as astute as the book was on what historians would later conceive of as evangelicalism, or born-again Protestantism, McLoughlin contributed little to start a field of born-again history. He definitely did not become a cheerleader for a new field of study by suggesting that his secular colleagues had ignored it because of bias. The closest he came to recognizing a need to assess the new evangelical identity that neo-evangelicals were laboring to construct was in the opening paragraphs of the book, where he framed his orientation to revivalism. McLoughlin believed that by 1959 the United States had experienced four religious awakenings. Accordingly, he located the endeavors of those whom he referred to as "neo-fundamentalists," or in today's vernacular, "neo-evangelicals," in the period of the Fourth Great Awakening, which included the neoorthodox rejection of liberal Protestantism. Still, he was uncertain whether Billy Graham was the climax of this post–World War II revival or a new phase of revivalism. So although McLoughlin brushed up against the presence of a new kind of born-again Protestantism and paused briefly to assess it, his overarching concern was nevertheless with revivalism, in which case, Graham and "neo-fundamentalism" were simply manifestations of deeper impulses in the soul of American society. In *Modern Revivalism*, then, as in *Revivalism and Social Reform*, if evangelicalism gained a hearing, it did so as a synonym for revivals and the kind of piety they inspired.

The one exception to this pattern of treating evangelicalism as the equivalent of revivalism was McLoughlin's 1968 anthology of nineteenth-century Protestantism. Its title, *The American Evangelicals, 1800–1900*, is indicative of an expanded notion of evangelicalism. The book's contents make the same point, including not simply revivalists such as Charles Grandison Finney and Dwight L. Moody but also New England Congregationalists such as Lyman Beecher and Julia Ward Howe, liberal or proto-liberal Protestants such as Horace Bushnell, Phillips Brooks, and Josiah Strong, authors such as Julia Ward Howe, and moral philosophers such as Francis Wayland. McLoughlin was clearly working with an understanding of evangelicalism that reached well beyond the camp meetings and anxious benches of itinerant evangelists. His apparently wider view went so far as to include nineteenth-century religious life in the United States. He opened by declaring that "[t]he story of American Evangelicalism is the story of America itself . . . for it was Evangelical religion which made Americans the most religious people in the world." Perhaps McLoughlin was beginning to see the neo-evangelical light, for his rhetoric matched the conception that neo-evangelical leaders sometimes expressed about the links between their faith and their nation's greatness. And when McLoughlin elaborated on his contention by stating that evangelicalism's history "must be told on three levels: first as philosophy, second as theology, and third as social history," those who hoped that twentieth-century evangelicalism would make a larger mark than it had before 1950 may have been tempted to think that McLoughlin was supplying them with a model for evangelical greatness.[24] But whatever evangelicals themselves made of this historian's argument, was McLoughlin's book a turning point for American religious history? Did it mark the transition from an older generation of scholars who thought of evangelicalism as another word for revivalism to a new body of scholarship, what Butler would later call "born-again history," that saw evangelicalism written large in the warp and woof of American politics, culture, intellectual life, and religious organization?

If McLoughlin's book did signal a shift in American religious history, it fooled the likes of Martin Marty, who fifteen years later was lamenting the dearth of literature on evangelicalism. More likely this book was a throwback to an older view of American church history that Protestants developed in the nineteenth century. In books such as Robert Baird's *Religion in America* (1844) and H. K. Carroll's *The Religious Forces of the United States* (1893), both of which were important efforts to make sense of America's religious diversity, evangelicalism was synonymous with Protestantism. After all, this was an era before the fundamentalist controversy, when Protestants, despite their denominational diversity, displayed remarkable fraternity and cooperation. The only real dividing lines in American religion were between Protestants and Roman Catholics, on the one side, and between trinitarian Protestants and Unitarians and groups such as the Mormons, on the other. In this context, evangelicalism was simply generic Protestantism. According to Carroll, evangelicals were found in those churches that affirmed the inspiration, authority, and sufficiency of the Bible; the Trinity; the deity of Christ; justification by faith alone; and the work of the Holy Spirit "in the conversion and sanctification of the sinner."[25] As much as that definition may have encouraged neo-evangelical leaders after World War II to regard themselves as the real mainline in American Protestantism, it was also a sufficiently broad and vague definition to include the likes of Horace Bushnell and Julia Ward Howe, Protestants whose lineage neo-evangelicals rarely if ever sought. Living as they did after the modernist-fundamentalist controversy, neo-evangelicals could not turn back the clock to a time when evangelicalism included liberals and conservatives. After all, they believed evangelicalism was synonymous with orthodoxy. Consequently, if they were going to find historians to write about the American Protestant past in ways that supported their own conception of evangelicalism, they would have to find someone other than McLoughlin. Indeed, they would have to wait for a new generation of historians, many of whom came from within their own ranks.

The Construction of Evangelical History

If evangelicalism was a distinct expression of American Christianity lost on most church historians prior to 1980, a decade later evangelicalism was hard to avoid in the study of American religion. One obvious factor was the rise of the Religious Right and its support of the Reagan presidency. Seemingly overnight, evangelicalism had gone from the backwoods of revivals and tent meetings to the nation's public square. Journalists and political commentators who wanted to know where people such as Jerry Falwell, Tim LaHaye, and C. Everett Koop had come from—hardly the backwoods—created a ready market for a new line of scholarship on American religion. Almost coincidently, Wheaton College, with some support from the Billy Graham Evangelistic Association, in 1982 established the Institute for the Study of American Evangelicals. This agency was hardly a response to the religious presence in American electoral politics. In fact, plans for the ISAE had developed from a successful conference held at Wheaton College in 1979, funded largely by the Lilly Endowment, on the Bible in American culture.[26] But the ISAE did bring together a group of evangelical historians who would become the chief interpreters of the neo-evangelicals' understanding of evangelicalism. The group consisted primarily of Mark A. Noll (Wheaton College) and Nathan O. Hatch (University of Notre Dame), who were the Institute's cofounders, along with George M. Marsden, then at Calvin College; Harry Stout, then at the University of Connecticut; and Grant Wacker, then at the University of North Carolina. Joel Carpenter, who was finishing a doctorate in American history at Johns Hopkins University with Timothy L. Smith, was the ISAE's first director. In turn, the Institute's first book, *Evangelicalism in Modern America* (1984), almost singlehandedly established evangelicalism as a force to be reckoned with, not just in Reagan's America but going all the way back to John Winthrop.

George Marsden, who edited and wrote the book's introduction, staked out what would become the working definition of evangelicalism for American religious historians. He identified three layers of meaning. The first, and the one that has become de rigueur among religion scholars, is a conceptual definition. An evangelical, according to Marsden, is one who emphasizes:

"1) the Reformation doctrine of the final authority of Scripture; 2) the real, historical character of God's saving work recorded in Scripture; 3) eternal salvation only through personal trust in Christ; 4) the importance of evangelism and missions; and 5) the importance of a spiritually transformed life."[27] As much as this conceptualization drew on the various lists of essential doctrines constructed by fundamentalists (for some it was five points, for others nine), Marsden slighted the fundamentalist contribution when he listed concrete examples of evangelicalism. Consequently, a second layer of meaning involved a common set of "heritages," "tendencies," "an organic character." Here Marsden rummaged through the Protestant past, starting with the Protestant Reformation and continuing with Puritanism, pietism, Methodism, and various shades of holiness, restorationist, and revivalist groups in the nineteenth and twentieth centuries. "Widely common hymnody, techniques of evangelism, styles of prayer and Bible study, worship, and behavioral mores," Marsden wrote, "demonstrate these connected origins."[28]

The third layer of evangelical identity in Marsden's introduction was arguably the most striking. He spoke of evangelicalism as a denomination, that is, "a religious fellowship or coalition of which people feel a part."[29] Marsden traced the roots of this sense of commitment back to pietism of the eighteenth century, which stressed a "common zeal for spreading the gospel" and ran all the way down to Billy Graham. Interestingly enough, this definition permitted Marsden to speak of "card-carrying evangelicals." These people had a sense, like their nineteenth-century spiritual grandparents, of belonging to a "complicated fellowship and infrastructure of transdenominational evangelical organizations."[30] Whether intended or not, this definition of evangelicalism played directly to the strengths of the neo-evangelical leaders who after World War II were trying to gather the different Protestant strands together into a coherent evangelical braid. Not only had Marsden granted the neo-evangelical project a much longer history than one going back to the fundamentalist controversy, but he had also essentially used the neo-evangelical definition of *evangelicalism* as the basis for studies of these kinds of Protestants. In effect, Marsden provided historical justification for the likes of Carl F. H. Henry, Harold John Ockenga, and

Billy Graham by making them the bearers of the evangelical tradition.

A few years later, ISAE historians produced two important books that further solidified the new definition of evangelicalism and linked it to neo-evangelicalism, though the usefulness of the definition also showed its limitations. The first was Mark A. Noll's study of evangelical biblical scholarship, *Between Faith and Criticism* (1986). Although the book began with nineteenth-century controversies prompted by the reception of higher criticism in American Protestantism, it ended by focusing on the Evangelical Theological Society (ETS), which initially was closely linked to the National Association of Evangelicals. In effect, after World War II the ETS became the professional home for conservative biblical scholars who were on the margins of mainline Protestant organizations such as the Society of Biblical Literature or the National Association of Biblical Instructors. So again, evangelicalism emerged as a synonym for conservative.

Noll's opening section of definitions is deft and shows his own discomfort with the hegemonic uses to which the label *evangelical* may be put. So, on the one hand, he acknowledges a theological or normative definition widely employed since 1980. The four cardinal convictions are a high view of Scripture, an affirmation of God's ongoing intervention in human history, the lordship of Christ and the sufficiency of his salvation, and the need for conversion.[31] Noll goes on to concede that such a definition lacks "conceptual clarity." He then turns to history for help. Evangelicalism is the progeny of Presbyterians and Baptists from the 1920s who fought in the fundamentalist controversy and later neo-evangelical leaders. These fundamentalists and neo-evangelicals "have been those most willing to be defined by the activities of the best-known evangelists"—Finney, Moody, Sunday, and Graham.[32] At this point, Noll's definition adds the newer neo-evangelical understanding of evangelicalism as conservative to the older study of American church history, which equated it with revivalism, an expansion that both adds and subtracts precision since revivalism is inherently innovative, not conservative. The ambiguity that results from such a historical rendering of evangelicalism is that it allows Noll to include under the evangelical big tent groups and schools as diverse as Disciples of Christ, Mennonites, Southern Baptists,

Dallas Theological Seminary, the Moral Majority, and African-American Protestants. To his credit, Noll admits this makes evangelicalism theologically sloppy. "The pieces . . . never fit together exactly, overall organizational discipline is practically nonexistent, and channels of communication can be a puzzle to outsiders." Such an admission should have given evangelical historians pause, since part of the point of academic work is to clarify, not to revel in ambiguity, especially if trying to explain things to "outsiders." But this admission did not keep Noll from adopting Marsden's notion of an "evangelical denomination" whose members "manifest the connectedness of a family grouping that is quite concerned about its immediate relatives."[33]

The following year Marsden cemented the ties between this definition and neo-evangelicalism with his fortieth-anniversary history of Fuller Seminary, *Reforming Fundamentalism* (1987). This book is as entertaining as it is insightful and uses the institutional history of Fuller Seminary to unravel some of the puzzles that Marsden found in his own study of fundamentalism. As such, the book has less to say in a definitional way about evangelicalism than it does about Fuller's place in the construction of evangelicalism. Even so, Marsden's opening chapter is instructive for the way the field of American religious history understands evangelicalism. At one point, evangelicalism is simply marked by "a zeal to proclaim the biblically revealed gospel of salvation through the atoning work of Christ."[34] Marsden admits that this conception applies as much to the mainline denominations, which "at one time" were evangelical, as it does to the trans-denominational enterprises most often erected by evangelists. Evangelicalism, then, extends beyond revivalism to American Protestantism as a whole.

The ambiguity increases when Marsden argues that neo-evangelical leaders confronted the question as to whether to return to pre-fundamentalist evangelicalism or to perpetuate fundamentalist antimodernism. In which case, neo-evangelicals were fundamentalists who did not want to be, but they found nothing in the older pre-fundamentalist evangelicalism to which to return.[35] So now four sets of evangelicalisms are possible, two pre-fundamentalist varieties (one denominational and one parachurch) plus a fundamentalist version and a post-fundamentalist version. Clarifications on this order might have been useful to the guild of religious historians, but they were as much the product of the ambiguities surrounding the definition of evangelicalism that was coming into vogue as they were the result of hard thinking. The confusion prompted Marsden to conclude his introduction by explaining how he was using the words *fundamentalist* and *evangelical*. But the quotation marks around different words could not hide the difficulty. Once fundamentalism split in the 1940s, he writes, "the 'new evangelicals' or 'evangelicals' came together as a party of former fundamentalists. Although they successfully reappropriated 'evangelical' as the primary designation for biblicist American Protestantism, by no means all 'evangelicals' had shared their struggles with fundamentalism."[36] Given Marsden's and Noll's difficulties in winning the evangelical shell game, it is not surprising that the "new" evangelical movement itself was unraveling at the very same time that the ISAE was taking off.

Yet the confusion surrounding the term did not stop religious historians from using evangelicalism as a catchall for a certain kind of Protestantism with the reputation chiefly of being on the conservative side of the fundamentalist-modernist divide. Here a brief acquaintance with representative works will have to suffice as an analysis of publishing trends. Three books on nineteenth-century United States history, all from the mid-1990s, reveal the triumph of the neo-evangelical definition of evangelicalism beyond born-again historians, a victory that ironically made the so-called secular academy, at least a portion of it, the handmaid of religious adherents most fearful of intellectuals.

Two representative books that picked up and ran with the label of evangelical identity are William R. Sutton's *Journeymen for Jesus* (1998) and Christine Leigh Heyrman's *Southern Cross* (1997). The former is a study of nineteenth-century artisans and the way evangelical convictions informed their class consciousness. The latter, which won Columbia University's Bancroft Prize, examined the appeal of evangelical religion in the South and its transformation from a liberating to a repressive faith. Whatever the merits of each book, and they are numerous, the important feature to observe is the way each historian chose the evangelical label to categorize what was essentially a Methodist story. Sutton's book begins with the assertion that it is a study of artisans who were "evangelical Protestants." Yet his sources are almost entirely Methodist workers in Baltimore. In fact, the next two chapters, "Methodist Dissent and the Limits of Christian Submission to Authority" and "The Institutionalization of Methodist Protestantism, 1827–1835," reveal that Sutton's study is actually a contribution to Methodist church history. The popularity of evangelicalism as a tool of analysis among American religious historians, however, prompted him to use the subtitle *Evangelical Artisans Confront Capitalism in Jacksonian Baltimore* rather than the narrower *Methodist Artisans Confront Capitalism in Jacksonian Baltimore*. (No doubt, publishers have their own reasons for preferring the evangelical label to a denominational label, since the former promises a larger readership.) Likewise, Heyrman's study of southern folk religion attempted to include Presbyterians, Baptists, and Methodists, but her sources were primarily Methodist. Here the problem is not one of false advertising. Instead, it is a climate of scholarly opinion that disregards differences among Baptists, Methodists, and Presbyterians and reduces them to an evangelical core. The triumph of evangelicalism as a definite identity allowed historians to lump all Protestants who believed in a set list of doctrines and stressed the need for conversion together as evangelicals.[37]

Richard J. Carwardine's *Evangelicals and Politics in Antebellum America* (1993) reflected the extent to which evangelicalism could obscure the diversity of Protestant expressions. In an otherwise landmark study of the cultural factors that shaped antebellum American politics, Carwardine, as his title indicated, located practically every Protestant tradition, aside from Unitarians and Transcendentalists, in the evangelical category. This is all the more remarkable because Protestant diversity was arguably strongest during the six decades before the Civil War than during any other period of United States history. Carwardine followed the lead of religious historians in defining evangelicalism as a creed that included the Trinity, human sinfulness, the atonement, regeneration, and the final judgment. Evangelicalism also required "a moral life and a personal experience of salvation." To be sure, Carwardine did not ignore differences among those whom he called evangelical. He noted disputes over church government, infant baptism, Calvinism versus Arminianism, and revivalism. He even asserted that for many American Protestants "their attachment to denomination meant more to them than being part of a wider evangelical community."[38] In addition, the differences Carwardine observed also had important political implications, with northern evangelicals adopting a public theology that fused religion and politics in a way that southern evangelicals resisted.[39] Even so, the divergences among evangelicals that denominational identities could well have explained drowned under a flood of historical literature attesting a separate evangelical identity. Indeed, what for an earlier generation of historians would have been a testimony to either the uniqueness of American religion (e.g., denominationalism) or the acculturation of American Protestantism (e.g., the churches' baptizing American political ideals) had become proof of the presence and strength of evangelical Protestantism.

The latest sign of the evangelical paradigm in American religious history is the one-man encyclopedia by Barnard College historian Randall Balmer. His *Encyclopedia of Evangelicalism* (2002), published by Westminster John Knox, demonstrates the way the study of evangelicalism has dissolved older Protestant categories while also showing the infiltration of neo-evangelical self-understandings into the mainstream academy. This book is unexceptional in uniting diverse Protestant groups that in the day-in day-out duties of denominational life never cross paths. In Balmer's categorization, therefore, both the hard-core Calvinists in the Orthodox Presbyterian Church, who believe speaking in tongues ended when the last apostle of Christ died, and members of the Assemblies of God, a Pentecostal denomination that makes such Spirit-filled language a sign of genuine Christianity, are evangelicals. Never mind that each denomination has no formal link, other than an affirmation of the church universal. Nor does it seem to matter that as Calvinistic and Wesleyan denominations, these groups occupy fairly distinct positions on the Protestant spectrum. By waving the wand of conversion and Christian essentials, these Calvinists and Pentecostals became evangelicals.[40]

What is particularly interesting is that Balmer's specific entry on evangelicalism recounts the same narrative that neo-evangelicals constructed over thirty years earlier. It begins with the First Great Awakening, extends to the revivals of the Second Great Awakening, and highlights the activism of evangelicalism's perfectionist side. After the Civil War, evangelicalism adopted a defensive posture in reaction to liberalism and the social gospel, a stance that precipitated the fundamentalist controversy of the 1920s. After that stormy decade, fundamentalists, in Balmer's telling, regrouped to mount the political initiative associated with the Religious Right and the Reagan revolution. Surprisingly, this account leaves out the very neo-evangelicals who first argued for an evangelical tradition extending back beyond the 1920s and representing the orthodox Protestant position. Instead, Balmer places the neo-evangelical initiative in a separate entry that leaves dangling the relation of institutions such as the National Association of Evangelicals, Fuller Theological Seminary, and the Billy Graham Evangelistic Association to the wider evangelical movement.[41]

Despite the irony of ignoring neo-evangelicals in a dictionary article on evangelicalism, Balmer's narrative does follow closely the one that Bruce Shelley, a professor of church history at Conservative Baptist Theological Seminary, constructed to celebrate the twenty-fifth anniversary of the National Association of Evangelicals' founding. His book, *Evangelicalism in America* (1967), was as much a justification for the neo-evangelical project as it was a history of the organization and its religious roots. Even so, in the chapter on American evangelicalism prior to the 1940s, Shelley started, as Balmer does, with the awakenings of the eighteenth and nineteenth centuries, followed by the social reforms of the benevolent empire and opposition to liberalism in the form of fundamentalism. The only differences are that where Balmer concludes with evangelical support for Ronald Reagan, Shelley wrote before the emergence of the Religious Right, and while Balmer overlooks neo-evangelicalism, for Shelley the NAE is the culmination of American evangelicalism.[42]

To be clear, the point here is not to imply that the recent recovery of evangelical history is a sinister plot by historians who grew up born-again or that recent historical scholarship, though gussied up with footnotes and bibliographical essays, is simply repeating an argument already made by evangelical leaders from the 1940s and 1950s. In other words, the issue is not whether Balmer had a copy of Shelley's *Evangelicalism in America* when he wrote his *Encyclopedia of Evangelicalism*. Instead, the point is simply to note the parallels between the construction of an evangelical identity by neo-evangelical spokesmen and the subsequent categorization of Protestantism by the religious history guild. Evangelical academics may have read and been influenced by the works of Carl F. H. Henry and may have listened to the radio sermons of Billy Graham. A better explanation of this coincidence is the rise of the Religious Right and the presence of evangelicalism in American electoral politics. Whatever the explanation, after 1980, religious historians were not defining evangelicalism as an older generation of church historians had, as a revivalistic form of Protestantism, but as *the* preservation of orthodox or conservative Protestantism. The similarity between that understanding and the one neo-evangelicals had articulated during the intra-Protestant squabbles of the 1950s should have given scholars pause. That it did not may be one of the more significant ironies surrounding debates about the place of Christianity in the secular, postmodern, and politically correct university.

The Loss of Church History

The success of born-again history, described here all too briefly, should not lead to the conclusion that religious historians have created a cardboard figure that lacks three dimensions, let alone a pulse. The literature on American evangelicalism, as mentioned at the beginning of this chapter, is immense, and much of it is very useful for understanding trends and developments within American Christianity. The intention here has been simply to open a few of the books produced since 1980, the period of evangelical history's renaissance, and see how scholars use evangelicalism as a category or designation in their description not only of recent Protestant history but also of American Protestantism, at least since 1776 if not going back to 1620. Even so, the shelves that hold all the books on evangelicalism are numerous, so many in fact that librarians need reference works to keep track of those shelves' contents. Consequently, even though this literature may and in some cases does reflect greater nuance and variety than what is suggested here, the point stands that religious historians have generated a class of literature that did not exist forty years ago. What to an older generation of "seminary historians" looked at most like an expression of revivalism or a "third force" today has become a full-blown designation for understanding one group of American Protestants.[43] What is more, historians have come to understand these evangelical Protestants as *the* conservative ones.

Nevertheless, indicative of some of the variety in assessments of evangelicalism is a book by Paul K. Conkin, an intellectual historian who taught at Vanderbilt University for many years. His 1995 work, *The Uneasy Center,* is interesting at the very least because Conkin offers a somewhat different definition of evangelicalism than many religious historians. Conkin locates evangelical origins in John Wesley and the Methodist movement, a conclusion that is not entirely surprising given that he was trained during a period when the Meads, Hudsons, McLoughlins, and Smiths dominated the study of American Protestantism. Nor is his description of the "fuller and deeper religion" that Wesley advocated unusual. It consisted of four traits: conversion, earnest devotion, evangelism, and holiness.[44] What is unusual about Conkin's estimation of evangelicalism, compared to the work being done by religious historians, is that he contrasts this form of religiosity with Reformed Christianity, a label he attributes to a strain of the Christian religion with roots in the Reformed branch of the Protestant Reformation (e.g., Zwingli, Calvin, Bucer, Knox, and Cramner). The American descendants of these Reformers, Conkin argues, comprised the center of American religion before the Civil War and included mainly the denominations of British origin, such as Anglicans, Congregationalists, Presbyterians, Baptists, and Methodists.

Although Conkin includes Methodists in this Reformed mainstream, he does so because they started in the Church of England, not because they were Calvinistic. In fact, his grid for understanding nineteenth-century Protestantism also involves a recognition of evangelicalism's changing identity. The revivals of the eighteenth century had prompted some to call themselves *evangelical* and to use this in a "restrictive" sense, one that designated a subclass of Protestants. These evangelicals differed from the Reformed center, according to Conkin, because their piety embraced a narrower range of ideals than that in the denominations. He goes on to acknowledge that by the twentieth century *evangelical* would take on an even narrower understanding.[45] In fact, in his conclusion, Conkin reflects on the twentieth-century heirs of the Reformed center and argues that the legacy of nineteenth-century Reformed Christianity is modern-day mainline Protestantism. This apparently leaves the Protestants affiliated with the National Association of Evangelicals as the religious descendants of Wesley and the Methodist revivalists. Despite the outward similarities, Conkin concludes that the evangelicalism of the neo-evangelical movement is actually distinct from the evangelicalism of either the eighteenth or nineteenth centuries. The older evangelicals "were the innovators, the most creative and at times most prophetic of Christians." Today's evangelicals, in contrast, "are reactive and atavistic. . . . [A]nd the result is a type of evangelicalism that seems very different from the early nineteenth-century Methodist variety."[46]

Conkin's understanding of evangelicalism could likely be confusing for the purposes of argument here. First, he asserts that evangelicalism did exist before neo-evangelicals offered it as an alternative to fundamentalism. Second, he concedes that evangelicalism is a legitimate category for understanding contemporary Protestantism even if its resemblance to older strains is distant. Yet as much as Conkin adds to the ever increasing literature on evangelicalism, his book is important for what it reveals about an older style of religious history. His concern throughout is not with individuals who espouse certain doctrines or talk about specific life-changing experiences. Instead, his object of study is the church or, more specifically, denominational life. Consequently, Conkin's book represents what happens to scholarly assessments of evangelicalism when they look more at church structures and patterns of affiliation than at individual doctrines or individuals' religious experiences.

Conkin's different approach to American Protestantism is a reminder that the study of evangelicalism during the last twenty-five years occurred at precisely the same time that the study of American Christianity shifted from church history to religious history. In a thoughtful essay about changes within the study of American Christianity, David W. Lotz, historian at Union Theological Seminary (New York), posited that a shift took place between 1965 and 1985. During this period, the study of Protestantism switched from the history of the church to the history of the more generic entity, religion. Church historians prior to 1965 regarded their work as part of a theological enterprise, with a recognition that the church was the institutional embodiment of divine grace. The religious historians who soon elbowed aside their older colleagues "secularized" the study of Christian history. They concluded that theology was out of place in university history and religious studies departments. Religious historians were also embarrassed by the parochial character of church history. American religion was much more diverse than Protestantism or even Christianity.[47] Consequently, the recovery of American religious history that Henry May applauded in 1965 was actually in the process of winding down, for he had noticed the work of seminary historians who were performing church history, work that looked primarily at the denominations considered part of the Protestant mainline. The real recovery of American religious history would not occur until historians discovered the vitality of Americans' faith outside the Protestant establishment. In effect, this shift from church to religious history was the academy's rejection of Protestant hegemony in the United States.[48]

Ironically, the recovery of American evangelical history would not have had nearly the visibility it has achieved had it not been for this significant shift in the study of American religion. On one level, neo-evangelicals, as heirs of the fundamentalist controversy, stood to benefit directly from the field's rejection of the oppressors, mainline Protestantism, and its delight in the victims of such oppression. Although neo-evangelicals and the identity they constructed were as Protestant and predominantly white as anything the mainline churches could muster, they were also outsiders who, according to one spin, had been forced out of the mainstream. To study evangelicalism, then, was to contribute to the exploration (read: celebration) of America's religious diversity and of those groups previously regarded as unimportant or bizarre.

On another level, the history of evangelicalism played precisely to the strength of the new model of religious history. Institutions, formality, official representatives—these phenomena were for many religious historians the antiquated subject matter of church historians. They did not embody America's genuine religious vitality. So the profession moved from the pew, the pulpit, the church assembly, and the denominational periodical to signs of religious influence on culture, politics, economics—all walks of life where religion made a difference for the way ordinary people lived daily. It would be hard to imagine a recipe easier to follow by students of the new evangelical identity. After all, evangelicalism was a religion not confined to formal and bureaucratic denominational structures. Instead, it was a faith that gave ordinary believers the courage to get things done, whether on the farm, in the gym, in the public square, or on the mission field. In effect, born-again faith typified the mood of the new religious history; it was pluralistic, egalitarian, and utilitarian.

But it may not have been good for the understanding of either American religion or Christianity more generally. As much as Americans may participate in a variety of parachurch activities and support them with their hard-earned dollars, statisticians of United States religious life continue to make claims about American religiosity on the basis of church attendance. America is, according to pollsters, the most religious of Western democracies because roughly 40 percent of its citizens are in church every Sunday. If this is true, and if it is truly as significant as many interpreters suggest, then finding out what these Americans do every Sunday and what goes into that decision to attend or the consequences of such participation might be worthwhile pursuits for religious historians and other religious scholars. But the academic hostility to religious forms and institutions, a sort of scholarly pietism, has left the church out. In turn, the study of evangelicalism has profited from this rejection of denominational and congregational life. The history of evangelicalism has thrived while denominational history has atrophied. Yet if the Christian religion involves rites, offices, and creeds, then saying these things don't matter does not make it so. Still, the construction of an evangelical identity has yielded the conviction that a faith freed from churchly affairs is *the* conservative expression of Christianity.

Either way, the expansion of interest in evangelicalism has been a mixed blessing. It has produced scholarship that obscures as much as it brings to light, and its assumptions about Christianity are as novel as the neo-evangelical project itself. Yet whatever one's judgment about the born-again history of the last twenty-five years, it is reasonable to assert that the neo-evangelical effort to reduce Christianity to bite-size portions in the interest of creating a Protestant party to rival the mainstream looks remarkably similar to the way religious historians have defined evangelicalism and read it back into the American past in order to make larger claims about a bigger constituency than denominational or church history allows, ironically, by conceiving of the Christian religion as a short set of doctrinal truths and devout activities outside the church.

2

Evangelicalism and the Revival of Social Science

Claiming that social scientists became enamored with evangelicalism at roughly the same time as religious historians is to state the obvious. The major books by American sociologists before 1980 reveal little awareness of evangelical Protestants as a segment of the United States' citizenry. This ignorance raises again the interesting question as to whether scholars were blind to something that today is widely regarded as a solid piece of American history and culture or whether evangelicalism itself had yet to make sufficient waves to generate scholarly interest.

Of the classic works in the sociology of religion, Will Herberg's *Protestant, Catholic, Jew* (1955) offers an interesting reading on early impressions of neo-evangelicalism and its effort to carve out a niche different from both mainline and fundamentalist Protestantism. Herberg's argument that religion in America lacked authenticity must have been heartening to evangelicals, since spokesmen such as Carl F. H. Henry, Billy Graham, and Harold John Ockenga had been saying something similar. "Americans think, feel, and act," Herberg wrote, "in terms quite obviously secularist at the very time that they exhibit every sign of a widespread religious revival. It is this secularism of a religious people . . . that constitutes the problem posed by the contemporary religious situation in America."[1] In this context, Herberg's brief reference to Billy Graham's revivals is noteworthy. Evangelists such as Graham and Charles Templeton, Herberg wrote, "for all the power and fervor of their crusades, still speak the language of individualistic piety, which in lesser men frequently degenerates into a smug and nagging moralism."[2] The evangelical initiative of the 1940s and 1950s, then, could not compare to the one form of evangelicalism that Herberg did recognize, namely, the revivals of the antebellum period that Christianized the United States by "bringing religion to the frontier."[3] For that reason, he showed no interest in evangelicalism beyond this passing reference to Graham and the "fringe" sects, which was an oblique reference to Pentecostals and fundamentalists.

A little over a decade later, a book written by prominent sociologists of religion was as silent on evangelicalism as was Herberg's. If *American Piety* (1968) by Rodney Stark and Charles Y. Glock was any indication, denominational analysis still dominated the field. Throughout the book, the statistics indicated that sociologists were exploring mainline Protestants and Roman Catholics. Several of their graphs did make room for a "sects" category in which they placed many of the largest denominations in the National Association of Evangelicals, from the Assemblies of God to the Christian and Missionary Alliance.[4] The one place in which Stark and Glock acknowledged a diversity within the Protestant fold other than along denominational lines was in a chapter on Americans switching denominations. Here they explored the traffic not simply among the denominations but also among liberal, moderate, and conservative Protestants. Yet these categories all referred to specific Protestant groups: Liberals were Congregationalists, Episcopalians, and Methodists; moderates were Presbyterians and Lutherans; conservatives were all Baptists. As quirky as this view of American religion may have been, it revealed once more that evangelicals had yet to show up on the social scientists' radar screen.

One last book to prove the point is Andrew M. Greeley's *Denominational Society* (1972). This Roman Catholic priest, who was one of the preeminent interpreters of American religion only four years prior to "the year of the evangelical," barely detected signs that 1976 would be such a watershed in the minds of journalists. Instead of discussing evangelicals, Greeley examined fundamentalists or "revivalist fundamentalists." At one point he did appear to differentiate between evangelicals and fundamentalists when he wrote, "The evangelical and fundamentalist groups on the right successfully resist the temptation to liberalism, but at a high price."[5] But this was basically a distinction without a difference. Greeley regarded fundamentalism as a recurring expression in American Christianity, a generic insistence that "religion and its ministers return to the doctrinal and political foundations on which the society was built."[6] When he turned to the uniqueness of evangelicalism, he located it, just as the seminary historians had, in the experiential Protestantism of revivalism. The First Great Awakening, Greeley argued, was a landmark event because it "inserted into the bloodstream of American Protestantism a mixture of enthusiasm, fundamentalism, and pietism." "The distance from George Whitefield to Billy Graham," he added, "is not, after all, such a great one."[7] Even here, however, Greeley also saw in Graham not so much a distinct Protestant type as a representative of American religiosity, a "high priest" of folk religion, offering "simple solutions to complex social problems."[8]

A decade later, social scientists would find it impossible to write about American religion without devoting a large section to evangelicalism. Again, part of what changed was the emergence of evangelicalism as a force in American electoral politics. Equally if not more important was a new generation of social scientists, many of whom would claim to be evangelical or to have grown up evangelical. For these academics, the public prominence of evangelicals was a gold mine. Almost overnight they possessed an insider's perspective on one of the hottest topics in social science. The work of these sociologists and political scientists deserves closer scrutiny, then, as another important piece in the construction of evangelicalism. Whatever their interests in the debates about public policy, the importance of religion to American society, or the definition of evangelicalism, these scholars were carrying on the work of the neo-evangelical leaders, for their social science was putting flesh on the bones of evangelical theology. This scholarship was (and still is) the study of evangelical adherents whom neo-evangelical leaders had persuaded to join their movement.

Conservative but Compromised

Religious historians, having accomplished the task of defining evangelicalism, left the more difficult task of describing evangelical adherents to social scientists. Historians, of course, engaged in some description, but their subjects rarely included the living. The work of charting the contemporary evangelical movement, the iceberg, as it were, underneath the tip of such circumstances as "the year of the evangelical," remained. David F. Wells and John D. Woodbridge edited a 1975 book whose ambitious title was *The Evangelicals: What They Believe, Who They Are, Where They Are Changing.*[9] But that book, like much of the literature emerging on the movement, was slim on the "who they are" part. Here the guild of social scientists stood prepared, and the particular sociologists and political scientists who rose to the occasion were themselves products of religious groups that identified at least loosely with modern American evangelicalism.

The initial exploration of evangelicals came from University of Virginia sociologist James Davison Hunter, himself a graduate of Gordon College, an evangelical liberal arts institution in Massachusetts. A student of one of the sociology of religion's masters, Peter Berger, Hunter used evangelicalism more as a way to apply his mentor's theories than to do justice to one of the most visible religious movements of the late twentieth century. Indeed, Hunter established the early social scientific line on evangelicals, regarding them as a seven-point underdog in their contest with modernity. If numbers alone could not interest researchers, and Hunter estimated that as many as 22 percent of Americans were born-again, evangelicalism was appealing simply as a conservative religion that had battled secularization better than other faiths.[10]

Hunter began by taking for granted the definition of evangelicalism that neo-evangelicals had been promoting for almost three decades. It was a conservative form of Protestantism, "deeply rooted in the theological tradition of the Reformation," Puritanism, and revivalism. At the core of evangelical identity was doctrine. Hunter's list included only three: "(1) the belief that the Bible is the inerrant Word of God, (2) the belief in the divinity of Christ, and (3) the belief in the efficacy of Christ's life, death, and physical resurrection for the salvation of the human soul."[11] This was a sparse set of affirmations, amazingly silent on the Trinity, for instance, and so conceivably giving the impression that evangelicals could be Unitarians of a Christ-only-God variety. The fact that Hunter did not have this in mind became clear when he identified four types of evangelicalism according to a social-scientific perspective. The "four major religious and theological traditions" in contemporary evangelicalism were the Baptist, Holiness-Pentecostal, Anabaptist, and Reformed-Confessional traditions. Although this way of defining evangelicalism allowed for greater diversity within the movement, thus avoiding a reduction of all parties to "conservative Protestantism," Hunter's analysis did follow neo-evangelicalism's approach in that these were precisely the denominational traditions that had been stitched together in the National Association of Evangelicals' quilt of church membership.[12] In addition, Hunter filled out his definition matter of factly with a recognition that evangelicals "behaviorally" required a conversion experience. Evangelism and missions were also parts of the group's identity. Even so, his goal of studying how evangelicals maintained their beliefs in the face of modernity and secularism tilted the balance of his definition toward the cognitive aspects of Christian faith.

Having cleared the thicket of religious boundaries, Hunter went deeper into the evangelical movement to see precisely which Americans found evangelicalism's tenets appealing or useful. Here he found curious details that did not match the impression created by the surging evangelical presence in American electoral politics. According to the data from which Hunter worked, evangelicals were predominantly white, often female, middle-aged, and married. The gender factor was not overwhelming, but women did comprise 20 percent more of the evangelical constituency than men. Geographically, evangelicals were more likely to be found in the rural South, and statistics indicated that evangelicals lagged behind other religious groups in income and education. Hunter found that evangelical households typically registered in the middle and lower rungs of annual income figures and that born-again Protestants composed the "only group that exceeds the average of the national sample *not* completing the eighth grade (8.6%) or high school (28.9%)."[13] These statistics contradicted the impression created by evangelical political involvement that the movement was evolving into a solidly middle-class, suburban, and better educated constituency. Even more challenging to the image of evangelicals climbing the social ladder were Hunter's findings on these Protestants' political orientations. The survey he used indicated that 30 percent of evangelicals were Republican, 43 percent Democrat, and 27 percent independent. In other words, Hunter's conclusion that the evangelical community "as a whole" was "perhaps more than any other major American religious body sociologically and geographically distant from the institutional structures and processes of modernity" almost entirely reversed the image of evangelicals as savvy media personalities and political strategists.[14] At the same time, the evidence reinforced the caricature of evangelicals as unsophisticated boobs.

Part of the reason for the disparity between Hunter's figures and the contemporaneous image of evangelicals on the rise was the survey data on which he relied. It came from a poll conducted in 1978 and 1979 by the Princeton Religious Research Center to be used by *Christianity Today*. Consequently, the data came from a time in between "the year of the evangelical" and the formation of the Moral Majority (later in 1979). As such, the number of respondents identifying themselves as evangelical may not have been as great during this time as when Hunter wrote, namely, after the victory of Ronald Reagan, when the evangelical bandwagon looked roomier. Plus, a survey conducted for the purpose of marketing a set of magazines could conceivably generate results different from one aimed at identifying a political constituency.[15]

Even so, the import of Hunter's first book was not to correct popular impressions of the stereotypical evangelical but to figure out the effects of modernity and secularization on faith. For this reason, evangelicalism provided a test case for the sociological study of religion, not an excuse to use sociology to understand evangelical Protestantism better. The baseline for Hunter's study was the effect modernity's "structural forces and symbols" had on a religious worldview. He was particularly interested in functional rationality, cultural pluralism, and structural pluralism, the building blocks of modernity, from sociology's perspective, as corrosive agents on faith. Hunter's main point concerned the plausibility of religion in a social setting in which faith is implausible. The "deinstitutionalization" of religion forced on modern men and women "an increasing number of choices" as to how to conduct their daily affairs. "The picture of the world presented in religious doctrine and symbols is not necessarily denied as a result of these structural tendencies." Instead of *denial*, the word Hunter chose to describe the effects of modernity on faith, in keeping with sociology's infelicitous jargon, was *disaffirmed*. This meant that religion "becomes less plausible in the minds of those confronting these forces." In the end, religious truth is reduced to a "matter of individual choice" or preference.[16]

Because evangelicals, as the demographics indicated, were farther removed from the institutional structures of modernity (e.g., the rural South), they were more conservative or "orthodox" than other religious groups in the United States. At least this was implied in Hunter's analysis. The better educated and the more affluent religious adherents became, the more likely they were to leave behind inherited religious convictions and practices. This premise helps to explain the significance of Hunter's dated data. If evangelicals were less backward, if they were more affluent, suburban, and Republican, his conception of the relationship between religion and orthodoxy would have required a different account. He would have needed to show how a believer could be socially modern and religiously traditional.

Even so, Hunter did detect ways in which evangelicals, despite their distance from the bulldozer of modernity, were making straight the path of equivocation. "Cognitive bargaining" was the name he gave to the process by which evangelicals accommodated their beliefs and practices to the modern situation. The hearty and sober understanding of vocation that informed Puritanism, according to Hunter, had thinned out under evangelical auspices into a set of "principles," "rules," "codes," and "guidelines" for successful Christian living.[17] He also found that evangelicals had adopted a posture of civility when confronted with a society in which their views were marginal. Hunter opined that the sentiment "No offense, I am an evangelical" had replaced an older outlook that was "rough-hewn, stern, and ungracious." Even in the way evangelicals tried to convert nonbelievers Hunter detected a discomfort with historical Christian notions about sin and hell.[18] Evangelicalism's cognitive bargaining also involved a turn toward the therapeutic. The claims of the gospel, Hunter argued, had acquired a new emphasis on "achieving 'psychological balance' and 'emotional maturity.'"[19] Although the subjective turn toward psychological wholeness among evangelicals was still oriented toward serving God and loving neighbors, Hunter believed that it had nevertheless "displaced" Protestantism's "traditional asceticism." As such, "the old-style nineteenth-century Evangelical, rigidly ascetic, brashly intolerant of other faiths, and somewhat irrational about his approach to spiritual life, has given way to the new-style Evangelical, technical about his faith, civilly intolerant with those of other faiths, and contemporary."[20]

This accommodative spirit of late-twentieth-century evangelicalism became the subject of Hunter's second book, a study of evangelical adherents who were not so distant from the forces of modernization. From the outset, *Evangelicalism: The Coming Generation* (1987) promised to be a depressing book for those who looked to born-again Protestantism as the lone defender of Protestant orthodoxy. Hunter's argument, in a nutshell, was that in its theology, understanding of work, morality and the self, teaching on the family, and politics, evangelicalism had begun to change significantly, so much that "the world of the coming generation of Evangelicals may bear little resemblance to the Evangelical world of many previous generations."[21] In other words, the "costs and consequences" of evangelicalism's survival as a form of religious orthodoxy were clearly unfavorable. At the same time, Hunter conceded his ambivalence about these changes. "I am not convinced that all of the changes . . . are all that bad," he wrote in his preface, but "neither am I convinced that they are all that good."[22] Hunter would leave such value judgments to the evangelical leadership. Interestingly enough, aside from Os Guiness, whose endorsement on the back cover praised Hunter for his contribution to the subject of "religion and the future of the republic," the Gordon-Conwell theologian David F. Wells was the only evangelical gatekeeper to endorse Hunter's book, a work that foreshadowed Wells's own assessment of evangelicalism's fortunes a few years later in *No Place for Truth* (1993).

The cracks in evangelicalism's foundations, from Hunter's evidence, were most noticeable in the realms of work and morality and the self. He concluded that "the Protestant legacy of austerity and ascetic self-denial is virtually obsolete in the larger Evangelical culture and is nearly extinct for a large percentage of the coming generation of Evangelicals."[23] "Virtually" and "nearly" gave Hunter some wiggle room, but these were by far the gloomiest of his assessments. In doctrinal matters, his findings showed slippage, thanks to "philosophical rationalism, even shades of positivism,"[24] in such teachings as biblical inerrancy, salvation and hell, and the social gospel. But here Hunter conceded that evangelicals had maintained "cognitive boundaries" even if not perfectly. On the family front, evangelicals continued to emphasize the institution's importance, while they also showed increasing dependence, along with the rest of American society, on social and psychological experts to maintain functional relationships. In politics, Hunter's data indicated an older generation still motivated by conservative causes, though more tolerant of other perspectives, and a younger generation moving to the left.[25] Each of these changes added up to a movement that in Hunter's estimation was still vital and worthy of respect in its effort to preserve orthodoxy yet resembled "less and less what earlier generations understood" this orthodoxy to be.[26]

For Hunter's purposes, evangelicalism functioned as a case of orthodoxy under siege. This form of Protestantism had once possessed what he called "binding address." "The strength of culture . . . is measured by the power of its address on people." Without it, "the moral energy necessary to motivate men and integrate communities" disappears.[27] From the sixteenth century until the latter decades of the nineteenth century, Protestantism maintained such "binding address" on its adherents. Fundamentalists perpetuated these claims through a sectarian circling of the wagons. Contemporary evangelicalism, however, was showing signs that the older zeal and combativeness conflicted with tolerance and civility. Hunter conceded that fundamentalism's defensiveness may have also reflected the loss of binding address for conservative Protestantism. But in evangelicalism the harm was nearing completion. Hunter concluded by drawing an analogy between evangelicalism and the pilgrim of John Bunyan's *Pilgrim's Progress:*

[W]hat our pilgrim (Evangelicalism) endures and Bunyan's does not is a long and sustained season in the Labyrinths of Modernity. Not only does he emerge a little dizzy and confused, but out of the experience our traveler is transformed. The pilgrim becomes a tourist. Though still headed toward the Celestial Country, he is now traveling with less conviction, less confidence about his path, and is perhaps more vulnerable to the worldly distractions encountered by Bunyan's pilgrim.[28]

As clever as this analogy was, Hunter's analysis of evangelicalism did beg a significant question: Was evangelicalism actually the modern equivalent of orthodox Protestantism? By assuming that evangelical Protestantism was the conservative option among American Protestants, Hunter missed internal factors within the post–World War II movement that may have been as responsible for evangelicalism's cognitive bargaining as modernity was. Of course, his studies were more concerned with larger questions about religion and modernization. This explains why the last three chapters of *Evangelicalism: The Coming Generation* explored the maintenance and preservation of orthodoxy in modern times, an examination that involved non-Christian religions and also planted seeds for Hunter's next book, *Culture Wars: The Struggle to Define America* (1991). Consequently, even though this University of Virginia sociologist who had once studied at an evangelical liberal arts college may have had personal reasons for understanding the evangelical movement better, his work gave evangelicalism's internal struggles broader significance.

Even so, by being one of the first sociologists of religion to study evangelicalism as another piece of the American religious mosaic and, more important, by accepting the convention that evangelicalism stood for Protestant orthodoxy, Hunter confirmed the impression that was quickly taking root throughout the academic study of religion in the United States: Evangelicalism was *the* conservative faith.

Conservative and They Vote

Because Hunter's interests were in the survival of orthodox faith in the modern world, his books on evangelicalism were slanted to the movement's theology and religious practice. Yet he could not ignore the political resurgence of evangelical Protestants, since he was writing during the Reagan presidency. In his first book, *American Evangelicalism*, Hunter explained the resurgence of evangelical political activism during the 1970s and 1980s as one of the chief examples of conservative Protestant resistance to modernity. "Modernity creates conditions in which 'immorality,' from the Evangelical perspective, is structurally engendered." In other words, "modernity fosters 'sin,'" and evangelicals were clearly on record as being opposed to such behavior. Hunter added that such wickedness, in the evangelical outlook, jeopardized "the moral covenant widely believed to exist between God and America." By opposing sin at the ballot box, evangelicals were standing up to the forces of secularization.[29]

In his second book, *Evangelicalism: The Coming Generation*, Hunter went somewhat deeper to comment on evangelical politics from a longer historical perspective. Organizations such as the Moral Majority, he concluded, were different from previous evangelical initiatives. Before, evangelicals had not been inclined to translate their beliefs into political action. But throughout the twentieth century, evangelicals had been eager to preserve a certain form of culture, one that was moral and devout. As such, the Religious Right was part of a longer tradition of "political and cultural intolerance."[30] This politically conservative posture thus functioned as the bascline for Hunter's charting of the next generation of evangelicals' capitulation to the forces of tolerance and civility. Whether it was a form of declension or not, evangelicalism as a form of conservatism was running out of gas, as evidenced by the upcoming generation's politics.

Of course, writing during the heyday of evangelical political success, Hunter could not avoid the Religious Right, even though it was more or less beside the point. However lackluster the sociology of religion's analysis of evangelical politics, political scientists were quick to fill in the gaps in Hunter's conclusions. In fact, the dramatic influx of religion into the public square provided students of American politics with a cache of data in need of interpretation. In a series of books and articles, the four horsemen of the evangelical electorate, John C. Green of the University of Akron, James L. Guth of Furman University, Corwin E. Smidt of Calvin College, and Lyman A. Kellstedt of Wheaton College, discovered a mother lode of statistics that they believed required political scientists to rethink their assumptions about the fate of religion in modern society. They also reinforced the conservative identity of evangelicalism, this time with statistical precision.[31]

The key to their success in carving out a professional niche for their study of evangelical politics was the meticulous detail they added to the study of religion and American politics. Prior to 1990, the major social science questionnaires did not make adequate provision for religion. This is not to say that social scientists asked no questions about the faith of American citizens. But they generally followed the scholarly consensus in thinking that if their questions left room for Protestant, Catholic, and Jewish responses, they had done an adequate job. Green and his colleagues recognized early on that the Protestant category did not do justice to evangelicalism. Consequently, one of their first triumphs was developing measures for distinguishing among Protestants and conducting surveys that reflected differences between mainline and evangelical Protestantism.[32]

In the fall of 1993, these scholars surveyed roughly twenty-eight hundred Americans on the basis of core beliefs and affiliation with sectarian religious movements. The markers of core belief included commitment to personal evangelism, the inspiration and inerrancy of the Bible, life after death through faith in Christ, and the applicability of the term "born-again Christian." A respondent's proclivity to sectarianism depended on the degree to which he or she identified with the labels "evangelical," "fundamentalist," "charismatic," or "Pentecostal." These questions yielded a conceptualization of evangelicalism that was both scientific and reinforced the movement's image as the preservation of historic Protestantism. At the core of evangelical identity, according to this survey data, was the importance of personal evangelism, belief in eternal punishment or reward, salvation through Christ alone, the authority and reliability of the Bible, and conversion. Also important to being an evangelical was actually saying so, that is, self-applying the label.[33]

The four political scientists were not simply trying to show that their peers in political science had been remarkably ignorant of Protestant diversity; they were trying to show that faith correlated directly to political behavior. What is more, these political scientists were convinced that by adding greater precision to survey questions, they could identify evangelicals and determine how they voted. For instance, on the issue of abortion, Green and his colleagues provided numbers that showed that the most committed evangelicals were opposed to it and tended to vote Republican on the basis of that conviction. The same was true for the politics of homosexuality. "The most committed Evangelicals oppose gay rights and tend to be conservative Republicans," they wrote, "who turned out in large numbers to vote for Bush in 1988."[34] To some, this sort of conclusion, coming as it did in the mid-1990s, may have looked like the usual social scientific quantification of the obvious. In this particular case, the links these political scientists traced between evangelicalism and the GOP did little but reinforce the conservative credentials of born-again Protestants. Yet because these results came packaged with the kind of statistics that political scientists preferred, Green, Guth, Smidt, and Kellstedt throughout the 1990s continued to trumpet the conservative bona fides of evangelicals.

The timing of this data was ironic for a couple reasons. First, the publication of these interpretations coincided mainly with the Clinton presidency. Instead of being able to weigh in with their findings on the GOP's success, these political scientists were forced to explain the importance of evangelicals to the Republican party despite Clinton's ability to outmaneuver his religious foes in a number of key contests. Yet Green and his colleagues continued to argue, on the basis of evangelical beliefs and votes, that religion was important to electoral politics. This scholarship's timing was also ironic in that not all evangelicals marched lockstep with the Moral Majority or the Christian Co-alition. In fact, the faculty at the evangelical colleges where two of the men taught would likely have viewed the Religious Right with skepticism. At the same time, evangelical media outlets such as *Christianity Today* did not endorse the sort of politics that these scholars believed were highly correlated to conserva-tive theology. In addition, some evangelicals on the left, such as Jim Wallis, were quite vocal in distancing themselves from Ralph Reed, Pat Robertson, and Jerry Falwell. These examples pointed to a visible and articulate evangelical party of dissent and suggested that some evangelicals did not vote Republican. One of the more arresting implications of these findings was the notion that the less inclined an evangelical was to vote for a GOP candidate, the more likely such a person was to be less religious. In other words, conservative politics was emerging as an indication of evangelical devotion.

Yet despite these anomalies, Green, Guth, Smidt, and Kellstedt found editors who were eager for their evaluations of presidential and midterm election results. The appeal at the *Christian Century* must have been in part a way to keep tabs on sectarian Protestants and their meddling in public affairs. The only victory for Republicans in the 1990s came in 1994 when the GOP took control of Congress. Green and his colleagues stressed the importance of evangelicals to Republican success and reported that the Christian Right "probably mobilized 4 million activists and reached 50 million voters."[35] It was not a victory for "angry white men" but for the Religious Right, since this was the first election in which a majority of evangelicals identified themselves as Republican. Even in Republican defeat, evangelicals showed their political clout. In 1992, when George Bush lost to Bill Clinton, the spin was that the loss would have been greater had the Republicans abandoned family values.[36] Likewise, the election in 1998, when Democrats made history by gaining House seats in an off-year election, showed the Religious Right's weaknesses but not its demise. The Democratic victory was "just a defeat, not a debacle. The Religious Right remains a potent force in Republican politics."[37]

These political scientists' articles for *First Things* said less about the resilience of evangelical politics and more about the importance of religion for public affairs, a conclusion that fit well with the journal's editorial policy. In 1992, Green, Guth, Smidt, and Kellstedt faced the difficulty of explaining a successful presidential campaign that insisted, "It's the economy, stupid!" Clinton's election suggested that markets mattered more than values, an implication at odds with these political scientists' arguments. Their response was, "It's the culture, stupid!" The point was that religion and values had always been key to the formation of political parties in the United States and that the 1992 contest did not upset this pattern but actually confirmed it. The problem was that most interpreters of the election had yet to look beyond pocketbook issues to the emergence of "more-religious" and "less-religious" coalitions.[38] The same stress on the importance of culture and religion came through in their assessment of the 1996 presidential election, another apparent defeat for evangelicals and victory for economics over religion. Green, Guth, Smidt, and Kellstedt conceded the importance of economic factors in the results but added that cultural values were more basic, the presuppositions, as it were, with which voters regarded the economy. "This emphasis on values will influence the ways in which short-term economic forces are interpreted politically," they wrote, with modernists, the "less-religious," evaluating the economy "from the perspective of social reform" and the traditionalists, the "more-religious," assessing it on the basis of "personal responsibility and social order."[39]

In an election that was more agreeable for evangelicals, the 2000 highly contested victory for George W. Bush, the closeness of the election prevented glib pronouncements about the influence of the Religious Right. But these political scientists, following the lead of Hunter's book *Culture Wars*, interpreted the division in the United States between its blue and red districts in terms of the modernist-fundamentalist controversy. "Clearly, there is a new religious order in American electoral politics," they concluded, one in which conservative Protestants voted opposite modernist Protestants.[40] In effect, the conservatism of evangelicals had prompted these social scientists to employ the language of theological controversy to explain electoral politics in the United States.

Although the case these scholars made for the importance of religion for voting behavior was more interesting than their observations about the Religious Right's reasons for voting, which were fairly obvious, the net effect of their writings was to attach the label conservative all the more firmly to the evangelical movement, almost to the point of making it look like the extreme right. Of all the analogies these political scientists used to describe evangelicals' influence, the one perhaps least flattering was that the Religious Right was the Republicans' most conservative core constituency. The Religious Right was "a significant voting bloc, and is probably as important to the [Republican] party as black Protestants, Jews, and secular voters are to the Democrats."[41] This comparison was intended as a compliment, a testimony to evangelicals' strength, a constituency without which Republicans would necessarily fail. But this comparison also removed chances for judging evangelicalism as a movement of moderate and sensible proportions. Ironically, it rendered evangelicals as little more than just one more disgruntled interest group to which the major political parties were captive. Clearly, the reputation for orthodoxy, when transferred to the political sphere, came with disadvantages. Despite that inconvenience, the study of the Religious Right by political scientists added another floor in the construction of evangelicalism.

Conservative but Nice

With the work of productive political scientists throughout the 1990s firmly fixing evangelicalism on the right end of the cultural and political spectrum, the movement could well have profited from a treatment that showed how mainstream and moderate it was. Hopes for such an approach were realized in two impressive books by Christian Smith, a sociologist of religion at the University of North Carolina. In some respects, his *American Evangelicalism: Embattled and Thriving* (1998) and *Christian America? What Evangelicals Really Want* (2000) culminated a period of social scientific investigation of evangelicals started by Hunter. Smith's books concluded an almost twenty-year effort by social scientists to chart the strengths, size, and character of the movement hatched almost a half century earlier by the neo-evangelical movement. Although Smith's aim was to portray evangelicals in less garish hues, the picture he drew still enhanced the movement's reputation as *the* conservative wing of American Protestantism.

In his first book, *American Evangelicalism,* Smith simply attempted to gauge how the movement was faring. A number of books written by observers of and participants in the movement had begun to question whether evangelical Christianity was actually living up to its reputation as a repository of orthodox Protestantism. Smith's findings, based on in-depth interviews and national surveys, revealed that evangelicalism was still the engine that could, this time with a lot more horsepower. "Contemporary American evangelicalism," he wrote, "is thriving. It is more than alive and well. Indeed, we will see . . . that it appears to be the strongest of the major Christian traditions in the United States today."[42] Smith's measures included doctrinal affirmations, the salience of faith to evangelicalism's adherents, confidence in convictions, participation in church life, recruitment of new believers through evangelism, and retention of group members. The importance of correct theology for this study's respondents was especially useful for proving the conservatism of evangelicalism. "Fully ninety-seven percent of evangelicals," Smith found, "believe that the Bible is God-inspired and without error." Born-again Protestants were equally committed to a lower estimate of human nature, though only 34 percent agreed to describe it as "sinful," with 48 percent preferring "good and sinful." Numbers were high for those who believed that only faith in Christ could provide salvation (96 percent), while they dipped some on the question of moral absolutes; 75 percent affirmed the existence of such moral standards.[43] Indicative of evangelicals' theological soundness was one woman's response in an interview:

> As an evangelical, I believe that the whole Bible is true. I believe that Jesus Christ is the Son of God, and that He came into the world to save us, and He died on the cross and rose again from the dead, and He is sitting at our Father's right hand. I also believe it's important to stand up for what you believe.[44]

Smith then attempted to explain the resilience of evangelicals' conservative convictions. Contrary to what Hunter argued, that the forces of modernity were wearing away evangelical resolve, Smith argued that precisely in wrestling with cultural pluralism born-again Protestants were thriving. This involved a fairly dense exposition of various sociological theories. The one that emerged the winner was the "subcultural identity" interpretation of religious strength. What it proposed was a way for faith to persist in modern settings thanks to its capacity to embed *"itself in subcultures that offer satisfying morally orienting collective identities which provide adherents with meaning and belonging."* According to Smith, this theory went on to explain that a pluralistic society could enhance a religious tradition's strength by forcing it to employ *"the cultural tools needed to create both clear distinction from and significant engagement and tension with other relevant outgroups, short of becoming genuinely countercultural."*[45] This way of conceiving evangelicalism was a stroke of genius because it made it possible to interpret evangelical dissent as a sign of the movement's strength. If born-again Protestants were no longer certain of their religious convictions, it was a sign of healthy tension in the movement. Even so, Smith recognized plenty of features in those whom he surveyed that demonstrated a resilient faith, including a heightened sense of boundaries with non-evangelicals, a commitment to objective truth, an awareness of "moral superiority," a different way of life, a drive to convert nonbelievers, and a feeling of being displaced by hostile forces.[46] These factors added up to an evangelical movement that had constructed and maintained "its collective identity largely by its members drawing symbolic boundaries that create distinctions between themselves and relevant outgroups."[47]

Smith did point out areas in which evangelicals faced obstacles. Their sense of identity could at times be so imposing that it came across to other Americans as a threat. He found that evangelicals were "generally not leaving particularly good impressions on those they are proselytizing," nor did they know "how to communicate their message in a manner that will be well-received."[48] This was a point to which Smith devoted his second book on evangelicals, *Christian America?* As he indicated in his introduction to this book, "Many nonevangelicals view evangelical Christians with deep suspicion, as enemies of freedom and liberal democracy."[49] Smith responded to this perception with surveys of evangelicals regarding politics, cultural pluralism, education, and gender relations that indicated that these believers were "diverse, complex, ambivalent, and inconsistent," uninterested in "cultural warfare."[50] Nevertheless, Smith concluded in *American Evangelicalism* that "far from necessarily undermining the strength of orthodox faith, modernity creates the conditions in which traditional religion may thrive."[51] And even if the tension that conservative Protestants felt over the secularization of American society sometimes resulted in evangelical leaders who spoke of a "Christian America," rank-and-file born-again Protestants were simply "thinking about morality and faithful witness in their personal lives."[52] As such, evangelicalism was a conservative religion, not a political agenda.

The social scientific study of evangelicalism had come a long way since its inception in the early 1980s with the work of James Davison Hunter. What he began as a means of testing the viability of orthodox religion in a context of modernization and secularization grew into various testimonials, all of them cloaked in scientific garb, to evangelical Protestantism's conservatism and vitality. The proverbial icing on the cake came with a 2002 book from two political scientists at Calvin College, James M. Penning and Corwin E. Smidt, *Evangelicalism: The Next Generation*. With the advantage of almost twenty years intervening between their own work and Hunter's first book, these social scientists set out to see whether Hunter's findings, which indicated a decline of adherence among evangelical college students, were in fact the case. As they indicated in their conclusion, their data provided "reassurance to many in the evangelical world, particularly leaders of evangelical institutions of higher education," because it indicated "stability over time."[53] In fact, the theological views of evangelical college students in the 1990s mirrored those of students and adults from the early 1980s.

These results allowed Penning and Smidt to make a number of generalizations and comment on debates within evangelicalism. For example, they acknowledged that certain developments within the movement suggested that it was losing its center as traditional, and reformist evangelicals squared off on various theological and practical fronts. But these authors ended up fairly optimistic about evangelicalism's future. Their reasons involved the ongoing sense among its adherents that evangelicalism constituted a subculture. During the middle decades of the twentieth century, evangelicals considered themselves "a minority, outside the mainstream of American social and cultural life." Evangelical college students in the 1990s also believed they were part of a religious subculture. As such, the future of evangelical Protestantism was bright because the tension that accompanies struggles between minority and majority points of view and ways of life has tended in the case of conservative Protestantism to strengthen its identity. Consequently, evangelicalism's capacity to authenticate faith through individual choice and association with like-minded believers "should provide American evangelicals with grounds for optimism concerning the future of their tradition."[54]

One of the remarkable features of Penning and Smidt's treatment of evangelicalism involved the use of the word *tradition*. The study of born-again Protestantism throughout the 1980s and 1990s, combining the labors of religious historians and social scientists, hammered away at evangelicalism's status as an orthodox expression of Christianity, thus making "tradition" a fitting description of the movement. Even so, this was an ironic choice of words for a form of Christianity that, owing to its dependence on revivalism and pietism, was in fact hostile to tradition. Penning and Smidt were alert to this when they concluded that evangelicalism's strength lay precisely in its appeal to individual choice rather than a reliance on patterns of ascription or inheritance, which characterizes traditional religions. Unlike older forms of Christianity that pass on the faith to new generations through the family and churchly means of birth, baptism, catechism, and worship, evangelicalism locates the primary mechanism of religious identity in the sovereign individual, a move that is about as modern and antitraditional as can be. Still, evangelicalism's theological fragmentation was not enough to raise doubts about the movement's conservative credentials. Instead, with the assistance of graphs and statistical methods, social scientists proved that evangelical Christianity was as orthodox and traditional a faith as modern times had to offer.

The Evangelical Friendly Academy

In the 1940s, when the leaders of the emerging neo-evangelical movement called for a scholarly renaissance among evangelicals to rescue the demise of Western civilization, men such as Harold John Ockenga and Carl F. H. Henry did not likely have in mind the social scientific study of religion. Indeed, the establishment of seminaries such as Fuller in Pasadena indicated that these evangelicals were pinning their hopes on traditionally religious subjects such as theology and the study of the Bible. Yet Mark A. Noll, in his provocative book *The Scandal of the Evangelical Mind,* identified social scientists as the scholars showing some hope of correcting evangelicalism's anti-intellectual reputation. Noll had in mind specifically the political scientists who had used "sophisticated techniques from the academy" to explore a subject—"the actual political behavior of evangelicals and how it differs from those in other religious traditions"—that the church and academy had ignored.[55]

The contrast between neo-evangelicalism of the 1940s and evangelical scholarship of the last two decades of the twentieth century is important to keep in mind for reasons central to this book. After World War II until the 1970s, evangelicals constantly looked over their shoulders to see who was going to accuse them of fundamentalism. Some changes in perception occurred during these years, but the greatest public relations victory for evangelicals was having academics with respectable degrees saying in equally reputable scholarly publications that born-again Protestants composed the orthodox party, the embodiment of Protestant tradition, in the religious life of the United States. What made this coup all the more arresting was that the academic imprimatur of evangelicalism occurred during a time when born-again Protestants were increasingly critical of American universities and colleges for abandoning the nation's religious heritage in favor of multiculturalism and political correctness.

The ironies accompanying the recent social scientific and historical scholarship on evangelicalism could well raise questions about the rigor and hostility of the secular academy. The religious identity—mostly evangelical—of many of the scholars who have made the strongest case for evangelicalism's conservatism invites other questions about the obstacles facing Christian scholars in the apparently antireligious university. Nevertheless, as interesting as evangelical scholarship may be for assessing the ethos of American universities and colleges, the more important point concerns how a group of social scientists and religious historians not only created evangelicalism as one of the more forceful tools of analysis within the contemporary academic study of religion but also vindicated the efforts of neo-evangelical leaders from a previous generation. By measuring the beliefs and behaviors of Americans who identified with the evangelical label, these academics demonstrated how successful the coalition-building strategy of the 1940s was in creating a religious group to rival the mainline churches. In addition, by polling the average evangelical on the core doctrines of their faith, these social scientists established that born-again Protestants were the rightful heirs to Protestant orthodoxy. Whether these are the best ways of assessing a religious movement's conservatism, the academic rigor undergirding these findings clearly worked to evangelicals' benefit in ways that evangelistic crusades, Christian musicians, and evangelical publishing firms had not.

3

Measuring Evangelicalism One Question at a Time

To discern the strength of Lutheranism in the United States, someone might reasonably go to the statistics of the largest American Lutheran denominations. There a student of American Christianity could find membership statistics, the number of congregations, information on regional structures, financial data, and even reference to Lutheran creeds and forms of worship. When attempting to discover the influence and significance of evangelicalism, a researcher faces an altogether different situation. Because the movement is not ecclesial—in fact, no particular denomination in the United States claims to be the Evangelical Church of America—a scholar needs to figure out a different strategy for assessing evangelicals' significance. Of course, a historian or sociologist could look at the records of any number of born-again Protestant parachurch organizations, if such documents were accessible to the public. But because of a lack of a formal mechanism for belonging to evangelicalism, the subject of born-again Protestantism in the United States requires measurements other than what religion scholars typically use to study churches. Opinion polls and national surveys have generally been the solution to this predicament. The standard practice, as reflected in scholarly articles and monographs, is to devise a set of questions whose responses will identify people belonging to the evangelical camp. To be sure, to be fully scientific, those who survey the American public need to conduct polls in an impartial manner. Consequently, a poll examining the religious views of citizens of Wheaton, Illinois, would not necessarily be representative of the entire American population. At the same time, surveys prepared to allow researchers to correlate religious convictions to social views need to be crunched in ways that make computing skills essential. Still, arguably the most important part of collecting survey data is developing an adequate set of questions, questions that somehow get at the distinctive ideas and practices of a religious group but do so in a way that does not lead those answering.

The apparent objectivity of recent opinion polling on religion in the United States has contributed mightily to the impression that evangelical Protestantism is one of the most influential, fastest growing, and conservative faiths in the nation. Ever since the 1970s, when pollsters and social scientists began to ask questions that probed beyond the standard Protestant-Catholic-Jew categories, evangelicalism has claimed between twenty and forty million American citizens. The curious aspect of these recent efforts to count evangelicals is the assumption that asking a few questions about the inerrancy of the Bible or a conversion experience will uncover those born-again believers formerly hidden by blunter survey instruments. What if, for instance, pollsters were as intent on discovering, to use the example that opened this chapter, the Lutheran presence in the United States? What if telephone surveys asked respondents about the real presence of Christ in the Lord's Supper or about the imputed righteousness of Christ? Here the findings might not be all that encouraging, either to researchers hoping to chart a Lutheran element in American society or to Lutheran church officials who believed their pastors were training church members well, for the relatively more complicated teachings of the Lutheran confessions would likely not be as intelligible to the American public. Neither would questions about Lutheran doctrine and practices generate the numbers that questions about the general and fairly domesticated articles of evangelical faith do. This example helps to illustrate another way in which evangelicalism is a construction, this time of pollsters and the science of public opinion. No good way exists for counting evangelicals other than surveys. Those curious about the appeal of evangelicalism are stuck with interviewers, multiple-choice questions, and regression analysis. These tools for measuring public opinion have created an evangelical identity in two important ways. First, opinion polls and surveys use questions that academics or pollsters devise. In effect, these scholars arrive arbitrarily at an idea of what the Bible teaches, without reference to what theologians teach or churches confess. Second, these measurements of public opinion apparently chart a segment of the population that is evangelical. These statistics can appear very impressive and have undoubtedly influenced politicians and religious enterprises in search of Americans who share certain values. Still, the measurement of public opinion is a strange way to show the strength of a religion that emphasizes the supernatural workings of God on the human heart and that divine truth matters more than human ingenuity.

In Search of Evangelical America

The rapidity with which pollsters began to track evangelical beliefs and practices after 1976 was pronounced. It might be useful to remember what kinds of questions about religion sociologists of religion asked Americans during the earlier decades of the twentieth century. One of the earliest and most frequently cited studies of American devotion based in part on survey questions is Robert S. Lynd and Helen Merrell Lynd's *Middletown: A Study in American Culture* (1929). What is interesting to notice in this account of middle America, conducted in Muncie, Indiana, is the sort of beliefs that attracted the Lynds' attention in the section on religion. Rather than using the multiple-choice format common in later opinion polls, the Lynds relied on true-false questions. The questions they asked of children were: (1) "Christianity is the one true religion and all peoples should be converted to it";

(2) "The Bible is a sufficient guide to all the problems of modern life"; (3) "Jesus Christ was different from every other man who ever lived in being entirely perfect"; and (4) "The purpose of religion is to prepare people for the hereafter."[1] The Lynds also added a few questions to gain further insight into religious life in Muncie: (1) "What are the thoughts and plans that give you courage to go on when thoroughly discouraged?" (2) "How often have you thought of Heaven during the past month in this connection?" (3) "What difference would it make in your daily life if you became convinced that there is no loving God caring for you?"[2] Although the Lynds' conclusion, based on the responses to these questions, was somewhat gloomy—"one infers that doubts and uneasiness among individuals may be greater than a generation ago"—the numbers showed widespread belief in the exclusiveness of Christianity (83 percent of the boys, 92 percent of the girls), the reliability of the Bible (58 percent of the boys, 68 percent of the girls), the uniqueness of Christ (76 percent of the boys, 81 percent of the girls), and the reality of heaven and hell (48 percent of the boys, 57 percent of the girls).[3]

A sequel to the Middletown project, conducted fifty years later by a team of sociologists, illustrates that the generic questions used by the Lynds continued to dominate the construction of opinion polls and surveys. *All Faithful People* (1983), by Theodore Caplow (University of Virginia), Howard M. Bahr (Brigham Young University), and Bruce A. Chadwick (Brigham Young University), was a follow-up to the Middletown study and was devoted to the religion of Muncie's inhabitants. Although evangelical Protestantism had grabbed national headlines and was apparently experiencing a revival during the same years (1976–81) that these researchers conducted their investigation, an older orientation that divided the religious landscape among Protestants, Catholics, and Jews still prevailed. To be sure, for a comparison of results to be meaningful, Caplow and his associates needed to ask the same questions. So, for instance, the questions put to Muncie's 1970s high school students to measure orthodoxy still involved views about Christ, the Bible, Christianity's supremacy, and the afterlife. The headings under which the new team of researchers placed these questions did reflect an effort to account for the growing prominence of evangelicalism. The questions about Christ and the Bible were listed under "orthodoxy." The one on the afterlife measured "religion's objective." And the query as to whether Christianity was the one true religion to which all people needed to convert was in a section on "evangelicalism."[4] Never mind that adherents of Roman Catholicism, Protestantism, and Eastern Orthodoxy would have had little trouble answering this question affirmatively as well. The conviction that Christianity was exclusively true by the late 1970s had become a belief associated with evangelical Protestantism. The one question that indicated that evangelicalism was a factor in Muncie was a repetition from the 1924 survey, not a new one that asked with greater precision about differences among Protestants. As such, this study was one of the last gasps of an older approach to surveying American public opinion on religion.

The new order of opinion polling that replaced the older paradigm of Protestant-Catholic-Jew emerged at roughly the same time that the team of researchers was updating the Middletown study. One indication of the newer perspective was the partnership between George Gallup Jr. and *Christianity Today* in a 1979 poll that measured levels of religious belief and practice among Americans. Only a decade or so before, the neo-evangelical editors of *Christianity Today* had been forced to track their movement's strength by reading between the lines of the major denominations' statistics. For instance, in a 1967 news item, the first that the magazine devoted to Gallup's findings, evangelicalism was a black hole in the leading polling organization's universe. The breakdown of American religion still followed the predictable lines of denominational affiliation, with Episcopalians outdistancing Presbyterians, Lutherans, Methodists, and Baptists on measures of education, employment, and income.[5] These results mirrored those of the Middletown project. But by the late 1970s, when, according to Dean M. Kelley, conservative churches were growing and evangelicals were becoming more prominent in public life, the old survey questions about denominational affiliation and status were much less plausible.[6] By then evangelicalism appeared to be a phenomenon that pollsters would need to chart if their comments on American society were to appear reliable. The partnership between Gallup and *Christianity Today* was more than coincidental; it signaled the demise of the mainline churches and the rising fortunes of born-again Protestants, a group that to outsiders appeared to be full of promise.

Of course, George Gallup Jr. was no stranger to public opinion and could clearly spot changes in American religion that demanded certain adjustments in his own endeavors. Gallup's father, George Gallup (1901–84), had been a pioneer in gauging public sentiment and turning that information into a marketable commodity. Gallup Sr. had started in journalism and then moved to advertising. He combined both fields for a Ph.D. dissertation at the University of Iowa in which he developed a method of charting newspaper readers' interests. For a while, Gallup Sr. taught journalism at Drake, Northwestern, and Columbia Universities. But he returned to advertising by the 1930s and developed the American Institute of Public Opinion, an organization that applied the techniques of market research to people's perceptions of social and political life in the United States. In 1958, that institute became the Gallup Organization.

George Gallup Jr. was the one responsible for channeling his father's advertising and market research endeavors in spiritual directions. A graduate of Princeton University, where he majored in religion and wrote a senior thesis on the reasons people gave for believing in God, Gallup Jr. had planned on studying for the priesthood in the Protestant Episcopal Church. For a summer after college he even taught at a summer Bible school for African-Americans in the South. But when offered a job in the family business and granted the freedom to measure public opinion on religious questions, Gallup Jr. gave up on the priesthood to pursue what he would later consider another form of ministry. As he explained in one interview, "The most important purpose of polls is to explore people's response to God and indicate ways to strengthen that response."[7] When asked by his partners at *Christianity Today* about his own religious preference, Gallup responded, "I am evangelically oriented. I feel very strongly that a conversion experience is absolutely focal, whether it is gradual or a sudden growth experience." He added, "I would say I tend to be orthodox. In terms of creation, for example, I accept the authority of the Bible, but I would stop short of a literal interpretation."[8]

Gallup's self-understanding may have been a factor in his decision to collaborate on the *Christianity Today*–Gallup Poll.

He was a mainline Protestant with a clear sense of devotion who had little acquaintance with evangelicalism. Through polling he discovered believers with a similar zeal and sense of religious purpose. Gallup's own devotion may also explain why the poll he conducted jointly with *Christianity Today* used a definition of evangelicalism that was less doctrinal than the one that either historians or social scientists applied. The 1979 poll actually reflected two outlooks. One was the generic aim of the Gallup Organization: "What are the beliefs of the American people? Which specific Christian doctrines do they accept and which do they reject? How does this affect their social and political and ethical views?"[9] The editors and likely the marketing staff of *Christianity Today* supplied the other point of view: "Who are the evangelicals? Where are they to be found? How pervasive are evangelical beliefs in American religious life? How do evangelicals' convictions affect their conduct?" The people at *Christianity Today* admitted to having a hand in designing the questions. After much discussion of and internal debate over the meaning of evangelicalism, they arrived at two kinds of evangelical adherents. One they called "orthodox." These were Protestants who believed Christ was fully divine and fully human, affirmed him as the only hope for salvation, regarded the Bible as the Word of God whose contents were mistake free, read Scripture regularly, and attended religious services at least once a month. The other variety of evangelical was the "conversionist" type. These evangelicals read the Bible, attended religious services at least once a month, and "had a particularly powerful religious experience that is still important to them, which they understand as a conversion experience that included an identifiable point at which they asked Jesus Christ to become their personal Savior."[10]

Combining orthodox Protestants and born-again evangelicals under the evangelical tent resulted in big numbers. Among the findings that the magazine's editors thought readers would perceive as most surprising were the following:

- One out of every five adults eighteen years old and older—31 million people—is an evangelical.
- Better than one-third of the adult population has had a life-changing religious experience. For 50 million people,

the experience involved Jesus Christ, and for 39.5 million
people, it was a conversion that included asking Christ to
be one's personal Savior.

- Almost half of those surveyed—69 million people eighteen
  and older—are hoping to go to heaven only because of their
  personal faith in Jesus Christ.
- More than eight out of every ten people believe Jesus Christ
  is divine.
- Sixty-five million adults believe the Bible is inerrant.
- A "whopping" 84 percent—more than eight out of every
  ten people—believes the Ten Commandments are valid
  today.[11]

The word *whopping* may have indicated that the editors were
as surprised and even encouraged as they believed readers
might be. But figuring out how *Christianity Today*'s executives
interpreted the data did not take detective work. In a separate
article, "Who and Where Are the Evangelicals?" the anonymous
author began by declaring that evangelical Protestants in the
United States, by virtue of constituting one-fifth of the population, "are clearly a powerful religious force in society."[12] George
Gallup Jr. himself was no less resolute about evangelicalism's
vigor. "From the variety of survey evidence," he told the magazine in an interview, "the 1980s could be described as the decade
of the evangelicals, because that is where the action is."[13] The
magazine echoed Gallup's opinion less colloquially and more
verbosely: Because evangelicals "already comprise one-fifth
of the population, contribute much more to the church than
nonevangelicals, understand their own faith better, are far more
ready to speak out to others about their faith, and place high
priority on winning others to their evangelical faith, it is hard
indeed to escape George Gallup's conclusion that evangelicals
will have much to do with how religion shapes up in the United
States during the 1980s."[14]

A harder look at the evidence, even in the light of Gallup's
and *Christianity Today*'s spin of it, did not necessarily lead to the
cheerleader-like sentiment that "what was inconceivable 25 years
ago is now a reality by the grace of God."[15] Whatever the neo-
evangelical movement's faults, its aims were much more heady

and doctrinal than the mushy American religiosity, according to the poll's findings, into which evangelicalism had so well blended. For instance, the editors took much encouragement from the statistic indicating that 94 percent of Americans believed in the existence of God. This was a clear refutation of the trends that sociologists and other intellectuals had cited to vindicate secularization. Yet the editors went on to note that responses to the poll also showed little understanding of divinity. "The precise nature of the Supreme Being is another matter," one article conceded, but it clearly did not follow "that the more education a person has the less likely he is to believe in God."[16] By relegating "the precise nature of the Supreme Being" to the low priority of "another matter," *Christianity Today*'s editors were softening the hard edges of a movement that forty years earlier was not only willing to refer to God with more specificity than "Supreme Being" but also insisted, contrary to the mainline churches, that essential doctrines were necessary for salvation.

Whatever cheer *Christianity Today*'s evangelical readers and editors took from the poll, the data also raised a number of questions about the industry of public opinion monitoring. Gallup was no less optimistic about the survey's results. He interpreted the data in a way that countered claims about the self-centeredness and hedonism of the so-called me generation. American society was experiencing a "spiritual surge," "strong trends toward spirituality," in which case, as long as evangelicals could avoid some of their worst offenses, they could tap that surge and continue to experience "great success." Still, what the poll failed to clarify was whether evangelicalism as a body of belief and practice actually existed or whether the questions had been posed in such a way as to elicit answers that might sound evangelical but could as easily indicate a vague warm feeling about closeness to a being bigger than those responding to the poll.

For example, many of the answers to questions about bedrock doctrines that might indicate orthodoxy on closer inspection looked highly ambiguous. On the matter of Christology, thirty-nine million adults were willing to affirm that Jesus is "fully God and fully man." Yet the data also indicated "confusion in the mind of the average person as to *precisely* who Jesus is." The glass-half-full take on this imprecision came in glowing terms: "We Americans may not know exactly who he is, but we know who he is not: he is not *just* another one of us. . . . Jesus continues to be The Man, par excellence, the One who eludes our definitions."[17] Such evasion of precision could, of course, call into question other findings, especially those concerning the experience of Christ that Americans said was so important to their faith. "Personal faith in Christ" was the only hope of heaven for 45 percent of the population, a number that supposedly indicated "how pervasive basic doctrine is in American society." But if this Christ were basically an iconic figure, the subject of "pop musicals, hit songs and the number one 'Hero' to many college students," not the Second Person of the Trinity as defined in the orthodox categories established at the Council of Chalcedon, then how extensive was such basic doctrine in the United States? Or if evangelicals were so great in number and if they represented the "orthodox" party in American Christianity, why did understandings of Christ run more in the direction of hero than of divine worship? Indeed, if Gallup had asked questions about Christ with words taken from the Chalcedonian Creed, such as, "Do you believe that Christ is 'very God of very God,' 'begotten not made,' 'by whom all things were made?'" the glass would likely have been considerably less full, perhaps bordering on empty. *Christianity Today* allowed that even "the barber on the street in ancient Constantinople had a sharper understanding of the deity of Christ than does the average evangelical today."[18]

The numbers on attitudes toward the Bible were equally equivocal. As much as the inerrancy of the Bible proved to be a popular belief among Americans, the *Christianity Today*–Gallup Poll also indicated that many of these respondents spent little time inspecting the contents of such an authoritative book. For instance, only 60 percent could identify the speaker of the phrase "ye must be born again," a Bible verse that hardly appeared in an obscure passage of Scripture—only thirteen verses away from John 3:16, the evangelistic mantra.[19] Only five out of ten respondents, moreover, could identity as many as five of the Ten Commandments, a finding that did not mesh well with the poll's tabulation that 80 percent of Americans believed the Decalogue was still relevant for the present. Both *Christianity Today*'s editors and Gallup himself believed that the poll showed America to be a place where biblical moral standards held firm. But again, if Americans did not know the Bible's summary of God's law, why were the poll's results so encouraging both about the place of religion in the United States and the vitality of American evangelicalism? A skeptical interpretation of the poll and its joint sponsorship might plausibly conclude that the design of the questions reflected an agenda, one that combined Gallup's mainline Protestant sense of the church's duty to society and *Christianity Today*'s responsibility to promote evangelicalism. In evangelical Protestantism and its chief periodical, one of the nation's oldest authorities on public opinion found a growing faith that could fill in for the declining old-line Protestants.

The *Christianity Today*–Gallup Poll was an initial stage in the shift among those measuring religious public opinion toward a recognition of evangelicalism's importance. This change was discernible in Gallup's own books, in which notice of evangelicals took almost a decade to surface. In *The Search for America's Faith* (1980), for instance, a book that was likely based on polling conducted at the same time as the *Christianity Today* study, born-again or conservative Protestantism was not noticeably evident. Instead, the book discussed differences between the churched and the unchurched and paid some attention to the older concern of spotting variations between Protestants and Catholics. Still, although Gallup did not designate an evangelical identity, he clearly discovered responses that fit the findings written about in *Christianity Today*. In one section of the book's conclusion, "The Return of an Orthodox Faith," Gallup revealed trends indicating a "powerful return to the conservative tenets of religion."[20] This traditional faith received additional momentum from a younger generation that had had a "conversion experience" and looked to Jesus Christ as "the central shaper of their lives." Evidence of this conservative faith also came from questions that described the Bible as "the word of God, . . . not mistaken in its teachings and statements," and Jesus Christ as "both fully God and fully man, or . . . the Son of God."[21] Yet indicative of the older style of polling that evaluated American opinion on the basis of denominational affiliation, Gallup broke down responses to these questions along Episcopalian, Presbyterian, and Methodist lines. In fact, in another line of inquiry concerning how people felt about their faith, Gallup again used the historic American Protestant denominations, with the additional category of Catholics, to make sense of the data.

By the time of *The People's Religion* (1989), Gallup's interpretation of religious public opinion proved that his prediction that the 1980s would be the decade of the evangelicals was prophetic. The triumph of evangelicalism as an identity for which to look in surveys of Americans was evident not simply in the sorts of questions Gallup asked. Notions about the deity of Christ or the inerrancy of the Bible had not been on the radar screen of social scientists or pollsters prior to "the year of the evangelical," but during the 1980s, students of public opinion, aware of a revival of evangelical Christianity, went out in search of it.[22] Still, what was most striking about the shift in polling was that evangelicals had become a separate constituency in the American religious public. In addition to the Christian groups that Gallup sought to measure—Catholics, Baptists, Methodists, Lutherans, Episcopalians, Presbyterians, and "other" Protestants—were evangelicals. Gallup's reasons for singling out evangelicals as a separate group stemmed from a definition that by 1989 required greater precision. Beginning in 1976, he explained, his polling methods had defined an evangelical as someone who "had had a born-again experience," "held a literal view of the Bible," and "had attempted to lead someone else to Christ."[23] By that standard, born-again Protestants accounted for 18 percent of the population in 1976 and had grown to 22 percent by 1984. For his 1989 book, however, Gallup opted simply for self-identification. Consequently, an evangelical was someone who answered affirmatively the question, "Would you describe yourself as a born-again Christian, or not?" This question was not only the "most likely to get an accurate response" but also followed "Gallup's practice of accepting religious self-identification."[24] By this measure, evangelical Christians made up 31 percent of the American population.

At the same time that Gallup expanded the definition of evangelicalism to include anyone who identified with the phrase "born-again Christian," he narrowed the scope of his investigation mainly to political and social issues. This made sense in the context of the late 1980s, when Jerry Falwell and Pat Robertson were carving out a constituency for the Republican party. But it did not contribute much to an understanding of the relationship between evangelical religious convictions and public attitudes. On abortion, for instance, Gallup found that evangelicals were more opposed than even Roman Catholics, whose church clearly forbade the practice. In fact, evangelicals' opinions were almost exactly the opposite of those of the non-evangelical American public: Born-again Protestants supported legislation that restricted abortion by a 62 to 32 percent majority, while non-evangelicals *opposed* such legal restrictions by 60 to 32 percent.[25] On the less controversial issue of smoking, though no less a matter subject to legislation, evangelicals were in the ballpark of American public opinion. In regard to the question of whether or not to smoke, evangelicals finished last, with only 23 percent saying they had smoked within the past week compared to 35 percent of non-evangelicals. But on the matter of banning advertisements for cigarettes, evangelicals were closer to the average American: Born-again Protestants favored such restrictions (50 to 44 percent) by a slightly larger number than non-evangelicals (48 to 50 percent).[26] On questions about international affairs, evangelicals were clearly different from other Americans. Born-again Protestants, Gallup found, were the greatest supporters of Israel; 37 percent of the evangelical respondents could be classified as "strong" supporters compared to 20 percent of non-evangelicals. Evangelicals also were the Americans most suspicious of the Soviet Union. Of those surveyed, 54 percent of born-again Protestants believed it was a greater risk to the United States to trust the Soviet Union (compared to 33 percent who thought it was a greater risk to be suspicious of the Soviet Union). Non-evangelicals were evenly divided, with 43 percent saying it was a greater risk to trust the Soviets and 43 percent indicating it was more dangerous not to trust them.[27]

Measuring evangelical identity primarily through stands on public issues, on the one hand, allowed Gallup to offer fairly firm conclusions about the ways in which evangelicals stood out from the rest of Americans. He wrote that they were "the most conservative group in the country on social issues—abortion, the women's movement, gun control, race relations, homosexuality, tolerance of atheists."[28] On the other hand, Gallup explained that on many of these same issues evangelicals were closer to the mainstream "than they or others realize." They believed abortion was permissible in certain instances, and they supported the Equal Rights Amendment, gun control, and government social programs. At that point, Gallup may have let his own interests become an obstacle to sober analysis. After all, how could evangelicals be the most conservative group on women's issues and yet support the ERA?

Gallup's preference for evangelicals came through in another interview conducted by the editors of *Christianity Today* after the release of *The People's Religion*. Asked about his earlier prediction that the 1980s would be the decade of the evangelicals, Gallup responded that even though their numbers had not increased, their influence had "extended way beyond their numbers."[29] He added that this influence was not simply a matter of presidential candidates professing to be evangelical or of renewal movements in some of the mainline denominations. Gallup declared that the strongest adherents in the United States were those who had had a direct experience of God, people who feel "that there are miracles, that there are meaningful coincidences, that there is a pattern to their lives, that God has a plan for their lives."[30] At the same time, he indicated that much of this experiential religion lacked "a sturdiness of belief." "There is a lack of knowledge of Christianity, a lack of awareness of Christian doctrines of atonement, redemption, and grace."[31] Still, despite the gap between experience and faith, Gallup told *Christianity Today*'s reporter that the 1990s would again be a bullish decade for evangelicalism.

Surveying the Religious Landscape (1999), Gallup's next checkup on the religious pulse of the United States, confirmed his 1989 prediction. The responses to questions about religious experience revealed that 39 percent of Americans claimed to be evangelical. This identity involved more than simply a feeling or a sense of divine presence. For Gallup's purposes, an evangelical had to "regard the Bible as the actual word of God," endeavor "to lead nonbelievers to a personal conversion," and have the experience of being born-again. The size of the evangelical population, he admitted, had remained constant since his pollsters had begun asking questions sensitive to born-again identity. What had changed during the 1990s was the number of Roman Catholics who claimed to be evangelical—21 percent, up from 12 percent in 1988.[32] In the meantime, the largest Protestant denominations continued to show a decline in membership: Methodists dwindled from 14 percent in 1967 to 9 percent in 1999, Presbyterians from 6 to 3 percent, Lutherans from 7 to 5 percent, and Episcopalians from 3 to 2 percent.[33] These statistics did not lead Gallup to conclude that evangelicalism was America's best hope for meaningful faith. In fact, his 1999 book opened with a fairly sober description of the disparity between the popularity of religion in the United States and the inability of organized "faith communities" to channel the public's religiosity into "deeper commitment" and "social outreach."[34] Even so, over the course of two decades, Gallup had been a trailblazer in helping journalists and pundits find the path to American evangelicalism. What was once at best a sectarian form of Protestantism had through Gallup's help become the faith of ordinary Americans.

A Quantitative Prophet

George Gallup Jr. may have been the most respectable pollster, but he was not the only one who established the prominence of evangelicals. George Barna, the man for whom the Barna Research Group is named, has emerged as the pollster of evangelicalism, the one whose research is clearly designed to strengthen born-again Protestantism. To be sure, Gallup was not averse to offering advice to churches, but he did so mainly in interviews. Barna, however, has quickly moved beyond statistics, graphs, and pie charts to recommendations for the health of evangelical congregations.

The president of Barna Research grew up a Roman Catholic and majored in sociology at Boston College. Barna gained some acquaintance with marketing and public perceptions when, after graduating from college, he took part in the campaign of a local Boston politician. But the young man's idealism prompted a decision to leave the seamy world of politics for graduate degrees in urban planning and political science at Rutgers University. This was Barna's formal exposure to the science of monitoring public opinion. His first job in the industry was in a Los Angeles media research firm where his efforts involved fund-raising for the televangelists Oral Roberts and Rex Humbard. This led to similar work for a Christian firm in Wheaton, Illinois. Barna explained to a *Christianity Today* reporter, "I loved the people, loved the ability to get out of bed in the morning and do some-thing . . . [more significant than] another ad to sell Kleenex." This job also exposed him to the links between research into public opinion and church ministry. Barna attended the mega-church Willow Creek in the nearby Chicago suburbs, pastored by Bill Hybels. The application of marketing to church work gave Barna "a whole new understanding of what the local church could be."[35]

That understanding of the church helped Barna launch his own marketing research firm, a company he started in 1984 in the bedroom of his home in Ventura, California. As circum-stances unfolded, the Disney Company effectively subsidized Barna's early days on the West Coast. He conducted market re-search for the Disney Channel for seven years, but in 1991, when Barna's contacts at Disney asked him to devote all of his market-ing savvy to the company, Barna decided instead to go full-time with his own company. Part of the reason behind this decision was the discouraging results produced by his own research on evangelical public opinion. Barna believed the church was in bad shape and that armed with an analysis of contemporary society, pastors and church leaders could make congregations more effective and evangelicalism more influential.

Barna's prophetic zeal to reform the church was evident even before he moved to California to found his own company. His first book, *Vital Signs* (1984), coauthored with his Wheaton colleague William Paul McKay, demonstrated the marriage of marketing research and gloomy estimates about the future of Christianity in the United States. Based on "data from national public opinion surveys and behavioral research studies," the book was an "attempt to present an objective analysis of the cur-rent condition and likely prospects for Christianity in America." Barna's findings indicated that "the integrity of the Christian faith . . . [was] being severely tested by a social transformation of massive proportions."[36] He pointed to a number of statistics that showed that evangelicals divorced as often as nonbelievers, were turning "liberal on abortion, and [were] increasingly prone to materialistic, hedonistic and secular outlooks." Such evidence also pointed toward a body of believers who were unprepared to meet the challenges of "godless humanism."[37] Barna's inflated rhetoric notwithstanding, George Gallup Jr. endorsed the book as being "right on the mark." Over the last two decades, Barna has rarely departed from that original assessment. Around the time that he decided to devote his full-time energies to being pollster-as-gatekeeper, Barna wrote three books that fleshed out his negative estimate of evangelical Protestantism and showed the usefulness of his work in marketing research. *The Frog in the Kettle* (1990), *User Friendly Churches* (1991), and *The Power of Vision* (1992) reiterated the assertion that evangelical Christians had in chameleon-like ways taken on the spots of their surrounding environment. Barna responded with recommendations for churches that required leaders to set visions and priorities for congregations and members to adopt a welcoming and inspiring lifestyle. From that time on, Barna switched to Gallup-like reports with more statistics and less cultural critique, though Barna issued these almost annually rather than every ten years. As his "ministry" became better known, Barna became in effect a consultant to the church growth/seeker church movement. His data offered inspiration and advice to congregations that hoped to be user-friendly and to transform American society.

The picture of evangelicals that emerged from Barna's reports could be both encouraging and unflattering. On the positive side, his research continued to beat the drum of evangelicalism's larger than life presence in American religion. For instance, in *The Barna Report, 1992–1993*, Barna said that 40 percent of the United States' adult population claimed to have made a personal commitment to Jesus Christ and believed they would go to heaven after they died because they had confessed their sins and accepted Christ as their Savior. This figure reflected a 5 percent increase from 1991, a jump that might have been related to the tumultuous national and international events surrounding the Gulf War. Equally heartening were statistics that indicated that born-again Christians were "not the down-and-out aged group of 'losers'" portrayed by some journalists. Income and education profiles revealed that "baby boomers are every bit as likely to be Christian as are adults from any other age group."[38] Barna did weaken some of this good news by arguing for a difference between evangelicalism, a classification of which "nobody" knew the definition, and born-again Christianity. According to Barna, an evangelical was a believer who had a fairly good understanding of the Christian religion and practiced it in meaningful ways. This segment of the population, Barna's evidence showed, comprised 12 percent of the population, a figure obviously not as rosy as the one for born-again Christianity. Even so, evangelicalism was still the largest segment of the Protestant world, leaving the historic denominations in the dust.

On the negative side, Barna continued to manifest a certain level of outrage at the spiritual and moral lapses of evangelicals. In *Virtual America* (1994), he predicted that evangelicals would be "increasingly isolated and disenfranchised from the mainstream culture because of their adherence to absolutes."[39] As much as this was a compliment, it also reflected Barna's data, which revealed that evangelicals were in decline, from 12 to 7 percent in a little more than a year.[40] With the faithful remnant in decline, Barna speculated, "Is the Church poised to attack the perversions that undermine people and organizations, and prepared to handle the overwhelming body of personal and corporate needs that exists [sic] in America today?" His answer, "Probably not," indicated that Barna had not lost his prophetic edge. "To create a society that not only recognizes God to be the King that He is, but that also seeks to serve Him with purity of purpose, we must establish firm spiritual foundations on which we may build for future growth."[41] This perspective explains in part why Barna refused to believe the hype about evangelical numbers and sought a narrower set of qualifiers. If evangelicalism really did involve the numbers that some polls indicated, then, according to his logic, America should have been in much better shape. That the nation was not proved to Barna just how weak and ineffective evangelical Protestants were.

Barna's disillusionment seemingly bottomed out in 2001. As a feature story in *Christianity Today* put it, Barna, who had become to evangelicals "what George Gallup is to the larger culture," had abandoned the project to reform the church through cultivating leaders with vision. "Most people in positions of leadership in local churches aren't leaders," he quipped. "They're great people, but they're not really leaders."[42] The article was not simply a report on Barna's emotional state. It also suggested displeasure within the evangelical movement's establishment over the pollster's angst. Tim Stafford, a long-time reporter for *Christianity Today*, noted how Barna's research reflected simply a marketing perspective. The implication was that this flawed outlook may have been responsible for Barna's equally erroneous picture of evangelical churches and their leaders. "Market research is not a neutral tool," Stafford explained. "It grew as a business technique, and reflects some of the biases of business. While missionary anthropology knows a lot about spontaneous revivals, business focuses on planned action." Stafford added that one could not understand Barna's assessment of American evangelicalism "without grasping that marketing forms its essential grid."[43]

Stafford's rendering of Barna was ironic if only because almost two decades earlier those same techniques had not troubled the editors of *Christianity Today*. The poll that George Gallup conducted in the late 1970s for the magazine, which undoubtedly informed marketing decisions in the periodical's business office, was equally susceptible to the charge of a skewed perspective. After all, the whole industry of public opinion polling, while projecting an image of scientific research, had emerged as a subfield within marketing and advertising. That is precisely the environment in which George Gallup Sr. learned the skills he passed on to his son. One difference, then, between George Gallup Jr.'s research from the 1970s to the 1990s and Barna's from the 1990s was that the former's data revealed a glimpse of evangelicalism that was much more upbeat and therefore more congenial to the magazine responsible for keeping born-again hopes alive. Indeed, the idea of evangelicalism as a large and vital presence in American society, one that neo-evangelical leaders in the 1940s had begun to promote, gained further credibility from the findings of pollsters such as Gallup and even the idealistic Barna, for without their numbers and subsequent crunching, many Americans would have had to rely on academics in the humanities and social sciences for information on evangelicalism. But with the steady stream of books from the likes of Gallup and Barna, along with news stories on their data, evangelicalism continued to be a force with which the nation would have to reckon.

Survey Says: "Evangelicals Defeat the Mainline"

When Dean M. Kelley's book *Why Conservative Churches Are Growing* (1972) appeared, it launched a soul-searching discussion among scholars of religion and mainline Protestant church leaders about the exhaustion of the largest Protestant denominations. Himself a senior administrator for the National Council of Churches, Kelley was by no means hostile to the mainline or its mission. Still, his argument, based on denominational statistics and sociological theory, was a discouraging one for the oldest denominations in the United States. Conservative or "strict" churches were growing, and the reasons appeared to stem from their zealous pursuit of evangelism and holy living. Meanwhile, "ecumenical" churches were in decline because, as Kelley argued, they were interested in matters secondary to strictly religious ones.[44] *Why Conservative Churches Are Growing* was released a few years before evangelicals gained prominent coverage in the press. Furthermore, the book's understanding of conservative churches was by no means synonymous with born-again Protestantism. Groups Kelley classified as conservative included Southern Baptists, Lutherans, Mormons, and Jehovah's Witnesses. Even so, when evangelicals emerged as a political force during the late 1970s and as students of public opinion began to quantify born-again Protestant strength, the plausible conclusion was that evangelicalism was winning the race with the mainline denominations. The effort by neo-evangelical leaders in the 1940s to build a coalition of conservative Protestants to rival the mainline was apparently paying dividends.

Of course, as the statistics of the pollsters would eventually show, evangelical numbers were large but not necessarily growing. Since 1976, when Gallup first asked questions designed to gauge evangelical adherents, the number of born-again Protestants had hovered between 40 and 12 percent depending on how strictly the interviewers framed their questions. Nevertheless, the timing of breast beating among mainline Protestants about the loss of church members and the results of public opinion polls worked to evangelicalism's advantage. Born-again Protestantism turned out to be the real story in American religion, not the mainline churches that now were cast in the role of the traditional fuddy-duddies in contrast to the vital and resilient evangelicals.

A spring 1993 cover story in Canada's news weekly, *Maclean's*, confirmed this impression and illustrated how crucial opinion polling was to the construction of evangelicalism's image of success. "God Is Alive" was the title of the article, and it reported on the findings of a nationwide telephone poll conducted in early 1993 by the Gallup Organization of Canada and the Angus Reid Group and funded in part by a grant from the evangelically friendly Pew Charitable Trusts. The results contradicted the image of Canadian society as agnostic and secular. As the *Maclean's* reporter put it, the poll portrayed "Canada as an overwhelmingly Christian nation, not only in name, but in belief."[45] What was old hat in the United States, such as the number of citizens who trusted in Christ, believed he was divine, or regarded the Bible as the Word of God, was stunning news in Canada. Eight out of ten Canadians believed in God, 67 percent affirmed the death and resurrection of Christ, one-third prayed daily, and over 50 percent read the Bible with a measure of frequency. The poll also revealed, as polls had done south of the border, that evangelicalism was surprisingly as alive as God. Angus Reid's results estimated that 15 percent of Canadians were evangelical, which indicated that they had had a conversion experience, read the Bible literally, and trusted in Christ's death and resurrection for salvation. Polls such as this one, just like the ones conducted by Gallup, may not have proved that evangelicalism was a growing religion. But these surveys did contribute to the growth of a sense that evangelicalism was a faith against which the gates of secularization could not prevail.

Stories such as the one in *Maclean's* suggest that, more than the research of historians and sociologists, pollsters' findings constructed the popular conception of evangelical Protestantism as a large and traditional faith. An important factor in the impact that surveys of public opinion made on public opinion is the aura of science such measuring devices radiate. Scholars who study the history and effect of opinion polls, such as Benjamin Ginsberg in *The Captive Public*, argue that the "pollsters' insistence on rigorous, precise measurement" helps to account for the public's confidence in opinion poll data.[46] The scientifically designed questions, along with the cold hard numbers they produce, come across as objective and free from bias. Susan Herbst, another author who studied the influence of opinion polling, this time on democratic politics in the United States, wonders whether polls and surveys should carry as much weight as they do. Instead of reflecting an accurate measure of people's ideas, she suggests that opinion polls actually narrow in harmful ways the range and character of public expression. It could be, Herbst points out, that opinion polls limit public debate first by reducing complex issues to simple questions and second by appearing to be scientifically accurate, thus short-circuiting discussion.[47]

The concerns Herbst raises about opinion polling and democratic theory also have relevance for evangelicalism and the understanding of Christianity. Has the construction of evangelicalism by opinion polls and the apparent popularity of born-again Protestantism narrowed discussions of what Christianity teaches and requires of its adherents? The Canadian sociologist of religion Reginald Bibby, quoted in the *Maclean's* story, argued that in modern society "[t]he gods of old have been neither abandoned nor replaced" but instead had been "broken into pieces and offered to religious consumers in piecemeal form."[48] A critical reception of opinion polls might very well see in them an example of what Bibby describes. Sound-bite questions end up breaking down profound religious truths into bite-sized portions to which those surveyed may respond positively with little reflection or conviction. Even so, as much as opinion polling raises questions about what counts as Christian and who may legitimately conduct the counting, surveys of religious public opinion in North America were a godsend for evangelicals. They placed hard numbers behind what evangelical leaders had been insisting on for three decades: Evangelical Protestants, not the mainline churches, were in the mainstream of the American public.

Part 2

The Unmaking of Evangelicalism

4

One, Holy, Catholic Movement

Christianity of the evangelical variety has historically struggled with the question of succession. How does the conversion experience become a model for nurture? Countless evangelical converts, having left behind a life of sin and irreligion, face a difficult task when thinking about passing on the faith to their offspring. Do they encourage their children to pursue the life they did, one of rebellion followed by the ecstasy of regeneration, so that their sons and daughters will come to genuine faith? Not likely. Much more common is the decision to rear their children in the beliefs and practices of the faith, even when such instruction and nurture flatly contradict the model of the conversion experience. After all, turning to God's mercy is much easier after a life of drugs and sex than it is after a wholesome upbringing of church attendance, family devotions, and Bible memorization.

The problem of succession in the spiritual hothouse of evangelical piety becomes all the more complicated when you are the child of evangelicalism's most celebrated figure. Franklin Graham, born in 1952 shortly after his father, Billy, came to national attention after a successful crusade in Los Angeles, struggled through the 1960s with the mores of evangelical religion and the expectations of his father's supporters. As *Time* magazine reported in a 1996 article on Franklin, "If Billy was the ultimate preacher, then Franklin made a run at being the ultimate Preacher's kid: fighting, taunting the police . . . into high-speed car chases and cultivating a fascination for firearms and rock music and a taste for hard liquor."[1] These were not the virtues Franklin's parents had hoped to cultivate in him, but they did make conversion much more plausible, which is what happened when Franklin was twenty-two years old. Neither were the pranks of this ne'er-do-well a fitting background for someone who might grow up to inherit his father's ministry.

In 1995, when Billy Graham anointed his son to be his successor as chairman of the board and chief executive officer of the Billy Graham Evangelistic Association, the organization numbered 525 employees and had an annual revenue of $88 million, a mailing list of 2.7 million active donors, a radio program called *Hour of Decision* that was broadcast on 660 stations, frequent television programs, feature films, and a monthly magazine called *Decision*. Part of what has made the Graham enterprise so successful has been its remarkable ability to avoid any hint of scandal. And that was what made Franklin Graham's succession so difficult for some of the BGEA's board members to accept as the best way to preserve the capital, physical and spiritual, that Billy had generated. Some talked about closing down the BGEA once Billy retired and turning the endeavor into a philanthropic organization. Others wanted to avoid Franklin, whose shenanigans even after conversion did not conform to evangelical sensibilities—he believes alcohol consumed in moderation can be a "good" thing. Yet how does a board of trustees simply end a highly successful endeavor once the founder is no longer capable of carrying on the work?

The problem that Billy Graham and his board members faced in appointing Franklin Graham as the head of the BGEA was not merely theirs. For good or ill, Billy Graham and the organization he shepherded had been crucial to the health and identity of the evangelical movement. In the words of David Van Biema of *Time* magazine, Billy Graham led "the revivalist, traditionalist branch of American Christianity . . . from obscurity in which it had languished roughly since the 1925 Monkey Trial . . . [to be] the most vital and aggressive spiritual force on the national landscape."[2] Mark A. Noll has written of Graham that he is "the most attractive public face that evangelical Protestantism has offered to the wider world in the half-century since the Second World War."[3] So attractive has Graham been that George M. Marsden has offered a jargon-free definition of evangelicalism: "anyone who likes Billy Graham."[4] All of this is a way of saying that Billy Graham has represented more than a man and his evangelistic efforts; he has also been the institutional center holding the evangelical movement together. The obvious question is whether evangelicalism can survive without Billy Graham no matter how effective his son may be.

Common sense suggests that putting all your eggs in one basket is not wise. Christian teaching also provides warnings about identifying too closely with one individual. When the apostle Paul chastised the Corinthians for forming factions identified with Apollos, Cephas, and himself, he was offering instruction about membership in the church, of which Christ is the head. To be a Christian is not to be a part of a movement but to be a member of the body of Christ. This is a lesson that the evangelical movement has not learned. Its recent history demonstrates the consequences of this learning disability. By relying on parachurch institutions instead of the church, evangelicals have put themselves in the awkward position of constituting a movement after Billy Graham without anyone at the center to like.

Not the Way It Was Supposed to Be?

The first important instance of the word *evangelical* as it has come to be used by scholars and pundits occurred in 1942. The scene was the founding of the National Association of Evangelicals (NAE), an event that was significant on several levels.[5] It signaled the emergence of the contemporary evangelical movement, for the NAE was the first organization founded by neo-evangelical leaders. It also stood for a reform of fundamentalism; neo-evangelicals were "progressive" fundamentalists who wanted to put behind the negativity of antimodernism and accent the positive of evangelical Christianity. Finally, the NAE demonstrated the perennial difficulties of putting the proverbial genie back in the bottle; the organization appealed to leaders of evangelistic and revivalistic "ministries" for whom the mildly ecclesial structures of the NAE were foreign. The prominence of parachurch organizations for born-again Protestants helps to explain why Billy Graham, not the NAE, would become the symbol for modern-day evangelicalism.

The NAE's first magazine was titled *United Evangelical Action*, and it said a good deal about the aims of the organization. It was an effort to unite conservative Protestants for specific activities that would lead America back to Christ. Harold John Ockenga, the founding president of the Association and pastor of Boston's Park Street Congregational Church, told the first assembly of the NAE that the questions they were about to address would "affect the whole future of evangelical Christianity in America."[6] The specific circumstances that gave Ockenga and fellow neo-evangelicals a sense of urgency were the Second World War and the reputation of conservative Protestantism.

On the most pragmatic of levels, World War II revealed the sort of handicap with which neo-evangelicals operated. If, for instance, a group of revivalistic Protestants wanted to send ministers to serve as chaplains in the United States armed forces, they had to work through denominational channels controlled by the Federal Council of Churches, which was the ecumenical arm of the denominations evangelicals considered to be liberal. A coincidental problem, though unrelated to the war, was the acquisition of time on the radio for religious broadcasts. Neo-evangelicals possessed some of the most popular radio preachers, for example, Charles Fuller, Paul Rader, and Donald Grey Barnhouse, but the Federal Radio Commission had recently delegated some of the administration of religious broadcasting to the mainline's Federal Council. Consequently, neo-evangelicals needed an organizational rival to the mainline ecumenical body, one that could coordinate and consolidate the various activities of conservative Protestants in cooperation with institutions such as the federal government.[7]

World War II, however, did more than demonstrate the organizational hurdles facing Protestants who were either on the margins of or had left the mainline Protestant denominations. It also proved the desperate nature of Western civilization and the need for the gospel. Again, Ockenga expressed evangelical alarm in his opening address at the first gathering of the NAE:

> Let us learn something from the Soviets and the Nazis. If the children of this world are wiser than the children of light, then it is time for the children of light to open their eyes and learn how to carry on God's work. This is the time, the day for offensive. Personally I am just as tired of defensive tactics in ecclesiastical matters as the Americans are tired of defensive tactics on the part of the United Nations. . . . Do not be so foolish as to think that though your own personal work is thriving at the present time you will escape.[8]

Ockenga elaborated on the three great threats to the United States and the cause of Christ: Roman Catholicism, liberal theology, and secularism. He believed, along with the other organizers of the NAE, that evangelicals needed to unite to combat these threats. In fact, Ockenga explained that the future of America as well as the West depended on the defense and propagation of the Christian faith as he and his fellow evangelicals understood it.

The nature of the evangelical faith resulted in the second set of circumstances that called for the founding of this new organization. At roughly the same time that the leaders of the NAE discussed a new venture to unite evangelicals in a common effort, Carl McIntire, the Presbyterian-fundamentalist who during the Cold War became synonymous with Christian anticommunism, beat them to the punch. In 1941, he formed the American Council of Christian Churches (ACCC). His aim was to make this a fundamentalist interdenominational association, one that required members to break all ties with the mainline churches. The leaders of the NAE actually considered throwing their support behind McIntire, but although the ACCC provided the organizational coordination that evangelicals needed, the leadership of the NAE thought McIntire's message was too negative. In effect, the decision to go with the NAE was a collective indication that the old fundamentalist habit of fighting modernism was not a sufficient basis for evangelical action. Instead, what the NAE would offer was a positive message with various evangelistic initiatives. As J. Elwin Wright, another of the NAE's founders, explained at the Association's founding meeting, evangelicals needed to steer a course between the indifference of Protestant liberalism and the hyper-negativity of fundamentalism. If they could rally behind a "spirit of cooperation," the NAE might lead the nation into a period of revival comparable to the previous Great Awakenings.[9]

Measured by numbers alone, the kinder, gentler NAE leveled an early round knockout against McIntire's American Council. By 1947, the NAE represented thirty denominations, totaling 1.3 million members. On its fiftieth anniversary, the Association had 4.5 million members. The NAE also took the lead in setting the agenda for the evangelical movement. It spawned several evangelical organizations such as the National Religious Broadcasters and the Evangelical Foreign Missionary Association. In addition, the NAE drew together members of the new evangelical intelligentsia, such as Ockenga and Carl F. H. Henry, and so indirectly fueled the founding of two other important neo-evangelical institutions: Fuller Theological Seminary (1947) and *Christianity Today* (1956). In contrast, it took the American Council almost five decades to reach 1.5 million members, and its fortunes were largely tied to those of McIntire, whose reputation for anticommunism scared away all but those most dedicated to the ACCC's almost manichean understanding of the world.

Nevertheless, the success of the NAE is deceptive, especially if McIntire's American Council is the only source of comparison. Another and arguably better gauge is the popularity of the NAE compared to that of ministries such as those associated with Billy Graham, Chuck Colson, Pat Robertson, Jerry Falwell, Chuck Swindoll, and James Dobson. Popularity may appear to be a subjective criteria, but the capacity to appeal to the people is precisely what makes evangelical broadcasters and institutions so successful. Put simply, evangelicalism thrives on parachurch "ministries" that function as sources of communication and recruitment not tied to a particular congregation or denomination. Therefore, it is much more likely that the average Assemblies of God church member (Assemblies of God is the NAE's largest denomination) has more familiarity with the *700 Club* than with any particular endeavor of the Association, whose membership comes primarily from the denominations that choose to affiliate with it.

The NAE's inability to compete with the charisma and direct marketing of celebrity-driven parachurch ministries was evident almost from the beginning of the organization's existence. Much of the support for and leadership of the new interdenominational agency came not from churches but from fundamentalist celebrities. Part of the motivation for the Association sprang from the fundamentalist ethos of the 1930s. In contrast to the religious depression that mainline denominations experienced thanks to fiscal and doctrinal malaise, born-again Protestantism flourished. Most of its chief outlets were parachurch agencies, with Bible schools and colleges providing the most direct forms of leadership. Some of these institutions, such as Moody Bible Institute, were founded in the final decades of the nineteenth century. Because of a fundamentalist lack of confidence in the institutional church, due in part to the controversies of the 1920s, Bible schools emerged as an alternative to denominational life.[10]

These institutions were designed to train lay workers for religious work such as foreign missions, urban evangelism, and Christian education. The influence of Bible institutes grew considerably through two related institutions. The first was the Bible and prophecy conference circuit, which attracted large numbers of lay Protestants to mass rallies throughout the late nineteenth century and into the first decade of the twentieth century. These conferences popularized the biblical interpretation that would be the backbone of the Bible schools' instruction. The second was radio. Bible colleges were among the first religious institutions to found their own stations and broadcast a steady stream of wholesome programming. In addition, Bible institutes and colleges often published educational material for Sunday school as well as magazines and books. The range of religious services these institutions offered, from graduates who could pastor congregations to Sunday school curricula and daily broadcasts, meant that Bible schools and colleges formed the infrastructure of born-again Protestantism. Believers who supported these schools or who benefitted from their services were likely to have identities defined as much by a school as by the Presbyterian or Baptist denominational title.[11]

Bible colleges reinforced the born-again Protestant identity through the form of devotion they enforced among students and promoted through publishing and broadcasting. In addition to abstaining from worldliness, Bible institute students learned a piety that demanded self-sacrifice and consecration for service. This scheme of devotion drew heavily on Keswick teaching, or Victorious Christian Living, which emphasized the renunciation of self in order to be filled with divine power, a strength that enabled believers to serve God in remarkable ways. Whatever its origins, this devotion stoked the parachurch agencies that helped born-again Protestantism thrive. It inspired many born-again teens and young adults to consider the foreign mission field and also generated the kind of energy and duty necessary to sustain the many services the Bible colleges provided.[12]

The point here has less to do with the success or ethos of the Bible schools and institutes and more to do with the parachurch character of born-again Protestantism on the eve of the NAE's founding. The original membership of the Association did consist primarily of denominations, but the leadership of the NAE came largely from the parachurch world of Bible colleges, evangelical publishing, Christian radio, and faith missions. The initial network for the Association ranged from J. Elwin Wright's New England Fellowship, which used Rumney Bible Conference in New Hampshire as a base of operations, to Will Houghton, who presided over Moody Bible Institute in Chicago, to Charles Fuller, whose *Old Fashioned Revival Hour,* broadcast from suburban Los Angeles, was one of the most popular programs in the United States. In other words, though the Association was formally denominational, its leaders worked mainly in parachurch settings. Indeed, the lesson taught by the controversies of the 1920s and 1930s was that the real vitality of American Protestantism was located in nontraditional outlets where entrepreneurial genius and the charisma of an evangelist or radio preacher was more effective than the staid and bureaucratic ways of denominations. The NAE tried to harness this energy, but ironically, its support rarely extended beyond the evangelical denominations to the mailing lists and financial resources of born-again Protestant parachurch organizations. The evangelical center could not be confined to a central agency, coordinating the work of its constituent members, for the heart of evangelicalism was in its decentralized and unregulated pockets that mixed evangelistic zeal with entrepreneurial know-how.

In many respects, the flurry of evangelistic, missionary, and educational activity that characterized born-again Protestantism in the 1930s was simply the default mode for Protestants hooked on revival-friendly devotion. This religious style had roots in German pietism of the seventeenth century and the revivals of the eighteenth century's Great Awakening. It looked more to the experience and actions of the individual believer for evidence of authentic faith than to the forms and order of the institutional church and her clergy. In fact, one of pietism's legacies, underlined by the revivals of the eighteenth and nineteenth centuries, was to regard ecclesial expressions of Protestantism as synonymous with nominal Christianity. If Protestants in the sixteenth and seventeenth centuries had looked to baptism, the Lord's Supper, preaching by an ordained minister, and a system of family worship and catechesis as the staples of Christian devotion, Protestants in the pietist and revivalist orbit questioned the authenticity of such church-based activities. Instead, private Bible reading and prayer, small groups, personal evangelism, and exemplary deeds of mercy became for born-again Protestants the way of genuine Christian devotion.[13]

During the era of the state church system, when Christian devotion was regulated as a public and formal enterprise, pietism and revivalism functioned as a means of pious dissent. But when Christendom lost the support of the state, as it did with the epoch-making changes following the American and French Revolutions, ecclesial Protestantism and pietism reversed roles, with the latter becoming the dominant faith, the former an acquired taste. In the United States, particularly, the separation of church and state created a religious free market. No longer did government regulate church life. Instead, the churches that recruited the most members and attracted the biggest givers were the ones that appealed directly to the people through charisma, organizational moxie, and sheer effort. In effect, the disestablishment of Christianity made plausible a faith that relied on voluntary assent and entrepreneurial genius. The United States, consequently, became the social experiment that proved the superiority of revivalist-style Christianity, at least in its capacity to attract adherents and solicit support. Church-centered Christianity was too formal, cumbersome, and elitist.

The moral of the story was that the parachurch promoted the Christian faith better than the church did.[14]

Moving from the revivals of the Second Great Awakening to the founding of the NAE requires a large historical leap, but the born-again Protestants responsible for attempting to unite conservatives in the 1940s were the direct heirs to almost three centuries of neglect of the institutional church. Revivalist Protestantism in the United States has historically relied on pious individualism, mass appeal, religious experience, and pragmatic techniques for communicating the gospel. As a result, although the leaders of the NAE saw membership in the organization shoot up thanks to the enlistment of several denominations, they did not understand or care to cultivate the traditional institutions and formal structures that had characterized church life. This defect was evident even to the Baptist church historian Bruce Shelley, who wrote the NAE's twenty-fifth-anniversary history. He observed that a "major area of need in the NAE is an in-depth study of the doctrine of the church." Shelley added that evangelicals had "produced so few works on the biblical doctrine of the church" because they "traditionally stressed those doctrines which bear directly upon the experience of the new birth."[15]

It is no wonder then that Billy Graham would emerge as post–World War II evangelicalism's poster boy, not the National Association of Evangelicals. Graham's work as an itinerant evangelist, unencumbered by ecclesiastical oversight, was much more in tune than were the NAE's denominational members with the structures that had allowed born-again Protestantism to thrive in a society in which the state had deregulated religion. Even more crucial to Graham's eventual notoriety, however, were the specific networks through which he emerged as the premier American revivalist. Those links and associations had few direct ties to the churches that originally joined the NAE.

Few evangelicals today are aware that before the Billy Graham Evangelistic Association there was Youth for Christ. Graham came to prominence first as an evangelist to teenagers during the 1940s in what Joel A. Carpenter has called "the dawning of an era." He explains that as important as the NAE may have been for supplying neo-evangelical leaders with a strategy, Youth for Christ was the first public sign that the 1930s "revival of revivalism . . . was finally breaking into public view."[16] Even more important, in Carpenter's estimation, is that the Youth for Christ movement was not your fundamentalist father's revivalism. Its leaders, a group of unknown revivalists, combined born-again faith with the "style" and "media" of Hollywood and radio. "From a fundamentalist perspective," Carpenter writes, "the rally leaders were borrowing from the very dens of the devil . . . to accomplish the Lord's purposes." This strategy revealed how evangelicalism "might win a valued place once more in the public life of the nation."[17]

Youth for Christ originated in Philadelphia and New York through the efforts of Percy Crawford, an unconventional evangelist who attracted youth from southeastern Pennsylvania to Pinebrook, his summer camp in the Pocono Mountains, and through his radio show, *Young People's Church of the Air.* One of Crawford's lieutenants was Jack Wyrtzen, an insurance salesman who performed in a jazz band and started youth rallies in New York City and another summer camp, Word of Life, set in the Adirondack Mountains. The up-tempo gospel music that characterized the crusades of Crawford and Wyrtzen was key to their success. As Torrey Johnson and Robert Cook, another pair of successful youth evangelists, explained in their book, *Reaching Youth for Christ,* professionally performed entertainment was necessary to hold teenagers' attention. "Dare to offer something shoddy and they'll shun your meeting."[18]

Eventually, the youth rallies that Crawford and Wyrtzen established in the Northeast spread to cities in the upper Midwest. Chicago Youth for Christ began in 1944 through the initiative of George Beverly Shea, an employee at WMBI radio who assembled a band and solicited funding for a rally at Chicago's Orchestra Hall. The speaker for the series of rallies was a twenty-five-year-old pastor from a church in Chicago's suburbs: Billy Graham. Whether arrangements for the speaker or the musicians came first, the rest is history.[19]

Actually, Graham's fame did not come for another five years, during the Los Angeles crusade that would be a turning point for his career and the fortunes of post–World War II evangelicalism. Between the 1944 Youth for Christ rally in Chicago and the headline-making evangelistic crusade in 1949, Graham continued to speak on the youth rally circuit, where he learned many of the skills that would make him successful. The choice of themes, the manner of delivery, the importance of music, the necessity of advance planning and local staff—Graham experienced firsthand through the auspices of Youth for Christ all the ingredients he would need to make his own evangelistic organization click. Graham even came to the attention of William Randolph Hearst. As early as 1945, Hearst endorsed the Youth for Christ rallies in an editorial and instructed his newspapers to give positive coverage. The publisher's 1949 directive to his editors, "Puff Graham," in their coverage of the Los Angeles crusade helped make Graham a national celebrity who could attract crowds on his own.[20]

In the larger scheme of evangelical history, the often ignored Youth for Christ movement was a much more important broker of religious authority than the National Association of Evangelicals. The parachurch style attracted more publicity and generated larger numbers than did the ways of the institutional church, which goes a long way toward explaining why born-again Protestants preferred the parachurch over the church.

Feudal Evangelicals

George M. Marsden has likened evangelicalism's dependence on the parachurch to the feudal system of the Middle Ages. "Leading evangelists built up empires that became focal points of loyalty," he explains. The theory was that everyone was serving Christ, "but in fact they often were rivals." Marsden attributes this sense of competition to evangelicals' "general disregard for the institutional church." While denominational loyalties were important to some of the movement's adherents, for many they were "incidental." This was especially true of evangelicals who identified with figures whose appeal was explicitly transdenominational. Marsden concludes that "little seems to hold [evangelicalism] together other than common traditions, a central one of which is the denial of the authority of traditions."[21]

In point of fact, the glue holding evangelicalism together has actually been the culture of celebrity, which is perhaps the flip side of denying the authority of traditions. Billy Graham managed to hold the movement together from 1950 until the 1980s by supplying it with a common point of reference. Accounts of his crusades functioned in the same way that stories from furloughed foreign missionaries did for fundamentalists; the hopes of evangelicals rose and sank depending on the size of the city where he evangelized, the length of the crusade, and the amount of television coverage. As Billy went, so went evangelicalism. Graham himself offered little in the way of instruction to born-again Protestants, though *Decision* magazine and some of the evangelist's own books may have yielded some insight into the teachings and practices of Christianity. But Graham himself was an evangelist first and foremost, and most of what the BGEA produced was designed to save the unsaved.

Someone with Graham's fame and public approval rating was clearly good for a movement trying to recover from the negative publicity of fundamentalism. But did such public relations provide evangelical adherents with a coherent religious identity? Is liking Billy Graham the stuff of serious devotion? And what happens when the most popular evangelist has to compete with other prominent evangelical celebrities? What is the substance of evangelical identity when it involves not only admiring and rooting for Billy Graham but also liking, for instance, James Dobson of Focus on the Family and Tim LaHaye, the coauthor of the publishing phenomenon Left Behind series? What beliefs and acts of devotion follow from such affections? If Marsden is correct, the feudal system of evangelical celebrity creates incoherence among individual born-again Protestants as much as it fuels evangelicalism as a religious phenomenon.

Comparisons among three of the most visible parachurch ministries and their celebrity figureheads reveal the problems attending evangelical identity in the wake of the movement's parachurch structure. Graham, Dobson, and LaHaye all share evangelicalism's penchant to articulate the Christian faith in the idiom of everyday affairs. Graham's evangelistic appeals use little theological jargon. Instead, Graham has consistently argued that the gospel meets the most ordinary of human needs, especially those of being loved and having purpose in life. Dobson, through advice to parents about rearing disciplined children and to voters about family-friendly politicians, has also domesticated Christianity. To the extent that he talks about the specifics of biblical teaching, Dobson's wisdom comes in pre-cooked, easily consumed portions. In a similar fashion, LaHaye has taken Christian notions about the end of time, which constitutes some of the most mysterious parts of the gospel, and has turned them into highly entertaining fiction set in the most familiar of settings. Beyond this ability to vernacularize the Christian message, Graham, Dobson, LaHaye, and their organizations send messages that taken together are more incoherent than conflicting. If, for instance, being an evangelical involves some kind of beneficial relationship with the work of men who are in some way responsible for what evangelicalism represents, what sorts of ideas and behavior are required to belong to born-again Protestantism? If, in other words, American Christians, on the basis of parachurch organizations such as those of Graham, Dobson, and LaHaye, respond to surveys and opinion polls by identifying themselves as evangelical (not a far-fetched proposition), what characterizes that identity? The BGEA web site does give specific advice in the areas of doctrine and practice. A page titled "Believe" has links to various messages by Billy and Franklin Graham on death, eternal life, fear, forgiveness, God, hope, peace, and the supernatural. Curious omissions from the list are Christ and the Bible, especially given that pollsters sometimes use such topics to quantify evangelicalism's numerical strength. On the "Christian Living" page the advice is more concrete and accessible, since surfers do not have to choose from multiple snippets of Graham columns or evangelistic messages. The way to live as a Christian involves reading the Bible and praying daily, depending on the Holy Spirit, attending church regularly, serving others, conquering doubts, learning to live one day at a time, recognizing the blessing of suffering, resisting temptation, and talking to others about Christ. BGEA also makes Bible study material available to assist with these duties. In so doing, the organization recognizes a responsibility to provide more for converts than simply a stimulus to walk the aisle. But this advice does raise questions such as, If people engaged in these activities, would they be more evangelical? Or if evangelicals did not perform these responsibilities, who would know?

LaHaye's ministry is accessible through a couple web sites, his own and that of the publisher of the Left Behind novels. The former is lean on information about the Christian life. It states that LaHaye is currently writing books and speaking and so unable to provide regular updates on the site. Evangelicals who want to know more about the rapture, however, can find information about the Pre-Trib Research Center, which enlists over two hundred prophecy scholars to spread the message of the rapture. The web site for the novel series contains more to encourage evangelical ways, the "Seek God" page providing the most advice on what it means to be a Christian. In the "Tools for the Journey" section, users can find resources on discipleship, how to witness, small group study, daily devotions, and a secure site where those who log in may keep a spiritual journal. Like the BGEA material, the Left Behind sources are heavy on affect and light on objective content. In the study section, for instance, the site includes instruction from Campus Crusade's Bill Bright on the life and teachings of Jesus. In fact, most of the instruction on the Left Behind web site comes through links to Campus Crusade for Christ, another of the many parachurch ministries that compete for evangelical affection and largess. Otherwise, the way to "go deeper" as an evangelical is to live by faith, pray with confidence, and "experience the adventure of giving."

Focus on the Family offers an incredible variety of resources for evangelicals. The material is segmented by age and often by sex and generally provides an interpretive grid for believers trying to make sense of the things they encounter daily either through mass entertainment or the news. The assumption is that people who want what Focus on the Family provides are already Christians, since instruction on conversion or finding out about God is not readily apparent. On the matter of Christian living, the web site's resource page is underdeveloped. Topics include homosexuality, abortion, Ronald Reagan, bi-vocational ministry, and "how to be a Christian without being religious," all of which are links to book advertisements.

An evangelical (with Internet access, at least) trying to make sense of his or her religious identity has much from which to choose thanks to the parachurch ministries of Graham, La-Haye, and Dobson. Yet an evangelical in the United States has no reason to hold or follow any of the teachings or practices recommended by the largest evangelical outlets in the country. Being an evangelical requires very little, and that is the nature of the parachurch. Parachurch ministries have no binding address. Instead, the relationship between them and those who buy their products or give to their works is largely analogous to that between a business and consumers. Parachurch organizations have the goal of adding to mailing lists to increase the chances of raising more revenue through direct mail appeals. Most of the books and tapes they produce become incentives for donors to give more. Of course, their effort is to further an awareness of Christ and to instruct people in the ways of Christianity. But the parachurch, by virtue of its size, sends a message about evangelicalism that may actually impede its religious objectives: To be an evangelical is to be in a perpetual frenzy of trying to get more—more money, more contributors, more access, more zeal, and of course more believers.

Very different is the sense one has when inquiring into what it means to be a Pentecostal or a Lutheran. The expectations are firmer, the identity clearer, and the requirements for belonging concrete. Churches, unlike parachurch entities, have creeds that let people contemplating membership know the content of the denomination's faith. Churches also have structures of governance that provide a mechanism of accountability that is very different from that of the market model, which determines which parachurch celebrities are the most popular and therefore authoritative. These forms of church government do more than set limits on church officers. They also provide rules, and members and non-members alike can determine whether a church is abiding by them. Because parachurch agencies are less public and more like a business, their decisions have the potential of being arbitrary. Churches also have a common set of liturgical resources, such as hymnals, that provide members with a common vocabulary for worship. Indeed, churches generally gather once a week for worship, thus counteracting the anonymity that characterizes mass-market entities such as parachurch agencies. Such local knowledge comes with a price. It means having to get along with other church members who may not be the best potluck supper companions. But its benefits include forms of discipleship and diaconal assistance that parachurch efforts can hardly provide, thanks both to the latter's international scale and steady pitches for support.

If being an evangelical means liking Billy Graham, with a spot in one's heart reserved for James Dobson and Tim LaHaye, then evangelicalism requires very little from its adherents. One would be hard-pressed to imagine how evangelicalism could take the concrete form of a church, with a creed, set order for worship, and rules for ordination. Historically, the evangelical creed has been minimalist, the liturgy has tended toward Top 40 musical forms, and requirements for ministry have been so broad that every believer can have some kind of ministry. As a result, evangelicalism leans toward abstraction rather than the concrete forms of give-and-take involved in congregational and denominational life.

This helps to explain why the number of evangelicals in the United States, based on polls, is much greater than the numbers based on church membership. For instance, the NAE's total membership, based on the communicant members in the denominations affiliated with it, was 4.5 million in 1992. In *Megatrends 2000: Ten New Directions for the 1990s* (1990), John Naisbitt and Patricia Aburdene estimated that the United States had 40 million evangelicals.[22] The disparity between the figures could mean that the NAE was doing a woeful job in recruiting the many Americans who believed in the things for which the Association stood. Another possibility, of course, is that evangelical identity is so easily appropriated and measured that it has little significance. Not that pollsters ever ask Americans questions about being Brethren or Disciples of Christ. If they did, the statistics on religion would look very different. As it stands, being evangelical costs very little. It is a constructed phenomenon that academics, journalists, and parachurch leaders endow with great meaning, but beyond the cameras, bright lights, and microphones, the meaning of evangelicalism is indefinite.

The original leaders of the National Association of Evangelicals are as much responsible for this problem as they deserve credit for trying to address it. Enlisting denominations to rally behind a united evangelical identity was a relatively easy way to gain a significant number of members. They also could have recognized that the church was a more effective institution for sustaining the identity of Christians than the variety of Bible conferences, Bible institutes, and radio broadcasts on which fundamentalists thrived in the 1930s. Whatever the motives and understanding of the situation confronting born-again Protestants, the NAE's effort to give evangelicalism specific meaning was a failure. The Association failed because evangelicalism itself is an abstraction that sustains parachurch organizations, agencies that prosper through generalities and charisma. As much as the celebrity culture on which parachurch organizations thrive may be a blessing for name recognition, it confronts rank-and-file born-again believers with an odd set of competing loyalties. The parachurch, therefore, has been evangelicalism's genius as well as its Achilles' heel. It has spread the evangelical label, leaving born-again Protestants with a sense of belonging to something big. But that feeling comes with an anonymity resembling that faced by frustrated shoppers at Home Depot: The wealth of goods is truly remarkable, but it is so hard to find assistance.

A Special Purpose Religion

In his important book, *The Restructuring of American Religion* (1988), the Princeton University sociologist Robert Wuthnow argues that one of the most significant shifts in United States religious life since World War II was the rise of special purpose groups. Wuthnow describes these organizations in the following way:

> Their causes range from nuclear arms control to liturgical re-newal, from gender equality to cult surveillance, from healing ministries to evangelism. They address issues both specific to the churches and of more general concern to the broader society. Yet they are clearly rooted in the religious realm. They take their legitimating slogans from religious creeds. And they draw their organizational resources, leadership, and personnel largely from churches and ecclesiastical agencies.[23]

Wuthnow goes on to observe that special purpose religious groups are not a new phenomenon. They are at least as old in North America as the American Bible Society, founded in 1816. What is new was their prevalence in the latter half of the twentieth century. This is especially evident when comparing their growth to that of the denominations. In 1900, Wuthnow estimates, denominations outnumbered special purpose religious groups by a ratio of 2 to 1. In 1950, that figure changed to 1.2 denominations for every 1 special purpose religious group. By the 1970s, special purpose religious groups outnumbered denominations. Wuthnow concludes that "special purpose groups have not only increased in prominence relative to denominations but have also become more distinctly separate from denominations in origins and sponsorship."[24]

Wuthnow credits special purpose groups with revitalizing American religious life. In a highly diverse and specialized social structure such as that of the United States, these organizations "constitute a valuable way of sustaining religious commitment." "People can participate in these organizations for limited periods of time," Wuthnow adds. "When their interests change, or when a more pressing issue emerges, they can switch to a different organization." He sees these switches taking place in "all sectors" of social life, from business and politics to romantic relationships.[25]

Wuthnow's argument about special purpose groups could well explain why evangelicalism did remarkably well over the course of the twentieth century. Because it was not a backward faith out of synch with science and social progress, evangelicalism did not die after the Scopes Trial. Instead, freed from the restraints of denominational structures, it adapted to the free market of religion, and its entrepreneurial leaders established a series of religious franchises better situated to provide consumers with religious goods and services.

Of course, one sociologist's sign of vitality is another's indication of enervation. Steve Bruce, a British sociologist of religion, tends to be less impressed by the apparent vitality of modern forms of religiosity. In fact, he sees the seeming vigor of evangelicalism in its various structures as proof not that Christianity is reversing secularization but just the opposite. In his recent book, *God Is Dead* (2002), Bruce counters recent revisions of secularization theory to argue that the ideas that gave shape to social scientists' account of religion's place in modern society were right after all. Simply put, the notion of secularization claims that religious beliefs and rituals in modern societies, or those undergoing modernization, experience "a long-term decline in power, popularity and prestige."[26] As a result, the end point of secularization is not the disappearance of religion. Faith is too deeply entrenched in the world's various cultures and societies simply to be no more. Instead, religion's importance declines along with the number of seriously religious adherents.

This point about the ephemeral character of modern faith is particularly important to Bruce's explanation of the popularity of evangelical forms of Christianity. He concedes that organized religion remains "much more vigorous" in the United States than in other industrial democracies. Yet at the same time that the mainline churches are declining, evangelicals "are losing their doctrinal and behavioural distinctiveness."[27] Indeed, one of the reasons for evangelicalism's numerical success is that its most popular forms make so few demands on its adherents. Bruce sees little difference between the requirements for belonging to New Age religions and those accompanying evangelicalism. He writes:

> Diffuse religion cannot sustain a distinctive way of life. Where there is no power beyond the individual to decide what should be the behavioural consequences of any set of spiritual beliefs, then it is very unlikely that a group will come to agree on how the righteous should behave. Although the specific behavioural consequences of the Protestant ideal of "getting saved" vary from one time and movement to another, sectarians believe there must be some. Evangelicals in the tobacco-growing counties of the Carolinas might be keener to give up drinking than smoking, but they gave things up. Little specifics need follow from involvement in the New Age. The language of discovering yourself and getting in touch with the God within can, and is, used to justify almost any sort of behaviour.[28]

Whether or not Bruce's comparison of New Age religion and evangelicalism makes sense of all forms of born-again Protestantism, his point is important when considering the effects of evangelicalism's dependence on parachurch institutions and the hopes of 1940s neo-evangelicals for a lasting evangelical identity. "Individual autonomy, the freedom to choose, competes with the power of the community," Bruce argues.[29] By becoming a synonym for conservative Protestantism, through the popularity of evangelical celebrities and their parachurch organizations, the evangelical movement forfeited the authority that the institutional church possesses. To be sure, churches are imperfect instruments for achieving a common purpose. Protestants since the sixteenth century have experienced the divisive consequences of not having a central institution such as the papacy. But at least churches require beliefs and practices, although imperfectly enforced, that cultivate the religious identity of their members. The neo-evangelicals of the 1940s had hoped to do precisely that—nurture a religious identity for Protestants who were at odds with the mainline churches' leadership. They failed in that endeavor in part because they did not recognize that evangelicalism was an abstraction. As such, it functioned as a label that parachurch organizations could don just as easily as could a denomination or a congregation; in which case, the stuff of what it meant to be an evangelical was fluid.

The National Association of Evangelicals tried but could not contain the gigantic puddle that evangelicalism had become—a mile wide and, depending on the consistency, maybe even less than an inch deep. Unfortunately for evangelicals, scholars and church leaders continued to be impressed by the breadth of the leak but seemingly unconcerned about the movement's formlessness and shallowness. But if evangelicalism is going to mean anything more than liking Billy Graham, someone or something needs to channel the seepage into a culvert with adequate depth and firm banks.

5

No Creed
but the Bible's Inerrancy

The Evangelical Theological Society (ETS) opened for business at year's end, 1949. This organization, which has functioned as the chief scholarly outlet for biblical scholars and theologians who identify themselves as evangelicals, arose in large measure thanks to the efforts of the born-again Protestants who constructed the National Association of Evangelicals (NAE). To speak of the ETS as the theological arm of the NAE would be to engage in overstatement. Still, the ties between the two enterprises looked especially strong when the ETS invited Carl F. H. Henry to give the keynote address for the new organization. Henry, who had served as the book review editor for the NAE's periodical, *United Evangelical Action,* and on an NAE task force on Christian education and had taught at Fuller Theological Seminary, was firmly in the bosom of neo-evangelicalism. His selection as the ETS's first plenary speaker indicated the religious sympathies of the new organization.[1] Henry would go on to distinguish himself as evangelicalism's most highly respected theologian. The culmination of his scholarly labors was a six-volume study and defense of special revelation titled *God, Revelation, and Authority*. This made the ETS's selection of Henry as its keynote speaker all the more fitting, since from its founding the organization has insisted on only one doctrinal affirmation for membership: "The Bible alone and the Bible in its entirety, is the Word of God written, and therefore inerrant in the autographs."[2]

Of course, the NAE's doctrinal platform was broader than inerrancy, but not by much. Of its seven articles of faith, inerrancy topped a list consisting of the Trinity, the deity and miraculous work of Christ, regeneration, sanctification, eternal life and death, and the spiritual unity of Christians. The specific article on the Bible did not mention inerrancy. It read, "We believe the Bible to be the inspired, the only infallible, authoritative word of God." By the end of the 1940s, when the ETS was formed, that affirmation of biblical infallibility had taken on the narrower meaning of inerrancy. In turn, this doctrine, more than any other, became synonymous with evangelicalism after World War II. In fact, when Harold Lindsell wrote extensive defenses of inerrancy in the 1970s during debates about the nature of scriptural infallibility and authority, he defined evangelicalism by biblical inerrancy. Without this doctrine evangelicalism was meaningless. Lindsell wrote:

> Forty years ago the term *evangelical* represented those who were theologically orthodox and who held to biblical inerrancy as one of the distinctives. The Evangelical Theological Society is one case in point. . . . It was not long before the evangelical camp was divided into two parties—the one holding to theological orthodoxy with respect to matters of faith and practice as well as to inerrancy, the other limiting the trustworthiness of Scripture to matters of faith and practice, thus excluding other matters. It was at that point that the term *evangelical* took on different meanings to different people. Those who gave up on inerrancy while holding to biblical trustworthiness in matters of faith and practice continued to think of themselves as evangelicals.

Lindsell went on to ask whether those who did not affirm inerrancy were evangelical. He did not think so. But Lindsell had no authority to prevent such non-inerrantists from continuing to use the label evangelical. As a result, he concluded, "We should abandon the use of the term *evangelical* as a label for it no longer tells the world what historic evangelicals believe."[3] Obviously, Lindsell's despair was overblown. If inerrancy had been the line in the sand for evangelical identity, then how does one explain Billy Graham, for whom the doctrine was not a slogan and in fact would have gummed up the evangelistic machinery? Even so, Lindsell's fears for the movement and his understanding of inerrancy did reveal how flimsy born-again Protestantism's ramparts were. The Bible had traditionally been an icon of American Protestantism, and it clearly separated the faithful from the Roman Catholic element.[4] *Sola scriptura* became synonymous with rational, autonomous Protestant Americans who did not have to check in with church authorities. Once mainline Protestantism came apart, due to the competing claims of fundamentalists and modernists, born-again Protestants needed to raise the stakes of "the Bible only" by adding an explanation as to what kind of Bible was the only authority. For almost a generation the strategy worked, but by the late twentieth century, not even the confession "no creed but the inerrant Bible" could give evangelicalism substance.

The Construction of the Evangelical Mind

Historians of evangelicalism in the United States generally cite the founding of Fuller Theological Seminary in 1947 as a turning point in born-again Protestantism's fortunes. From 1925 until the years after World War II, evangelicals labored under the burden of being anti-intellectual. To be sure, the Scopes Trial and specifically the nationally broadcast examination of William Jennings Bryan by Clarence Darrow, in which the great commoner fumbled the most basic of the libertarian attorney's village-atheist-like questions, did not help the reputation of God-fearing Protestants. Even beyond questions of science and faith, born-again Protestantism's dependence on the forms and cadences of revivalism did not strike the nation's intelligentsia as the timber from which to form strong minds. Richard Hofstadter's 1964 Pulitzer Prize–winning study of anti-intellectualism in the United States dismissed fundamentalists as enemies of intellectual life. In the introduction, in which he listed several exhibits of contemporary anti-intellectualism, he reproduced a long quotation from Billy Graham, which included the following:

> [In the place of the Bible] we have substituted reason, rationalism, mind culture, science worship, the working power of government, Freudianism, naturalism, humanism, behaviorism, positivism, materialism, and idealism. . . . [This is the work of] so-called intellectuals. Thousands of these "intellectuals" have publicly stated that morality is relative—that there is no norm or absolute standard.[5]

Although Graham may not have helped the cause, ever since the 1940s, neo-evangelical leaders had recognized that if their faith were to gain a hearing and influence American society, they would need to beef up evangelicalism's scholarly standing. This strategy was partly the genius of Harold John Ockenga, who had studied at Princeton Theological Seminary and was a graduate of Westminster Theological Seminary's first class. While pastoring a Presbyterian congregation in Pittsburgh, he finished a Ph.D. in philosophy at the University of Pittsburgh. In 1936, he transferred his ministerial credentials to Boston, where he succeeded the famous A. Z. Conrad as pastor of Park Street Congregational Church. Upon his arrival in Boston, Ockenga strove to restore evangelicalism's voice within the formerly Puritan stronghold. He took advantage of the church's proximity to the Boston Common by preaching weekday sermons from Park Street's outdoor pulpit. Ockenga knew that in a city dominated by some of the finest universities in the nation, if not the world, evangelicalism would need intellectual muscle.[6]

Ockenga could not do it alone. His vision depended on several factors for success. One was institutional strength, which came in the form of the New England Fellowship and the seeds its leaders planted in forming the NAE. Another key ingredient was academic talent. Evangelicalism needed scholars who could engage America's intellectuals. In this case, Ockenga benefited from an unlikely development, namely, the convergence of roughly a dozen born-again Protestant graduate students at Harvard Divinity School and Boston University's School of Theology. The list of these aspiring academics reads like a who's who of the evangelical biblical scholars and theologians who came to prominence in evangelical colleges and seminaries and set the agenda for the Evangelical Theological Society: Samuel Schultz, Kenneth Kantzer, and Merrill Tenney, who went on to Wheaton College; Burton Goddard and Roger Nicole, who taught at Gordon-Conwell Theological Seminary; Edward John Carnell, Gleason Archer, George Eldon Ladd, Paul King Jewett, Carl F. H. Henry, and Glenn Barker, who held teaching posts at Fuller Theological Seminary; John Gerstner, who taught at Pittsburgh Theological Seminary; and Terelle Crum, who assumed teaching responsibilities at Providence Bible Institute.[7]

This remarkable convergence was particularly significant in the formation of Fuller Theological Seminary, a school founded in 1947 and named after one of the most popular radio preachers of the time. It soon emerged as the think tank for the new evangelical movement. Charles Fuller, the voice of the *Old Fashioned Revival Hour*, was at the peak of his career. His radio show, which combined Fuller's own brand of biblical exposition, his wife's empathetic reading of letters from listeners, and musical numbers performed by the Goose Creek Gospel Quartet, consistently attracted the largest audience of any national religious broadcast. Fuller's success gave him leverage in attempting to found a school for evangelism and missions. When he invited Ockenga to meet in Palm Springs to discuss plans for a school, the Boston minister prevailed upon the radio evangelist to consider a seminary. Ockenga believed that evangelicals needed more than another Bible college or institute. A graduate-level institution would provide the necessary intellectual heft neo-evangelicalism needed. Once Fuller committed to the idea of a seminary, he delegated to Ockenga the responsibilities for organizing it. The first press release for the seminary advertised Fuller as a "research center for evangelical scholarship." At that point, some of the evangelical graduate students from Harvard and Boston University looked especially valuable, particularly Carnell, Archer, Ladd, Jewett, Henry, and Barker.[8]

The scholarly imperatives of the neo-evangelical movement may help to explain the content of Ockenga's convocation address at Fuller's founding. His theme was the crisis of Western civilization, not the importance of training ministers for local congregations. The task for the new seminary was "to redefine

Christian thinking" in order to reiterate the "fundamental thesis and principles of a Western culture." Ockenga took a page from the kind of analysis of the relationship between Christianity and culture that theologians such as Abraham Kuyper and H. Richard Niebuhr regularly practiced. Western civilization, he told the seminary's board, faculty, students, and well-wishers, was "born out of the Hebrew-Christian tradition."[9] By virtue of its Reformation heritage, Fuller was well positioned to assist in the fight to preserve Western civilization both at home and abroad.

Other evangelicals shared Ockenga's ambitious vision and were taking steps at roughly the same time to beef up born-again Protestantism's poor intellectual performance. The first of neo-evangelicalism's scholarly ventures involved the unlikely choice of natural science. In 1941, several prominent evangelists and scientists teamed up to start the American Scientific Affiliation (ASA). The new body's purpose was almost as grand as Ockenga's vision for the new seminary in Pasadena, California. The ASA sought to harmonize science and the Bible. What helped to launch such an ambitious enterprise was the revivalist zeal for which fundamentalists and neo-evangelicals were known. Two of the three men who hatched the idea for the ASA were from Moody Bible Institute. Will Houghton, Moody's president, provided institutional resources; as a prominent figure in the founding of the NAE, he also brought to the ASA a similar vision of transforming American society with the truth of the gospel. The other figure from Moody was Irwin A. Moon, who had become something of a novelty in fundamentalist circles with a new form of evangelistic itinerancy, this one employing Sermons from Science, a film series about the wonders of God's creation. The third member of the team responsible for organizing the ASA was F. Alton Everest, an electrical engineer teaching at Oregon State University who offset the evangelistic and apologetic plans for the ASA by giving it more of an academic orientation.[10]

Juggling the ministry and scholarly aims of the ASA's founders was something of a trick. This proved especially difficult once questions about human origins and the teaching of evolution came up. The theologians and evangelists in the ASA's early ranks were more intent on refuting Darwinism than were the organization's academics, many of whom had made their peace with a nontechnical reading of the first chapters of Genesis and the received wisdom of their respective academic disciplines. Indeed, one of the reasons for tensions between the religious and intellectual purposes of the ASA was its statement of faith, which each member was required to affirm. It read:

> I believe in the whole Bible as originally given, to be the inspired word of God, the only unerring guide of faith and conduct. Since God is the Author of this Book, as well as the Creator and Sustainer of the physical world about us, I cannot conceive of discrepancies between statements in the Bible and the real facts of science.[11]

Eventually, the ASA modified its creed to include four points, with the first affirming "the divine inspiration, trustworthiness and authority of the Bible in matters of faith and conduct."[12] Even though the organization did over time back away from an inerrantist position, its origins reveal the intellectual aspirations that evangelicals possessed during the 1940s. The doctrinal consensus of the movement, which involved a high view of Scripture, was most often articulated in the idiom of inerrancy.

Starting a little after the heyday of neo-evangelical ambition but equally rooted in evangelicalism's scholarly aspirations was the Conference on Faith and History (CFH). The informal origins of this evangelical historical association can be traced to 1959, when a number of born-again Protestants, attending the American Historical Association's annual meeting in Chicago, huddled over breakfast with Earle Cairns, prominent member of Wheaton College's history department. The contacts made and networks established at this meal were sufficiently solid to generate formal plans in 1967 for a professional body of evangelical historians. Although the CFH emerged as an association dedicated to the work of professional history, like the ASA, it initially straddled the two worlds of religious and academic work.[13]

The organization's purpose was threefold: "To encourage evangelical Christian scholars to explore the relationship of their faith to historical studies; to provide a forum for discussion of philosophies of history and to survey current scholarship and foster research in the general area of faith and history"; and "to establish more effective means of interaction between historians associated with religiously oriented and non-sectarian institutions of higher learning."[14] Because an evangelical identity was necessary for membership, the CFH attracted nonprofessional evangelicals who were nonetheless interested in theoretical questions about the philosophy of history. This may explain why the organization originally appealed to some of neo-evangelicalism's theologians, such as Carl F. H. Henry and Harold Lindsell. It also accounts for the organization's statement of faith, which, like those of the other evangelical scholarly bodies, emphasized a member's attitude in regard to the Bible. When the organization's officers drew up a constitution, they defined an evangelical as someone who could affirm that the Holy Scriptures are "the Word of God, the Christian's authoritative guide for faith and conduct," and that Jesus Christ is "the Son of God and through his atonement . . . the mediator between God and man."[15] Obviously, an affirmation of inerrancy packed less of a punch for historians studying modern China than for biologists or anthropologists studying human origins. Nevertheless, the CFH's constitution indicated once again the centrality of a conservative view of Scripture for evangelicalism, even for academics aspiring to make a difference in fields beyond the study of the Bible or theology.

The attention that evangelical scientists and historians gave to the doctrine of Scripture may help to put the ETS's creed of inerrancy in perspective. Though in hindsight the doctrine of inerrancy may appear to be slim grounds for membership and theological reflection, it proved to be a remarkably fruitful basis for an organization that emerged during the 1950s and 1960s as the best evidence of a reinvigorated evangelical mind. Although the ETS did not begin until 1949, it signaled the reversal of a trend among fundamentalists that had characterized the first third of the twentieth century. According to Mark A. Noll, a variety of circumstances, such as "the loss of institutional bases within the older denominations, a shrinking corps of active Bible scholars, the spread of dispensationalism, the ascendency of activism, the distrust of the university, the disruption of the fundamentalist-modernist controversies," all contributed to an "eclipse" of serious and rigorous biblical scholarship among evangelicals. That situation began to change with the founding of the ETS.[16]

In his study of evangelical biblical scholarship, Noll credits the neo-evangelical leadership for breathing new life into fundamentalism's corpse-cold mind. To be sure, he recognized important alliances between those who would eventually join the ETS and mainline Protestant scholars such as Bruce Metzger; Dutch Calvinists and their publishing firms in Grand Rapids, Michigan; and British evangelicals who achieved a similar scholarly reawakening through InterVarsity Christian Fellowship. Even so, the presence of Ockenga and those he hired at Fuller are central to Noll's explanation of a resurgence of solid evangelical biblical scholarship. In addition to Henry, who wrote widely and organized almost as much, Edward J. Carnell made scholarship his vocation, even while succeeding Ockenga as president of Fuller. Everett F. Harrison taught New Testament at Fuller for three decades and made professional biblical scholarship accessible to students and pastors. George E. Ladd, Harrison's younger colleague in New Testament at Fuller, wrote books that were so highly regarded that a 1985 poll revealed their author to be "the most widely influential figure on the current generation of evangelical Bible scholars."[17]

Although Noll's final evaluation of neo-evangelical biblical scholarship was mixed, he did credit the efforts of those associated with Fuller and the ETS with a significant "turnabout" since the doldrums of the 1930s, when "few could have imagined a day when theological conservatives would again become participants in the academic world."[18] Perhaps the greatest compliment to the scholarly initiative of the biblical scholars and theologians who joined the ETS came in backhanded form in Noll's 1994 indictment of the evangelical mind. "The problem for Christian thinking," Noll wrote, "does not rise from the academic quality of seminary faculties, which has been steadily rising since the Second World War." He added that "to this day, professors at evangelical seminaries enjoy the most thorough technical training of all professional academics identified with evangelical institutions, and their work is read far more widely in evangelical circles than work from professors in the evangelical colleges."[19] Such may have been faint praise in a book titled *The Scandal of the Evangelical Mind*, but to the extent that an evangelical intellect exists, it owes no small debt to the neo-evangelical leaders who believed academic life was crucial to born-again Protestantism's witness.

The Limitations of Evangelical Thought

Nevertheless, neo-evangelical dedication and diligence to scholarly ideals could not hide the hollowness of the movement's theological platform. Some of the movement's leaders themselves were aware of the predicament. In 1965, Carl F. H. Henry used his perch near the top of *Christianity Today*'s masthead to assess two decades of evangelical scholarship. He believed its strength rested "in its high view of Scripture." Having rendered the good news, Henry went on to say that the weakness of evangelical scholarship stemmed from "a tendency to neglect the frontiers of formative discussion in contemporary theology."[20] Some of the discussions among evangelical biblical scholars, Henry believed, were "out of touch with the frontiers of doubt in our day." Evangelicals needed to go beyond merely "retooling the past and repeating cliches." "Unless we speak to our generation in a compelling idiom, meshing the great theological concerns with current modes of thought and critical problems of the day, we shall speak only to ourselves."[21]

Henry's former colleague at Fuller, George E. Ladd, registered a slightly different verdict only two years later in introductory remarks to the book *New Testament and Criticism*. Ladd believed the problem was theological, mixed with questions of succession and continuity. He detected two schools of evangelical scholars, one clinging to a negative approach toward critical scholarship that was typical of fundamentalism. The others, more akin to the neo-evangelical movement, were "convinced of the truthfulness of the fundamentals of the Christian faith" but acknowledged their "indebtedness to critical scholarship." Ladd did not hesitate in revealing the group with whom he identified. "These modern successors of fundamentalism, for whom we prefer the term evangelicals, wish, in brief, to take their stand within the contemporary stream of philosophical, theological, and critical thought."[22]

The curious aspect of both Ladd's and Henry's assessments was a sense that the neo-evangelical achievement represented the way of progress for evangelicalism. What made this perspective odd was a twofold problem. First, in Henry's case, was the question of whether the evangelical doctrine of Scripture, which was more or less required of theological, humanistic, and scientific scholars, as the cases of the ETS, CFH, and ASA show, was a sufficient theological base for such a robust intellectual agenda. Second, in Ladd's example, was the question of whether the division between the fundamentalist and evangelical heirs of the 1920s controversies was the real line of demarcation. Answers of a negative variety soon emerged as an even younger generation of evangelicals, contra Ladd, raised questions about how progressive the neo-evangelical movement had been. These scholars did so by asking, contra Henry, whether the evangelical doctrine of Scripture was all it was cracked up to be.

Indications of inerrancy's ineffectiveness in promoting a renaissance of evangelical scholarship were nowhere more evident than at Fuller Seminary. Although Harold Lindsell's book *The Battle for the Bible* (1976) blew the whistle on scholars at the Pasadena school, it was clearly a late one, well after the palace coup. Early on, the seminary faculty had drafted a statement of faith that, according to George M. Marsden, contained a minimal set of affirmations that followed the outline of theology in the Westminster Confession of Faith. Eventually, Fuller faculty sensed a need for greater precision and added the school's affirmation of inerrancy. It read: "The Books which form the canon of the Old and New Testaments as originally given are plenarily inspired and free from all error in the whole and in the part. These books constitute the written Word of God, the only infallible rule of faith and practice."[23] This was the theological adhesive that held neo-evangelical scholars together and supplied theological identity for this new breed of Protestant conservative.

The author of the statement was Fuller faculty member Edward J. Carnell. He wrote with both his Westminster Seminary training and the threat of neoorthodoxy in mind. For the original faculty at Fuller, the statement settled the matter. But Carnell himself eventually became unsettled or at least appeared to be to hard-line inerrantists when he wrote *The Case for Orthodox Theology* (1959). He raised doubts about his resoluteness when he discussed different conceptions of inspiration, highlighting differences between Benjamin Warfield and James Orr. Carnell's complaint was against a situation that had cut off the "classical dialogue on inspiration" and had placed evangelical academics in fear of raising difficult questions about Scripture. "The founding of new ideas has apparently run dry, for what was once a live issue in the church has now ossified into a theological tradition." Carnell continued, "When a gifted professor tries to interact with the critical difficulties in the text, he is charged with disaffection, if not outright heresy."[24] Because of such muttering, Fuller Seminary faced a public relations battle for several years after the book's publication. According to Marsden, the seminary distributed twenty thousand brochures containing Fuller's statement of faith and fifteen thousand scrolls on which were printed its statement on inerrancy along with the signatures of faculty members.[25]

Carnell's questions about textual difficulties and how to harmonize them with inerrancy was not an isolated occurrence at Fuller. On the heels of the public relations campaign to rescue the seminary's evangelical reputation came a shake-up in personnel that left inerrantists such as Lindsell either in the minority or without jobs. In 1962, key board members, along with the founder's son, Dan Fuller, pushed for a resident president; Ockenga had always managed to preside over the Pasadena school from his home on the other side of the North American continent. This push also involved an effort to make Fuller's neo-evangelicalism even more progressive. The favorite candidate of many board members for the job of president was David Hubbard, an Old Testament professor at nearby Westmont College. What complicated an otherwise dicey political struggle was Hubbard's assertion that the Bible was spiritually and theologically reliable but not inerrant. He also questioned the Mosaic authorship of the Pentateuch.[26] Also causing difficulty were personal ties between Charles Fuller, who was alarmed by defections from inerrancy, and Dan Fuller, whose exposure to European scholarship during his doctoral studies had alerted him to the deficiencies of the evangelical doctrine of Scripture. Finally, not to be missed was the harm Fuller Seminary's negative publicity was having on the *Old Fashioned Revival Hour*.[27]

The result was a takeover by the even newer neo-evangelicals of Fuller Seminary. Ockenga decided not to leave Boston for Southern California, and Hubbard became president. Dan

Fuller became the academic dean. What made this transition easier was that Billy Graham, who served on Fuller's board and was on the presidential search committee, accepted Hubbard's affirmation of inerrancy. As Graham explained to one inerrantist professor who threatened to leave the school because of the changes, "[Hubbard] stated outright that he believed in the inerrancy of the Scriptures and that he could support the doctrinal statement. If words mean anything, then he must be a strong conservative."[28] Graham's acquittal did not entirely comport with the exit of several faculty who believed that they, not Hubbard, were strongly conservative. Wilbur Smith and Gleason Archer left to teach at Trinity Evangelical Divinity School, and Harold Lindsell left to succeed Carl F. H. Henry as editor of *Christianity Today*. These personnel changes also bore fruit in a revision to Fuller's statement of faith. The affirmation of inerrancy was softened to become, "Scripture is an essential part and trustworthy record of this divine disclosure. All the books of the Old and New Testaments, given by divine inspiration, are the written Word of God, the only infallible rule of faith and practice."[29]

These were changes that Lindsell obviously could not forget, let alone forgive. Although the redirection of Fuller had occurred almost fifteen years before the publication of *The Battle for the Bible*, Lindsell wrote as if the events at Fuller were recent. Perhaps a reason for writing was the emerging prominence of evangelicalism due in part to the movement's political involvement. If so, the timing of the book was highly ironic. In the same year that journalists anointed 1976 "the year of the evangelical," Lindsell questioned whether anything was left in evangelicalism's reservoir. In a sense, the nation's bicentennial year may have been the turning point for evangelicalism, with Lindsell's book marking the unmaking of the evangelical movement that had grown up during the 1940s, and the political prominence of evangelicalism indicating the making of a new evangelical identity, one defined mainly by academics, pollsters, and pundits.

Whatever the basis for Lindsell's sense of urgency, his memories of the changes at Fuller were evident for all to see. He dedicated the book to former colleagues Archer, Carnell, Henry, and Smith. For good measure he lined up Ockenga, by then the president of Gordon-Conwell Theological Seminary, to write the preface. Lindsell then launched into an argument in which inerrancy was the "watershed" not only for evangelicalism but for genuine Christianity. Admitting error in the Bible, he warned, ultimately resulted in "the loss of missionary outreach," quenched "missionary passion," undermined "belief in the full-orbed truth of the Bible," produced "spiritual sloth and decay," and led "to apostasy."[30] In some ways, Lindsell was doing little more than asserting the Protestant doctrine of *sola scriptura*. Since Protestants recognized the Bible as the only authority for deciding questions of faith and practice, it made no sense to admit that some of what Scripture teaches is dubious. Even so, for Lindsell, the best contemporary examples of evangelical defection from the doctrine of inerrancy were controversies in the Lutheran Church–Missouri Synod and the Southern Baptist Convention. To be sure, the size of these denominations, two of the nation's largest, made them noteworthy. But neither church had been a member of the NAE and so had only loose connections to the sort of evangelical enterprise represented by Fuller, the ETS, *Christianity Today,* or the NAE. The editor of *Christianity Today* could well have been accused of tilting at theological windmills.

Lindsell was actually in good scholarly company in drawing a line in the sand with the doctrine of inerrancy. By the time he wrote the sequel, *The Bible in the Balance* (1979), he knew it. James Barr, a reputable biblical scholar at Oxford University, had written on inerrancy in the book *Fundamentalism* (1977) and, though for different reasons, he had identified inerrancy as the doctrinal lynchpin of evangelicalism. He used *evangelicalism* and *fundamentalism* interchangeably because of the doctrine of Scripture that informed each group. When Lindsell read Barr's criticism of born-again Protestants, the former Fuller Seminary professor could not hide his glee. "From Professor Barr's perspective it is clear that he regards biblical inerrancy as one of the major doctrinal beliefs of evangelicals," Lindsell wrote. "So it may be said that any definition of what evangelicals believe must include biblical inerrancy."[31] Lindsell had been vindicated by an Oxford don not particularly partial to evangelicalism and had exposed his former Fuller colleagues' departure from the doctrinal platform that had launched the neo-evangelical movement. Just as important was Lindsell's act of calling into question the health of evangelicalism at a time when it was finally gaining the notoriety that many born-again Protestants craved.

In fact, Lindsell's book may have started a controversy where none had existed, except at Fuller Seminary a decade earlier.[32] Between 1976 and 1986, the publishers of evangelical books kept themselves busy with a series of titles that debated the merits of Lindsell's case for inerrancy. Inerrantists took the lead when in 1977 they founded the International Council on Biblical Inerrancy (ICBI), an organization that included in its ranks such evangelical leaders as Francis Schaeffer, J. I. Packer, James M. Boice, and Lindsell. In 1978, ICBI drafted the *Chicago Statement on Biblical Inerrancy*, which affirmed that the Bible is "infallible"—that is, "true and reliable in all the matters it addresses"—and "inerrant"—that is, "free from all falsehood, fraud or deceit."[33] The organization also urged evangelical organizations and schools to add inerrancy clauses to their statements of faith and explored the possibility of forming a coalition of "inerrancy seminaries" that would be doctrinally safe.[34] Finally, ICBI sponsored a number of books, five in all, that defended and promoted an inerrantist doctrine of Scripture along historical, theological, and philosophical lines.[35]

Then in 1979, as if publishers did not have enough to keep them busy, Jack B. Rogers and Donald K. McKim entered the fray with *The Authority and Interpretation of the Bible*. Written by two moderate evangelicals in the mainline Presbyterian Church (USA), one of whom (Rogers) taught at Fuller, this book was a crossover piece. It argued that inerrancy was not the historic teaching of the Christian church but rather the creation of late-nineteenth-century Princeton theologians who combined Protestant scholasticism with the epistemology of Common Sense Realism to formulate a "peculiar" view of Scripture unsupported by biblical teaching itself.[36]

The Rogers-McKim proposal, in turn, prompted responses from both mainline Protestants and keepers of the evangelical flame. Robert K. Johnston, a Fuller graduate and a professor at North Park Seminary, and William J. Abraham, a professor at Southern Methodist University, attempted to build on the shifting sands of the meaning of biblical authority. The former looked beyond inerrancy to find other possibilities for theological unity among evangelicals; the latter used the inadequacy of the twentieth-century doctrine of inerrancy to explore ways of understanding biblical authority culled from older expressions in the evangelical tradition.[37] From the other side of the spectrum came a review of Rogers and McKim's book that eventually became a book written by John D. Woodbridge, professor at Trinity Evangelical Divinity School, the home of Fuller inerrantists in exile. Woodbridge, displaying a familiarity with the historical record not demonstrated by his Presbyterian rivals, argued that the evangelical doctrine of Scripture showed more continuity with the historic teaching of the church than did the Rogers-McKim proposal. Woodbridge also turned the historicist tables on Rogers and McKim by arguing that their thesis, stemming as it did from twentieth-century neoorthodoxy, was even more novel than the position of nineteenth-century Princeton Seminary.[38]

Though Woodbridge wrote as much from his own theological convictions as from his training as a historian, a significant component of the battle for inerrancy was a historical debate about the precise origins of the doctrine of inerrancy. Was it merely the product of late-nineteenth-century Calvinist apologists at Princeton Seminary under the influence of Scottish philosophy, or was it the historic teaching of the Christian church? As a result, the argument about the nature of biblical authority trickled down to the historians. In 1980, George M. Marsden took up the issue in his magisterial *Fundamentalism and American Culture*. He argued, along lines similar to those of Ernest R. Sandeen, that the fundamentalist doctrine of inerrancy was largely indebted to the Princeton theology and that the philosophical foundation for the militant conservative defense of the Bible's truthfulness in matters of history and science was Scottish Common Sense Realism.[39] Though Marsden did not really take sides in the matter,[40] his conclusions added greater weight to the Rogers-McKim thesis that inerrancy was largely a modern construction.

Then the Institute for the Study of American Evangelicals, newly formed, weighed in with its first conference and book, *The Bible in America*, a collection of essays that further cemented the ties between fundamentalist views about the Bible and the philosophy of the Scottish Enlightenment. In three important chapters, Marsden, Timothy P. Weber, and Grant Wacker reiterated the close affinity between fundamentalist conceptions of inspiration and inerrancy and the epistemological foundations of early modern science.[41] Finally, Mark A. Noll seemed to have the last word for both theologians and historians with his 1986 book, *Between Faith and Criticism*. In a masterful survey of evangelical biblical scholarship since the rise of the modern research university, Noll supplied a valuable perspective on the tensions and assumptions within American evangelicalism that contributed to its distinctive approach to and regard for the Bible. He concluded that evangelicals were firmly committed both to a high view of the Bible expressed in the idiom of inerrancy and to a scholarly outlook heavily indebted to Enlightenment epistemology.[42]

Woodbridge and D. A. Carson kept up the discussion with two collections of intelligent essays on the nature of biblical authority, *Scripture and Truth* (1983) and *Hermeneutics, Authority, and Canon* (1986).[43] But the perception persisted that evangelical attitudes toward the Bible reflected sometimes misguided if not naive ideas about truth, the human mind, and scholarly investigation. As Noll concluded in the afterword to the second edition of *Between Faith and Criticism*, evangelical biblical scholarship, despite increasing sophistication, continued to be discounted in the academic establishment in part because among evangelicals "the influence of early modern science . . . remains strong, while in the university world modern and post-modern science . . . prevail."[44] The final verdict on Lindsell's accusation was decidedly ambiguous. On the one hand, the debate did prove his contention that inerrancy was a watershed in the sense that the controversy revealed great theological diversity among born-again Protestants, so much so that one could well conclude the movement was hollow at its theological core. On the other hand, the inerrancy debate was decidedly inconclusive because it raised more questions about historical origins of the doctrine than it answered.

The pronounced attention to history was ironic in one significant respect. For all the effort to determine whether Lindsell was simply masking Benjamin Warfield or whether Rogers and McKim were redacting the Bible's teaching through a Barthian grid, almost no one was looking at the historical origins of the evangelical movement after World War II and the way inerrancy was part of its constructed religious identity. To be sure, fundamentalists, Calvinists, Baptists, and some Wesleyans earlier in the century had insisted on inerrancy as one of the essential articles of the faith. But neo-evangelical leaders had gone a step beyond the older fundamentalist strategy by attempting to be less defensive and negative but still conservative. One way to do this was by reducing the list of essentials even further, all the way down to an assertion of the Bible's truthfulness in all it teaches. This tactic allowed evangelical leaders to avoid difficult questions about what the true teaching of the Bible actually involved. As long as someone could claim the Bible was inerrant, he or she could be included under the evangelical tent.

When Marsden wrote the fortieth-anniversary history of Fuller Seminary, he observed that the controversy over inerrancy revealed the way in which debates within evangelicalism were so often resolved: by appealing to popular opinion rather than to recognized authorities. "Whereas evangelicals appeal to the 'Bible alone' for authority," Marsden wrote, "they lack adequate mechanisms for settling differences on how the Bible is to be understood." As a result, the inerrancy battle demonstrated for Marsden the evangelical movement's lack of formal or ecclesiastical channels for determining the boundaries of evangelical identity. "Typically having weak views of the church or of central ecclesiastical authority, [evangelicals] cannot depend on synods or councils to adjudicate their disagreements."[45]

Perhaps even more important than evangelicalism's lack of an ecclesiology is what the battle for the Bible revealed about the place of creeds among born-again Protestants. "The Bible only" has long been a shibboleth among American Protestants, one often used to denounce "man-made" creeds.[46] Yet someone such as W. G. T. Shedd, who taught at Union Seminary in New York City in the late nineteenth century, recognized how meaningless the logic of "no creed but the Bible" could be. In a defense of the Westminster Confession of Faith, he wrote:

> Of course Scripture is the only infallible rule of faith. But this particular way of appealing to Scripture is specious and fallacious. . . . This kind of appeal to Scripture is only an appeal to Scripture as the reviser understands it. "Scripture" properly means the interpretation of Scripture; that is, the contents of Scripture as reached by human investigation and exegesis. Creeds, like commentaries, are Scripture studied and explained, and not the mere abstract and unexplained book as it lies on the counter of the Bible House. The infallible Word of God is expounded by the fallible mind of man, and hence the variety of expositions embod-

ied in the denominational creeds. But every interpreter claims to have understood the Scriptures correctly, and, consequently, claims that his creed is Scriptural, and if so, that it is the infallible truth of God.[47]

Following Shedd's logic, the leaders of neo-evangelicalism recognized the need for a creed. The Bible alone could not carry all the freight of born-again Protestantism because many mainline Protestants also believed in the Bible alone. Therefore, the Bible inerrant became evangelicalism's creed. It set the boundaries for an otherwise ill-defined religious identity, one geared more to action than reflection (after all, the NAE's magazine was not called *United Evangelical Reflection*). Inerrancy was the theological construction of evangelicalism. In the end, even this amount of creedal specificity would be more specific than what the goal of united evangelicalism could bear.

Open-Mindedness and Dogma

The intellectual renaissance for which neo-evangelical leaders during the 1940s hoped, strategized, and gathered eventually came to naught. The standard explanation of outsiders as to why evangelicals continue to be marginal in the academic world was stated well in an essay that Alan Wolfe wrote for *Atlantic Monthly*. The Boston College sociologist claimed that evangelical scholars had a "loyalty-oath problem." The requirement of evangelical colleges that faculty and students sign a statement of faith "would be rightly considered hostile to academic freedom." Wolfe conceded that evangelical scholars and many of the colleges that sustained them had made significant strides in becoming reliable conversation partners in American higher learning. But, he warned, "as long as evangelical scholars insist on drawing up statements of faith that shut them off from genuine intellectual exchange, they will find it difficult to become the kind of intellectually exciting institutions they hope to be."[48]

Several years before Wolfe's essay, Mark A. Noll offered different reasons for the failure, or, as he put it, "scandal of the evangelical mind." The Wheaton College historian identified the problem as one of having not too much theology but too little and the wrong kind. For Noll, dispensationalism and creationism stamped evangelicalism with a hyper-supernaturalism that prevented born-again Protestants from appreciating the God-given character of the phenomena that most humanistic, social, and natural scientific scholars study. Though he could have cited inerrancy as another factor that nurtured among evangelicals a measure of discomfort with the human and natural as sources of divine revelation, Noll's main complaint about inerrancy was that evangelical leaders were confused about the importance of a doctrine that was only distinctive rather than essential to the movement.[49] Even so, his concluding advice on ways to recover from this scandal did point in directions different from Wolfe's friendly recommendations as an outsider. Instead of abandoning statements of faith, Noll suggested that taking theology more seriously could alert evangelicals to the variety of ways in which they could love God with the mind. He wrote, "The effort to think like a Christian is . . . an effort to take seriously the sovereignty of God over the world he created, the lordship of Christ over the world he died to redeem, and the power of the Holy Spirit over the world he sustains each and every moment."[50]

In other words, if Noll's argument is on target, the mistake neo-evangelical leaders made in their designs for an intellectual awakening was putting all their money on the narrow doctrine of biblical inerrancy. The rest of the Christian creed, as Noll contends and as the neo-evangelical encounter with confessional Protestants in Reformed and Lutheran circles showed, has far more to offer academics who may desire a religious justification for their work as scholars. The problem for the post–World War II evangelical movement, however, was that the fuller the creed or confessional statement, the smaller the number of American Protestants who might rally behind it. As a result, inerrancy supplied doctrinal rigor to a movement desperate for the kind of clout that numbers apparently signify. The doctrine of Scripture did allow neo-evangelical leaders for a while to construct an identity for Protestants who were unwilling to identify with the mainline denominations or their brand of ecumenical Protestantism.

But coalition building is different from intellect formation. As the history of Fuller Seminary would eventually show, even inerrancy was too slim a hook on which to hang the whole question of evangelicalism's identity. Indeed, the doctrine that was supposed to distinguish conservative from liberal Protestants and would prevent the sort of theological slippage associated with liberal Protestantism proved to be not only insufficient for an evangelical scholarly initiative. Inerrancy also turned out to be divisive, a notion that in fact contributed to evangelicalism's deconstruction. The problem was neither the neo-evangelical recognition of a need for intellectual leadership nor the infallibility of the Bible. The problem instead was trying to make one doctrine, isolated from a broader theology of revelation and the rest of Christian dogma, do the work of holding diverse Protestants together *and* supplying them with a plausible academic agenda. Without a substantial theological core, evangelical scholarship proved to be ineffective in challenging the course of American intellectual life. Moreover, without a substantial creed to shape the movement, evangelicalism itself could not avoid fracturing.

6

Worship in Rhythm and Tune

In the October 2002 online edition of *ChurchMusicNow.Com News*, the editors interviewed George Beverly Shea, the man they described as having "sung to more people in person than anyone else in history." Television quiz show contestants, if asked to identify that musician, would likely have thought of Bono or Paul McCartney, both of whom have had lengthy careers. But in the arena of longevity, it would be difficult to imagine anyone outperforming Shea. As the reliable baritone soloist for Billy Graham's crusades in a career lasting almost sixty years, whose version of "How Great Thou Art" is likely etched on the memory of most born-again Protestants over the age of thirty-five, Shea easily beat his closest competitors in the race to sing in live settings to large audiences. In fact, during the period between July and October of 2002 alone, Shea sang to over ten thousand people. Since he had finally decided to slow down his commitments to the Billy Graham Evangelistic Association (BGEA), an interview with the ninety-three-year-old was no doubt timely and understandable. Equally plausible was a question to the veteran evangelistic crusade musician about his opinion of the state of Christian music, for one of the factors in his decision to reduce appearances may have been the BGEA's decision to use the talents of younger Christian musicians, whose music was vastly different from Shea's.

The contrast between the musical staples of the older Billy Graham team and the new performers was on display in a Cincinnati news story covering the summer 2002 Billy Graham Crusade in southern Ohio and northern Kentucky. The first line announced, "Billy Graham Presents the Monsters of Christian Music!" This was not the BGEA's publicity strategy, but it could have been, according to the Cincinnati *Enquirer's* reporter, because in order to attract young people, "the savvy evangelist" had surrounded "his message with some of the hottest acts in the booming contemporary Christian music industry." Some of those musicians included Michael W. Smith; Kirk Franklin, "a top-selling crossover artist"; and dc Talk, a group "with a strong teen appeal and a smooth mix of rock, rap and pop." Then there was George Beverly Shea, "a fixture of Mr. Graham's ministry." Part of the reason for the switch from Shea, Cliff Barrows, and the Crusade Choir, which still performed on one of the nights, to the younger artists was that BGEA executives "were smart enough to recognize that this popular music was the vernacular that people were speaking," according to Frank Breeden, president of the Gospel Music Association. One of the performers, Tai Anderson of the rock band Third Day, chimed in: "Right from the top of the organization they see music as a really necessary and vital way to communicate to the culture."[1]

No one, not even George Beverly Shea, doubted the BGEA's understanding of music's appeal to attract audiences. What was not clear was to which culture the newer musicians communicated. When asked in the *ChurchMusicNow.Com* interview about the state of music in the church today, Shea gave a curious response: "It makes my soul hurt. Sometimes I don't even want to attend. But I love the people who do the contemporary music. I love the guys from D.C. Talk—they've been in my home, as has Michael W. Smith. They're wonderful people." Did this mean that people in churches performed the new music poorly? Did it suggest that churches and church choirs were behind the times, still singing songs like "Great Is Thy Faithfulness" and "The Old Rugged Cross"? Was it the case of good contemporary Christian music and bad contemporary Christian music, with dc Talk and Michael W. Smith representing the former and unnamed musicians the latter? Or did Shea love the sinner—dc Talk and Smith—and hate the sin—contemporary Christian music? The ambiguity forced a subsequent issue of the newsletter to issue a statement written by Dave Leeman, president of International Music Net, Inc. He wrote:

> The question posed to him, "What do you think of the state of church music today?" could be seen as eliciting a condemnation against music other than the styles that Shea embraces. I want to assure you, readers, that this is not the case. Although it was no surprise that a man of Shea's generation would have a bias toward the traditional, we shared with you his response because of the wonderful spirit and attitude he expressed that we believe is the only and Godly answer to the undeniable divisions over style in our church music world. . . . We are a divided church over how we express our unified belief that God should be worshipped and praised. But we can be unified by love that respects and honors those with whom we have different opinions or preferences. Shea's spirit toward DC Talk and Michael W. Smith is a model for all musicians on both sides of the walls.[2]

Only a few years earlier, religious historian Michael S. Hamilton had written an article for *Christianity Today* about precisely this division among low-church Protestants over song in worship. Hamilton cast the split in generational categories. "Baby boomers," he wrote, "have abandoned the denominational loyalties of their parents. The generation that was crowded into maternity wards and grade schools and rock concerts now crowds into megachurches." In fact, Hamilton added, "Only a generation that loved Woodstock could love Willow Creek." As a result, the fans of dc Talk and Michael W. Smith were not about to be content with the mellow voice and gospel hymn standards of George Beverly Shea or Cliff Barrows and the Billy Graham Crusade Choir. "A generation at odds with the traditions it has inherited," Hamilton summarized, "is going to change the way it does church."[3] Thus, the worship wars that were dividing congregations into two or three services that reflected the diverse musical tastes of members were even affecting the mass rallies through which Billy Graham had established his reputation and cultivated an evangelical constituency.

As much as born-again Protestants over the last two decades of the twentieth century engaged in disputes over worship, these worship wars actually reflected greater continuity than most observers or participants imagined. Worship had not been explicitly part of the neo-evangelical movement's effort to establish a conservative alternative to fundamentalism and to transform America with the gospel. But it was indirectly. The born-again Protestants who rallied under the banner of neo-evangelicalism made few contributions to the practice of worship in the name of ecumenism, but they shared an unmistakable liturgical outlook that relied heavily on the ability of music and song to create religious identity. For that reason, the musical idiom of George Beverly Shea was only the tip of an iceberg of worship style that unified those Protestants at mid century who would be evangelical. The problem, however, was that the appeal of these musicians and their songs was generational. Consequently, the music that gave vitality to and conveyed the emotions of evangelical Protestantism was also inevitably a crucial component in the growing fragmentation of the movement.

Why Should the Devil Have All the Good Music?

When Harold John Ockenga spoke at Fuller Seminary's opening convocation in 1947, he tried to connect the mission of the new school to the cultural task of preserving Western civilization. His interests were especially theological. Shoring up the West's religious foundation was one particular way that Fuller could assist.[4] The words "Western civilization" also connoted the great literary and artistic achievements of the West, from Shakespeare and Milton to Bach and Beethoven. Ockenga's words must have rung a little hollow to those outside fundamentalist circles, however, when the convocation proceedings turned musical and the *Old Fashioned Revival Hour* choir sang. George M. Marsden, who writes about this odd combination in his history of Fuller Seminary, does not specify which song the choir sang. But if the recordings of Charles Fuller's choral accompanists are any indication, one of the listeners' favorites was "He Keeps Me Singing." As popular as the song may have been, the first stanza and refrain were not a good indication of the seminary's commitment to promoting the culture of the West.

> There's within my heart a melody
> Jesus whispers sweet and low,
> Fear not, I am with thee, peace, be still,
> In all of life's ebb and flow.

> Jesus, Jesus, Jesus,
> Sweetest Name I know,
> Fills my every longing,
> Keeps me singing as I go.

Even if the choral number sung at Fuller Seminary's opening was not as sophisticated as the aspirations in Ockenga's address, the *Old Fashioned Revival Hour* choir's presence and performance demonstrated well the importance of music to the constituency that would affiliate with the evangelical movement. Practically everywhere a Protestant who was disaffected with the mainline churches went, he or she encountered music. The songs were not simply the great hymns of Watts or Wesley or Bonar. They were texts and tunes with remarkable relevance to a young generation of Protestants who felt handcuffed by the constraints of Victorian Protestantism, whether liberal or conservative.

For instance, as noted in chapter 4, music of a "zippy" variety was crucial to the born-again youth movement in which Billy Graham learned some of his skills as a popular communicator and organizer of rallies. This is a point that Joel A. Carpenter effectively makes in his study of the neo-evangelical movement, *Revive Us Again* (1997). Not only did Youth for Christ leaders such as Robert Cook and Torrey Johnson strongly urge local rally directors to include musical entertainment that would compete with popular contemporary music from the secular world, but born-again Protestants were also apparently blessed with a range of accomplished contemporary musicians. Johnson himself was, according to one reporter, "the religious counterpart of Frank Sinatra" thanks to his "curly hair," attire that included flashy bow ties, and his ability to speak "the language of the bobby soxers." But this Chicago pastor's appeal was primarily in his delivery, not his musical talent.[5]

For musical accomplishment, however, Johnson did not have to look very far. According to Carpenter, many of those responsible for Youth for Christ rallies had experience playing in dance bands or working as disc jockeys and "liked music with contemporary flair." Jack Wyrtzen, the New York City YFC leader, illustrated this pattern by moonlighting with a twelve-piece dance band before his conversion. Wyrtzen's own song leader, whom one admirer said sang "like a cowboy," obviously preferred the stylings of country to big band jazz.[6] Still, despite a diversity of musical fashions, the emphasis of born-again Protestant song was not on traditional but on contemporary modes of expression. This was no less true of Billy Graham's sidekicks, Cliff Barrows and George Beverly Shea. Carpenter writes that at least in the early days of Graham's circuit riding, the feel of the crusades was "as much Saturday night gospel variety show as traditional revival meeting." The music that by 2002 sounded traditional had actually been in 1947 "up-to-date."[7]

Born-again Protestant reliance on music to appeal to audiences and as the basis for corporate expressions of devotion was not novel to the youth movement of the 1940s. In fact, as heirs of fundamentalism, the leaders of YFC were running in trails well worn by their religious ancestors. Paul Rader was one figure from the 1920s who established the importance of music and entertainment in the gospel ministry. A former cowboy, teacher, boxer, football coach, and oil speculator, Rader became a popular figure in Chicago's fundamentalist circles thanks to two institutions. The first was the Chicago Gospel Tabernacle, which held meetings on Sunday afternoons and functioned, according to Carpenter, "much like a local theater on the vaudeville circuit."[8] The second important component of Rader's work was a radio broadcast, *The National Radio Chapel*, on a powerful Chicago station that sent signals as far as the East Coast and Canada. Key to the evangelist/emcee's success was music. To the Tabernacle Rader attracted talented gospel musicians who performed a variety of music that ran from hymns and gospel choruses to John Philip Sousa marches. Music at the Tabernacle also became program material for broadcasts. Eventually, Rader's own company, Tabernacle Publishing, produced its own songbook, *Tabernacle*

Hymns, which became a favorite of many born-again Protestant congregations. Among the favorite songs in the book were "My Sins Are Blotted Out, I Know," written by Rader's pianist, Merrill Dunlop, and Rader's own "Only Believe, Only Believe." "Like radio jingles," Carpenter writes, these gospel choruses "had to be easy to memorize, with catchy melodies and rhythms that almost sang themselves, so that people would find themselves humming and singing them again and again."[9]

The hits kept coming with the next of fundamentalism's popular radio preachers, Charles Fuller. The Southern California radio evangelist was converted in 1916 at one of Rader's revivals at Los Angeles's Church of the Open Door. He acquired some of his communications skills by conducting a Bible study in his home and by studying at the Bible Institute of Los Angeles (BIOLA). He used his Bible study as the basis to plant an independent congregation, Calvary Church. In 1924, Fuller started a radio broadcast on BIOLA's station that differed little from the kind of instruction he conducted in his home Bible studies. By the late 1920s, the Sunday evening service at Calvary Church provided the programming for his broadcasts. During the 1930s, Fuller decided to leave the pastorate to pursue radio work on a full-time basis. He concentrated on local stations, some of them powerful enough to reach the entire West Coast, until 1937, when the executives at the Mutual Broadcasting System invited Fuller to be one of their nationally syndicated religious broadcasters. That year his show, the *Old Fashioned Revival Hour,* could be heard Sunday evenings during prime-time hours on eighty-eight stations across the United States.[10]

Again, music was an important part of Fuller's success. The show's choir opened every broadcast with the born-again favorite "Jesus Saves." The choir also had a set slot in the show for singing other fundamentalist favorites such as "There's Power in the Blood" and "Beulah Land."[11] Perhaps even more popular than Fuller's choir was Rudy Atwood and the Goose Creek Gospel Quartet, who regularly performed on the broadcasts and indicated that the evangelist knew the importance of music to his listeners. According to Carpenter, "The quartet's smooth renditions of old-fashioned gospel hymns and Atwood's bright and lively keyboard embellishments added a hint of contemporary styling to the program."[12] By 1944, the *Old Fashioned Revival*

Hour attracted a listening audience estimated at twenty million. The songs, music, and performers undoubtedly helped Fuller's broadcast achieve such a large market share. Nevertheless, the gospel music of the fundamentalist era that provided the dab of liturgical epoxy holding the neo-evangelical movement together could not appeal to the fundamentalists' and neo-evangelicals' children. Early signs of a shift in musical tastes among born-again Protestants occurred in the 1960s in the work of musicians such as Ralph Carmichael. Randall Balmer calls Carmichael "one of the pioneers in the remaking of 'church music' from the old standards of eighteenth- and nineteenth-century hymnody to the 'praise music'" of contemporary born-again Protestantism. The son of an Illinois Assemblies of God pastor, Carmichael grew up learning to play the violin, piano, and trumpet. The brass instrument may have accounted for his affection for jazz of the big band era. After studying briefly for the ministry at Southern California Bible College, Carmichael returned to his first love—music. He served as minister of music for five years in a Los Angeles Baptist church before beginning to write music for Christian films, from Moody Bible Institute's movies about nature to Billy Graham's initial ventures into first-run films with titles such as *The Restless Ones* (1965). He also did work for the mainstream media, writing and arranging music for the likes of Nat King Cole, Bing Crosby, Pat Boone, and Ella Fitzgerald. Even so, he never left church music entirely behind. His songs "He's Everything to Me," "We Are More Than Conquerors," and "A Quiet Place" became favorites in church youth groups and Christian summer camps.[13]

Many of these songs also became pieces of musicals that he wrote with Kurt Kaiser. In camps and churches, teens learned and performed a blend of rock 'n' roll and folk music in such productions as *Tell It Like It Is* (1969) and *Natural High* (1970). Carmichael himself admitted that he wrote with the younger generation in mind; by the time these musicals were popular in the late 1960s and early 1970s, he was middle-aged. As he explained to one reporter, "That was a period of time when the kids felt disenfranchised. They were hearing a new genre of music on the radio that was so different from what they heard in church, so they just rolled their eyes at it. So Kurt and I began experimenting. Soon it began to catch on with youth ministers across the nation."[14] Randall Balmer confirmed Carmichael's point when in a brief survey of Christian worship songs he noted that even though born-again Protestants were slow to embrace rock 'n' roll in the 1960s, musicians such as Carmichael and Kaiser "recognized that the strains of 'Make Me a Blessing' and 'Bringing in the Sheaves' . . . could no longer compete with 'Hey Jude,' 'Alice's Restaurant,' and 'I Can't Get No Satisfaction.'"[15] As much as Carmichael's music functioned as a wedge between a younger generation and the music their parents considered essential Christian listening, it still stemmed from the same impulse that had informed the older generation's musical tastes. Carmichael's music was "zippy" and designed to reach young people with a Christian alternative to music of the secular world. What constituted zippy in the 1940s had significantly changed by 1970. But the operative words were still *youth* and *up-tempo*. Even more basic was the way in which music and song solidified a devotional style that was from all appearances uniquely evangelical.

Born-again Protestants' full embrace of the new musical idiom of the 1960s, however, would have to wait until the 1970s, when Jesus Rock, also known as Christian Contemporary Music (CCM), made its debut. This was the opening skirmish of the worship wars, a conflict that Carmichael's songs had sidestepped in part because they could be segregated in the settings of youth rallies and summer teen camps.

The standard account of Christian Rock's rise to a robust share in the recording industry's market—in 2001 it accounted for $747 million in record sales—begins with Larry Norman. In 1969, Capital Records, the label that recorded and distributed the Beatles and Frank Sinatra, released Norman's first album, *I Love You*.[16] A product of Northern California youth culture, Norman had started with a band called People. But Norman would achieve his fame as a solo artist, being dubbed by the *New York Times* as "Christian rock's most intelligent writer and greatest asset."[17] His music caught on among Christian teens—the Jesus People—who had clear sympathies with the countercultural stance of the hippies and Woodstock but who were hesitant to embrace the other two members of the 1960's sex, drugs, and rock 'n' roll trinity. Norman was the first in a wave of Christian rockers that soon included Randy Matthews, Andre

Crouch, Petra, and Second Chapter of Acts. Norman's question, "Why should the devil have all the good music?" apparently made sense to teenagers and young adults with devout motives and, perhaps more importantly to record company executives, disposable income.

The appeal of Christian Rock was initially greater than its profitability. The problem was that CCM artists did not have easy access to rock 'n' roll's mobile billboard: the car radio. Christian Rock was too religious for Top 40 stations and had too much beat for Christian radio, which when not broadcasting preachers and evangelists was still playing the hits of songwriters such as Fanny Crosby sung by the likes of George Beverly Shea. The key to CCM's success as a money-making venture lay in the recognition by recording industry executives that Christian music had some appeal with mainstream audiences. The designation "Gospel Music" became a catchall for everything from folk to rock 'n' roll that contained religious themes or words (some evangelicals tried to claim the Irish band U2 as part of Christian Rock because of religious themes in their lyrics). The one singer who capitalized on and proved the success of this strategy of crossing over into "secular" markets was Amy Grant, CCM's first crossover artist. Her album *Age to Age* (1982) was the first from a born-again artist to sell more than one million copies and stayed at the top of *Billboard* magazine's "inspirational" chart for over 150 weeks. Her next production, *Straight Ahead* (1984), was number one in the same category for more than a year. Eventually, Grant proved unable to achieve the same success as a "secular" singer, but she did demonstrate that CCM, when marketed to the right niche, could be more than an artifact of a religious subculture.

Nevertheless, as important as artists such as Norman and Grant were to the success of CCM as a business enterprise, more significant was the spiritual foundation laid by the charismatic movement. Coincidental with the rise of Christian Rock was the phenomenon of Praise & Worship (P & W) music. These songs made worship less stuffy and more accessible to the 1960s youth culture. In some cases, the musical idiom was rock 'n' roll or a softer version thereof. But like the generic category of Gospel Music, P & W indicated that the song was generally contemporary. Furthermore, the P & W label stood for a style of worship in which music was not merely the filler between preaching, Bible reading, and prayer. It also functioned as the means by which worshipers entered the very presence of God.

The chief figure in the application of musical pop to evangelical worship was Chuck Smith, the founding pastor of Calvary Chapel in Southern California. Originally a minister in the Church of the Foursquare Gospel, Smith struggled with the denomination's Pentecostal ethos for almost two decades. In 1965, he began to minister to a struggling church, Calvary Chapel in Costa Mesa, California. Smith and his wife, Kay, decided to target the hippies and surfers in the vicinity. One of the devices he used was CCM in worship. His success with and reliance on this music led him to found a recording company, Maranatha Music. In turn, Calvary Chapel's style of worship caught on with a younger generation of born-again Protestants, leading to a network of congregations that took the Calvary Chapel name.

Much of P & W's significance lies in its domestication of Christian Rock for the average congregation's worship service. Prior to the advent of the P & W genre, CCM appealed primarily to teens seeking a safe form of rebellion. Many of the venues for early CCM musicians were coffeehouses or the concert stage. Worship in churches, no matter how indifferent to liturgy, was still wedded to the hymnal and therefore at odds with rock 'n' roll's intensity and edgy sensibility. But with the advent of soft rock and as the teens of the late 1960s and early 1970s became adults, the contemporary music of the era gained respectability. Part of its new status stemmed directly from the music's ability to generate feelings and emotions that worshipers and their pastors often associated with the movement or work of the Holy Spirit. Indeed, one of the primary engines driving the charismatic movement of the second half of the twentieth century was music. Protestant and even some Roman Catholic congregations did not have to experience the second blessing of speaking in tongues because an encounter with the Third Person of the Trinity was possible through music that animated believers. What became particularly clear in the spread of charismatic worship was how much better Christian Rock and its lighter versions were in stimulating such experiences than were the gospel music standards of the late nineteenth or early twentieth centuries. In the words of Michael S. Hamilton, "Rock 'n' roll was simple. It engaged deep emotions and it portrayed itself as free of hypocrisy." He adds, "Praise and worship music focuses on intensifying the individual's experience of God," thus aligning perfectly with the 1960s generation's "luxuriant self-concern."[18]

Donald P. Hustad, a veteran church musician, picked up on the significance of musical style to the new forms of worship to emerge since the fusion of rock and charismatic Christianity. In the foreword to Barry Liesch's *New Worship* (1996), Hustad observed that "charismatic believers have a right to develop their own theology and exegesis, and they have done this well." After all, it's a free country, and in the United States that freedom especially gives believers the liberty to design worship and forms of devotion geared to popular sovereignty rather than beholden to an official church or governmental liturgical agency. The trouble, however, as Hustad explained, is that charismatic forms of worship are not readily compatible with non-charismatic religious traditions. For this reason, he warned that "noncharismatics should not thoughtlessly copy or imitate [charismatics'] worship formulae, unless they expect to enter the same 'Holy of Holies' in the same way." Instead, religious adherents of historic Protestant traditions "should develop their worship rationale based on their scriptural understanding, and then sing up to their own theology."[19]

As Hustad implied, the triumph of praise songs over gospel music and traditional hymns established a different understanding of worship among evangelicals. Even though older Protestant convictions about worship assumed that God was present with the saints gathered on Sunday through an act as simple as invoking God's presence at the beginning of the service, the popularity of CCM nurtured a different conception. Access to the "Holy of Holies" for many evangelical Protestants now depends on the praise band, overhead projectors (or their high-tech equivalent), and worship modelers stationed behind microphones at the front of the church. One indication of this shift comes from George Barna's 1994 survey, *Virtual America*. He asked survey respondents whether they find worship "inspiring," "refreshing," "Spirit-filled," "participatory," or "traditional." Barna interpreted the results as evangelicalism's "Great Report Card."[20] But in a footnote he qualified his interpretation by admitting that when respondents heard the phrase "Spirit-filled," they likely thought it meant "full of energy, vigor and spirit" instead of "permeated by God's Holy Spirit."[21] The addition of contemporary music to evangelical worship cultivated by charismatic styles undoubtedly contributed to the new understanding of "Spirit-filled." But the worship experience of born-again Protestants both before and after the neo-evangelical attempt to reform fundamentalism had always been dependent on music that borrowed heavily from the idiom of youth culture and its music. The reason had to do with the ability of up-tempo music of celebrity performers to stimulate the emotions better than the staid hymnody sponsored and approved by denominational committees. The difficulty for born-again worshipers was how to maintain some semblance of continuity and liturgical coherence with a younger generation that no longer found its parents' music "refreshing" or "Spirit-filled." This problem is particularly nettlesome if worship is supposed to yield some shared understanding and sensibility of the faith once delivered. With a worship vocabulary that changes every generation—maybe even every decade—thanks to the importance of popular music, born-again Protestants face a task not unlike that of all the king's horses and all the king's men who tried to put Humpty Dumpty back together again.

Youth Ministry Goes to Church

As much as P & W stems from older born-again Protestant habits of singing to the beat of a contemporary drummer (or even to worship practices Pentecostals perfected during the 1920s), journalists and pundits generally did not take notice of the phenomenon until it became embodied and institutionalized in the megachurch. In a 1996 article for the *Atlantic Monthly*, for instance, reporter Charles Trueheart gave some indication that mainstream media outlets had finally detected something that pastors, worship committees, and the born-again laity had been aware of for at least a decade. His piece began with a description that illustrated what those outside born-again Protestant circles found so startling about the apparently new forms of worship:

No spires. No crosses. No robes. No clerical collars. No hard
pews. No kneelers. No biblical gobbledygook. No prayerly rote.
No fire, no brimstone. No pipe organs. No dreary eighteenth-
century hymns. No forced solemnity. No Sunday finery. No collection plates.

Trueheart granted that this list had "asterisks and exceptions,"
but its meaning was clear. "Centuries of European tradition and
Christian habit are deliberately being abandoned, clearing the
way for new, contemporary forms of worship and belonging."[22]
Never mind that Billy Graham—one could also cite revivalists
going all the way back to George Whitefield, who first introduced
some of those "dreary" eighteenth-century hymns—had been
cultivating a novel form of worship well before Bill Hybels or
Rick Warren were even conceived. With the advent of religious
complexes such as Hybels's Willow Creek Community Church
and Warren's Saddleback Church, the "newer" style of evangelical
worship became a phenomenon with which to be reckoned.

Trueheart's article included more information about these
churches than simply worship. He noted the importance of their
size, their financial resources, their variety of activities, their
nonthreatening approach, their buildings and grounds. But in
most cases what stood out for Trueheart was the new worship
these churches practiced and the kind of music that defined
such services. These congregations, he argued, were drawing
"previously unchurched or unhappily churched people by being
relentlessly creative about developing forms of worship—most
symbolically and definingly, music—that are contemporary,
accessible, 'authentic.'"[23] Trueheart even connected, if only implicitly, the new style of worship to the sorts of innovations in
Christian music that had occurred during his own adolescence.
At the conclusion of the article, he likened the rise of P & W to his
own efforts while a student at Phillips Exeter Academy in the late
1960s to implement and lead "experimental" worship services
in the school's chapel. "We tried," he wrote, "to break through
to . . . [fellow students] in worship services by singing Beatles
songs and performing scenes from Samuel Beckett and slipping
in as much Holy Scripture as we could."[24] Without saying so
directly, Trueheart traced the roots of evangelical contemporary
worship to the most recent effort to lure teenagers to church by

offering them worship in the idiom of youth culture. Michael S. Hamilton chimed in when he observed that baby boomers were responsible for setting into motion the "revolutionaries" who "starting from outside the church tradition . . . began adapting popular secular music for religious purposes."[25]

Bill Hybels, the pastor of Willow Creek, would hardly qualify as a revolutionary by 2003 standards. But as a young man he was one of those children of born-again Protestantism who bucked the apparent stiffness of church life and worship. In 1974, as a youth pastor who spearheaded a teen outreach program called Son City, Hybels acquired all the ingredients that would go into his later much grander project in Chicago's suburbs. According to *Christianity Today*, "The loud cutting-edge Christian music, the gritty realism of dramatic skits, and the use of multimedia were wrapped around Bible studies delivered without Christian jargon on topics that young people could relate to."[26] What was cutting edge in the mid-1970s for Jesus Rockers by 2000 had become in the words of *Christianity Today* "the newest establishment," "an institution in American life." The reason was that what had been considered revolutionary in 1975—seeker-sensitive focus and multimedia worship—had become common practice twenty-five years later. The other reason is that the baby boomers, the former radicals, grew up, moved to the suburbs, and became politically conservative but could not leave behind the music of their youth. Hybels supplied them with a church (or a model for it) where praise bands and overhead projectors triumphed over hymnals, choirs, and organs. The generation that grew up listening to George Beverly Shea by 2000 was less numerous and growing older. Its days were numbered. So were the days of those who thrived on Hybels's kind of worship; it's simply that the number of baby boomers' days is a lot higher (for now).

Rick Warren, the highly successful and much imitated pastor of Saddleback Church in the Los Angeles suburbs, does not quite fit the revolutionary mold that Hybels does, although the two successful pastors' vital statistics match in ways that demonstrate born-again Protestantism's knack for generation-specific appeal. Warren grew up the son of a Southern Baptist minister in Northern California. While his dad pastored a series of small Baptist congregations, Warren honed his skills as, in his wife's words, "a ham," "a goofball," the one who comes out "in an Elvis costume." These are precisely the skills necessary for youth ministry. Like Hybels, Warren trained for the pastorate while leading a youth group in Southern California. His antics gained sophistication in part from training at Southwestern Seminary, a Southern Baptist Convention school, but mainly while attending one of Robert Schuller's seminars on church growth at the Crystal Cathedral in Anaheim, California. In 1979, Warren put all the ingredients together—the SBC background, youth ministry, and Schuller-styled principles of church planting—to start a congregation in a small, unincorporated community that was just beginning a development and population growth spurt. The letter he sent out to local residents began by announcing, "A new church for those who've given up on traditional church services!"[27] As successful as Saddleback Church became, Warren's approach never appeared as cutting edge as Hybels's. The reason had something to do with Warren's unwillingness to play the radical entirely. His congregation remains part of the Southern Baptist Convention, though invisibly so. While Hybels abandoned his Dutch Reformed upbringing, Warren remained a "goofball" Southern Baptist.

Willow Creek and Saddleback represent the new wave of born-again Protestant worship. The style is designed to be user-friendly (read: seeker-sensitive) and relies heavily on musical fashions that are accessible to a generation that is losing its hearing on pop music. The stories about Saddleback have less to say about worship and music, partly because Warren focuses on the phrase "purpose-driven" to describe churches and, most recently, persons.[28] Still, in his first book, *The Purpose-Driven Church,* Warren devoted a chapter to the significance of music, conceding that he had made the mistake of "underestimating" its power. Music has the ability not only to shape character, he argues, but also to define a church. In a revealing paragraph, Warren writes:

> The music you use "positions" your church in your community. It defines who you are. Once you have decided on the style of music you're going to use in worship, you have set the direction of your church in far more ways than you realize. It will determine the kind of people you attract, the kind of people you keep, and the kind of people you lose.[29]

A survey of his congregation conducted in his early years at Saddleback indicated that 96 percent listened to radio stations that played "adult contemporary music," a form of late-twentieth-century American music that Warren praises as a "universal music style that can be heard in every country in the world." Once Saddleback turned down the contemporary music lane, people followed by the SUV-loads. Warren admits that the church has lost "hundreds" because of this decision. "On the other hand, we have attracted thousands more because of our music."[30]

Willow Creek, in contrast to Saddleback, has received more attention for its innovative worship.[31] But in their book on the history of the congregation, Lynne and Bill Hybels downplay the significance of music and the novelty of Willow Creek's services. They comment on questions of worship style on a mere two pages, and even there they stress the importance of the teaching of the Reformed theologian R. C. Sproul on the holiness of God for worship instead of Bill's later encounter with Pentecostal-influenced services. According to the authors, Sproul and Bill "nearly came to verbal blows" over different understandings of evangelism. But the Calvinist's teaching on God's holiness and sovereignty launched "a new era of worship at Willow Creek." Later, Lynne and Bill admit that "under the influence of Dr. Jack Hayford" the church took another, "even deeper, turn" toward "a more Spirit-anointed approach to worship. But it was first through the ministry of Dr. Sproul that worship came alive at Willow Creek."[32]

Yet other comments that Hybels has made indicate that music was likely more important than Calvinist teaching on divine sovereignty for Willow Creek's seeker-sensitive ministry. For instance, in a 1996 interview for *Worship Leader* magazine, Hybels admitted the importance of seeing Hayford's church worship. Hybels told the editor that he did not really understand worship until the mid-1980s, when he attended a conference at Hayford's Foursquare Gospel congregation, The Church on the Way. There the Illinois pastor saw a worship leader who was able "to take us from where we were, into the presence of God." After forty-five minutes to an hour of singing, which consisted of "adoring," "confessing before," and "expressing our absolute trust and devotion to" God, Hybels went back to his hotel room and said, "This changes everything!" "Every Christian should regularly experience what I did tonight."[33] Yet in their book on Willow Creek, Lynne and Bill trace their liturgical roots to Billy Graham's crusades, using a similar approach but a contemporary style. They write:

> Because we began in the mid-seventies, while Graham started in an earlier era, and because we were trying to reach a different generation, we've used cutting-edge communication methods: contemporary Christian music, drama, multimedia, video, and dance. But we have merely harnessed those art forms in the same way that Graham has used soloists, choirs, and testimonies. Our approaches may differ somewhat, but our driving values are identical.[34]

The difference Hayford may have made on Willow Creek was giving Hybels the vocabulary to talk about the new forms of worship as manifestations of the Third Person of the Trinity. In a 1994 interview with *Christianity Today*, Hybels responded to a somewhat threatening question about using entertainment in worship by saying that anyone who believed that Willow Creek put an inordinate stress on performance standards for their music and skits had "never experienced Spirit-anointed drama, multi-media, and contemporary Christian music." If critics of Willow Creek would only witness the church's service, "they would retract every single word they've ever written about it."[35]

To be sure, Hybels and Warren are only two—arguably the most visible—members of a generation of pastors who have played the role of generals in a war to update worship. Still, the influence of these baby boomer born-again Protestants, thanks to the phenomenal success of their congregations, has been enormous. According to Donald E. Miller, religion professor at the University of Southern California, because of these "New Paradigm Churches," "We are witnessing a second reformation that is transforming the way Christianity will be experienced in the new millennium."[36] Kimon Howland Sargeant, the author of *Seeker Churches* (2000), is no less impressed by the influence of congregations such as Willow Creek and Saddleback but is not as sure as Miller about the direction of the influence. Seeker churches have, he admits, set the standard for "the American religious landscape," but how much, Sargeant asks, has this benchmark come from the likes of Hybels and Warren or from American culture itself?[37]

In point of fact, the question of Saddleback's or Willow Creek's freshness and influence is moot once critics and advocates of contemporary music recognize, as Hybels himself does, that the reliance on youth music is a formula that born-again Protestants have been using for generations. Michael S. Hamilton captured the born-again-business-as-usual approach of the megachurches well when he wrote about Paul Rader's Chicago Gospel Tabernacle as part of a series of articles in *Christianity Today* assessing Willow Creek's significance. Like Hybels, Rader used a theater-like structure that accommodated five thousand "casually dressed" people, provided them with music that was "lively, contemporary, and professional," added a restaurant inside the Tabernacle, and throughout the week orchestrated activities for men and women, boys and girls. "The idea behind all this," Hamilton writes, "was to create a new kind of nondenominational church that would use an interesting program and comfortable surroundings to draw in the unchurched." Rader's efforts were so successful that they launched a "host of imitators in many parts of the country, who then formed an association of like-minded churches." As such, Willow Creek and Hybels are "not so much charting new territory as [they are] traveling along one of the main arterials of American evangelicalism."[38]

Hamilton's assessment may have been reassuring to readers who worried that Hybels and those like him may have been doing something that threatened the integrity of evangelicalism. Yet the idea that a series of religious geniuses who capitalized on music that appealed to young people had patched together twentieth-century born-again Protantism must have kept some of those same readers up at night. For starters, what did reliance on music that lasted no more than one generation and that was the favorite of less mature believers say about a religious faith that prided itself (in a good sense) on a message that endured from one generation to another precisely because of its abiding truths? Or what about the perpetual cycle of intergenerational warfare that such practices encouraged; how beneficial could the battle between gospel and rock 'n' roll be for sustaining a sense of participating in "one Lord, one faith, one baptism" (Eph. 4:5)? Furthermore, what kind of continuity did born-again Protestantism exhibit if the style or forms were constantly changing? Hybels and Rader, it appeared, were the same but different. The tensions embedded in that comparison and contrast were certain to yield a volatile mixture, a religious identity that was as unstable as it was divided by its adherents' demographics.

Like so many other features attributed to twentieth-century evangelicalism in the United States, the ability to cast the faith in the vernacular of contemporary (predictably youth) culture proved to be a winning formula, at least in the race for numbers and notice. But less successful was this formula in achieving a religious identity that was constant and routine. Those who followed it, like Hybels and Warren, chalked up figures, built edifices, and managed resources that clearly appealed to a wide swath of Americans and attracted the interest of church leaders and journalists alike. The question, however, is whether what became of Rader's Chicago Gospel Tabernacle will also be the fate of Willow Creek and Saddleback. Christ promised that the gates of hell would not prevail against his church. But will the turnstiles of contemporary music and youth culture overcome the megachurch?

Evangelical Schizophrenia

The generational swings of twentieth-century evangelicalism, or more specifically the reliance on cultural expressions that appeal to adolescents and young adults, may help to solve one of the movement's great riddles. Those American Christians who identify themselves as evangelicals emerged over the last quarter of the twentieth century as the party of traditional values. In James Davison Hunter's reckoning of the "culture wars," evangelical Protestants constitute an important segment of the "orthodox party." What distinguishes the evangelical, Roman Catholic, Jewish, and Mormon warriors in the "struggle to define America" is a commitment *"to an external, definable, and transcendent authority.* Such objective and transcendent authority . . . tells us what is good, what is true, how we should live, and who we are. It is an authority that is sufficient for all time."[39] Born-again Protestants easily qualify as orthodox in Hunter's analysis because of the way they approach such questions as abortion, women's roles in the home and society, the goals of public education, and government-funded art. The cultural orthodoxy (read: conservatism) of born-again Protestants looks fairly different, however, when students of American religion remember, which seldom happens, that these Protestants are also responsible for Jesus Rock and contemporary Christian worship. Even if the words of contemporary Christian artists' songs do not contain references to drugs or sex, the medium of rock 'n' roll itself does not embody the "objective and transcendent" cultural authority of which Hunter writes or the infallible and authoritative divine revelation that born-again Protestants profess to find in the pages of Holy Writ. Yet during the same decades that CCM and P & W emerged as the expressions of choice for evangelicals at church, family values and cultural conservativism became the calling cards of born-again Protestants in the public square.

One of the better explanations of born-again Protestantism's Janus-like countenance came almost a century ago from the typewriter of the Baltimore journalist H. L. Mencken. His devout friend Howard A. Kelly, a professor at Johns Hopkins University Medical School, twisted the writer's arm to see the evangelist Billy Sunday, who had included Baltimore on his preaching tour of the East Coast. Mencken captured a piece of Sunday's appeal that has generally characterized those versions of Protestantism heavily dependent on revivalism's techniques and excitement. Mencken wrote of Sunday that

> he comes down so palpably to the level of his audience, both in the matter and the manner of his discourse, that he quickly disarms the old suspicion of the holy clerk and gets the discussion going on the familiar and easy terms of a debate in a barroom. The raciness of his slang is not the whole story by any means. . . . It is marked, above all, by a contemptuous disregard of the theoretical and mystifying; an angry casting aside of what may be called the ecclesiastical mask, an eagerness to reduce all the abstrusities of Christian theology to a few and simple and (to the ingenuous) self-evident propositions, a violent determination to make of religion a practical, an imminent, an everyday concern.[40]

Part of what Mencken recognized is that the drive to evangelize, the search for seekers, prompts an effort to find ways of communicating Christianity that are intelligible to non-Christians. As much as the evangelistic motive may explain jazz band or rock 'n' roll inspired Christian music, it does not account for the inability of born-again Protestants to see the inconsistency of standing for religious values that transcend time and place while packaging those truths in forms that are singularly disposable.

Of course, inconsistency may be nothing more than the hobgoblin of small minds. The problem for evangelicalism though extends well beyond smoothing out the wrinkles in its conservative reputation. It involves the fundamental question of identity. To be sure, it is difficult to reconcile how born-again Protestants can be politically and culturally conservative and liturgically liberal. But if evangelical fashions change as often as those of Joseph Abhoud, then is it possible to identify a set of core convictions and practices that endow the word *evangelicalism* with a meaningful measure of coherence? The leaders of the neo-evangelical movement of the 1940s hoped to give new significance to the word and in so doing did not spend much time thinking about one aspect of the Christian life—namely, worship—that has remarkable power to unite believers across generations and cultures on a weekly basis. They relied instead on the repertoire of worship practices inherited from American revivalism, which depended heavily on music to rouse seekers to walk the aisle and believers to ratchet up their devotion. As a result, the strategy that worked so well in attracting young people and the unchurched to the faith became another stick of dynamite in the deconstruction of evangelicalism.

Conclusion

Enough Already

Ronald Wells, historian at Calvin College, began the year 1981 with a gripe against evangelicalism. Born-again Protestants were just starting to throw their weight around politically, or so it seemed, and Wells did not appreciate evangelicals' newfound shoviness. For that reason, Wells confessed that he had been "on the verge of writing a letter of resignation from the evangelical movement." As it turned out, Wells decided not to initiate such correspondence once he read a piece that described Christian Reformed believers like himself occupying a place on the fringe of evangelicalism, which was "more often an embarrassment than an asset."[1] And just where would he have sent such a letter had he penned it?

Wells's consideration of resigning from evangelicalism combined with the question implied in it is particularly important to the argument of this book. How can something like evangelicalism, which looks so real and has so many apparent outlets, be so difficult to leave? How does one, even if classified as a card-carrying member, receive the membership card? And if an evangelical decides, as Wells contemplated, to become something other than an evangelical, to what address does he or she return the card?

These rhetorical questions are the ones that have informed the preceding chapters. Evangelicalism is a seemingly large and influential religious body, but it lacks an institutional center, intellectual coherence, and devotional direction. It is so immense that many Americans cannot help but be an evangelical if they answer pollsters' questions a certain way or belong to a church that historians and sociologists somewhat arbitrarily identify as evangelical. It should not be so difficult to leave a movement for which the terms of admission are so generous.

The fact that some Christians in the United States may want to abandon a religious movement that has indirectly claimed them was one of the factors that led to the preceding chapters. Another was the coincidental popularity of evangelicalism as a category used with some precision by religion scholars. How is it that a religious movement, begun in the decade after World War II and now apparently running out of gas, caught on with people who would normally rank as some of the most skeptical and irreligious? One obvious answer is politics. Evangelicalism came to national attention when believers claiming that identity entered the drama (stage right, of course) of electoral politics. That occurrence gave academics who study religion in the United States lots of material to analyze. The emergence of evangelicalism as a political lobby may also have spelled the demise of this particular faith because it diverted born-again Protestants' attention from spiritual to temporal realities. The last claim is clearly contested and involves questions about the nature of Christianity and a believer's social duties. Still, the simultaneity of dissatisfaction among people in the pew (and some in the pulpit) with evangelicalism and born-again Christianity's value as a tool of scholarly analysis is striking. It is a coincidence that invites reflection on the way Protestant leaders and academics have used the evangelical label. First, it was a concept that less belligerent fundamentalists constructed to fashion an alternative to mainline churches (read: liberal Protestantism), and second, scholars eventually adopted it as a way to account for greater nuance within American Protestantism. As a construction, however, post–World War II evangelicalism has always been little more than an abstraction. It lacked the specificity of institutional life in which card-carrying members pay dues and live with the threat of penalties. It has no officials to enforce its teachings and practices. Abstractions have their usefulness, however. Over the last six decades of the twentieth century, evangelicalism proved its resourcefulness primarily as a category that signified numerical mass and therefore influence. For born-again Protestants, evangelicalism provided a sense of belonging to a movement much larger than a local congregation or even a national denomination. Evangelical Protestantism apparently represented the entire spectrum of conservative Protestants who would not bow to the memoranda issued by the National Council of Churches. It also stood for the faith of regular Americans, mainstream ones—in today's vernacular, Red America in contrast to the mainline's Blue America.[2] As a result, evangelicalism gave vigor to Protestants who lacked the Protestant establishment's considerable clout. It also motivated those Protestants who identified with the movement to band together and recover the United States' religious heritage. These were goals that obviously Lutheranism, Anglicanism, Presbyterianism, or Pentecostalism, for instance, could not achieve. Denominational labels left Protestants divided. The abstraction *evangelicalism* promised unity and more—unity *for action.*

For scholars, evangelicalism functioned in a similar manner. Why write about one slice of the American population, say, the Baptist piece of the pie, when evangelicalism could lead to larger claims about a broader cross section of United States citizens? The question that haunts most academics is "So what?" Is the subject of one's study really significant? One relatively easy way to answer this question is to find a topic that involves many people, meaning millions rather than thousands. By studying evangelicalism, a designation that was much larger than any of the denominational categories, with the exception perhaps of Roman Catholicism, historians, sociologists, and pollsters could write books and articles that made much bigger claims about the doings of American religion than if they interpreted religious life along narrowly denominational or congregational lines. Evangelicalism not only provided the basis for wider affirmations about American religion but also yielded a bigger audience. Even though Baptist and Methodist continue to top the lists of the largest denominations in the United States, imagine the difficulty of persuading a publisher to take a book on Methodism or Baptists when evangelicalism could work just as well and might attract not only Methodists and Baptists but also Presbyterians, Pentecostals, Congregationalists, and independents.

Evangelicalism, then, has provided a valuable service for believers, academics, and retailers. It has supplied a collective sense of identity to religious adherents and yielded a scholarly perspective on American religion with more nuance than previous interpretations. But as useful as evangelicalism may have been, its usefulness is no longer obvious. In fact, its harmfulness may be what has become most apparent.

Not Enough

In a recent collection of essays on evangelicalism, John G. Stackhouse Jr., theology professor at Regent College, uses the idea of perpetual adolescence to diagnose the problems with evangelical Christianity. Adolescents, he observes, are those recently free from parental authority (e.g., the difference between fundamentalism and neo-evangelicalism), addicted to popular culture (Christian Contemporary Music), venerate heros (evangelical celebrities), and have trouble behaving responsibly (e.g., using pious motives as an excuse for dereliction of duty). Because of its immaturity, Stackhouse argues, contemporary evangelicalism "has been fragmented a thousand ways."

> Loyalty to a group, especially a local congregation and denominational tradition, is now regarded as a quaint heirloom from Grandma and Grandpa's day. We are loyal to those organizations that suit us individually, whether World Vision, *Moody Monthly*, Mennonite Central Committee, Awana Clubs, InterVarsity Christian Fellowship, and so on. And when they don't suit us any longer, we move on to another option, another "brand" or "product."[3]

Stackhouse's recommendation for this predicament, interestingly, is not to return to an older generation's sense of loyalty to a tradition. Instead, he offers one question that if asked in every situation would "challenge radically our bent toward selfishness." The question: "How can I love God and my neighbor in this situation?"[4]

As warm a thought as Christ's summary of the law may be to professing evangelicals, it might also be as abstract a rationale for living as evangelicalism is a way of being a Christian. This may be why other writers who have identified at some point in their lives with evangelicalism have sought help in precisely those traditions that are more mature and require loyalty.

One of the first to point out the insufficiency of evangelical Christianity was Thomas Howard. At the time that he wrote *Evangelical Is Not Enough* (1984), Howard's evangelical credentials were impeccable. A descendent of the Philadelphia family that published one of conservative Protestantism's most influential magazines, *The Sunday School Times*, a brother of evangelicalism's favorite submissive woman, Elisabeth Elliot, and a professor of English at Gordon College, Howard had been well steeped in the culture and piety of born-again Protestantism. This may help to account for his increasing frustration with evangelicalism. As an expression of Christianity it was too fluid or insubstantial or abstract. "It is difficult for Christians with strong denominational loyalties, especially those with ethnic roots . . . to find the axis of evangelicalism," he complained. "No city constitutes a Holy See. . . . The words 'interdenominational' and 'nondenominational' are words of good omen, not bad omen, in this environment. We attached almost no importance to ancient historic credentials."[5]

Lest he upset born-again readers, Howard made clear that in claiming evangelicalism to be insufficient he was not saying that born-again Protestantism was wrong. The movement's articles of faith, its piety and zeal were all commendable. But Christianity offered so much more than the bare essentials of doctrine, a strict reliance on the Bible as opposed to the wisdom of the ages, or evangelicalism's strict morality. There were, for instance, phenomena such as liturgical worship, prayer books, religious images, the sacraments, and the church calendar that, according to Howard, could supplement and deepen the simple piety of born-again Christians. Accordingly, he ended the book with recommendations for evangelical Christianity to become "enough." First, he proscribed a "return to the episcopate." This was not a means for an ecclesiastical elite to lord over the laity but a way to ensure "unity and accountability" among the churches. Second, evangelicals needed to restore the Eucharist to its centrality in worship, and the way to do this was to administer the Lord's Supper "at least weekly." Third, Howard advocated the observance of the liturgical year, a practice that would help the saints have their "imagination filled with gratitude for these forerunners in the Faith and . . . be *helped*."⁶

As it turned out, Howard's recommendations were not enough to fix evangelicalism. Only a year after the publication of his grievances with evangelical Christianity, Howard became a Roman Catholic, and his book, formerly published by an evangelical press, Thomas Nelson, became a title in Ignatius' list, evidence that a former question about evangelical inadequacy had become a polemic for attracting born-again Protestants to Rome.⁷ So, too, Howard resigned his post at Gordon to teach at the nearby Roman Catholic seminary, St. John's. From Stackhouse's perspective, Howard's pilgrimage illustrates one of the common ways evangelicals have tried to overcome the trials of perpetual adolescence. Having gone through fundamentalism and then evangelicalism, some have become "high church types 'into' sacramental worship and the early church, with heroes such as Robert Webber and Peter Gillquist."⁸ Stackhouse may have left Howard off his list of liturgicalism's heroes because of his abandonment of evangelicalism for the "one *true* faith." Clearly, Howard's decision to become a Catholic and his later explanations indicated that he had no intentions of trying to harmonize evangelicalism and Roman Catholicism. His candor about these matters, in fact, raises a question about his initial strategy of adding polity, sacramental piety, and holy days to evangelicalism in order to make this born-again faith whole. Is it actually possible to combine the best of both Christian expressions, one modern and zippy, the other traditional and mysteriously ancient, and salvage a Christian faith that is coherent and disciplined?

As much as Howard's own actions suggest a negative answer to this question, a recent book from D. H. Williams, a Baptist minister and professor at Loyola University (Chicago), expresses a different response. In *Retrieving the Tradition and Renewing Evangelicalism* (1999), Williams argues a point that is similar to Howard's but puts firmer limits on where efforts to overcome evangelicalism's inadequacies may lead. Williams begins by attributing the incoherence of evangelicalism to "an acute problem of continuity."[9] He likens it to amnesia in which the afflicted person not only forgets family and friends but also "no longer remembers who he is." Evangelicals suffer from this condition, Williams argues, because they have forgotten "that the building of a foundational Christian identity is based upon that which the church has received, preserved, and carefully transmitted to each generation of believers." As a result, new techniques for church growth and seeker-sensitive worship have filled the vacuum of memory loss. Williams concedes that evangelicals are not intentionally disregarding the apostle Paul's final instructions to Timothy: "Follow the pattern of sound teaching. . . . Guard the truth that has been entrusted to you" (2 Tim. 1:13–14). But Williams does assert that evangelicals "are no longer sure what this 'deposit' consists of, or where it can be found." Even worse, for some born-again Protestants, "finding this 'deposit' does not matter anymore."[10]

Williams traces the origins of evangelicalism's historical amnesia to a faulty interpretation of the Protestant notion of *sola scriptura* that finds inherent antagonism between the Bible and tradition. Following Nathan Hatch's important book, *The Democratization of American Christianity,* Williams finds the seeds of contemporary evangelicalism's fragmentation in the United States' earliest Protestants. Their reliance on the Bible as the *only* legitimate authority in religion bred a form of antitraditionalism that also spawned anticlericalism and anticreedalism. This position had the feel of being democratic because "anyone with a Bible in his or her hands could hear God speaking directly."[11] But this democracy was no respecter of persons, nor did it allow for a demos that included dead saints. "Believers are urged to eschew creeds, confessions, or councils," Williams writes, "and are told to 'study the Word itself' since the truth is conveyed in simple terms known to all."[12] The situation facing contemporary evangelicalism, then, is "a loss of coherency within the church as the very content of the faith . . . no longer informs the central task of the church."[13]

Williams's recommendations to fix evangelicalism, as the title of his book indicates, involve "retrieving the tradition." He understands the word *tradition* as much as a verb as a noun. "It is *that* which Jesus 'handed over' to the apostles, and they to the churches, but it also meant the very process of handing over." Therefore, tradition signifies both the "acceptance and the handing over" of a full-orbed Christian faith that includes the Bible, Christ, and the "concrete forms" by which the apostles passed on what they received from Christ.[14] Retrieving tradition, then, consists of more than simply adding the Thirty-nine Articles to the Bible. It also involves worship and the workings of the church. Williams acknowledges that his fuller understanding of tradition appears to be at odds with such Protestant mainstays as the formal and material principles of the Reformation. Tradition, he writes, can be used to teach matters that have no biblical warrant. But as risky as tradition may be, its neglect is even riskier for born-again Protestants, for without self-conscious reflection on what has been passed down through the ages and the means for handing the Christian faith on, evangelicals throw out "the (Roman Catholic) baby with the (Tradition) bathwater."[15]

If the baby and the bathwater are inherently linked, as Williams argues, does the recovery of tradition inevitably lead, as it did in the case of Thomas Howard, to Rome? Williams does not think so. He concedes that for many evangelicals, the beginning of a dialogue with Christians across the centuries led to "more 'high church' oriented communions where orthodoxy is celebrated in historically sensitive settings."[16] The fact that so many have abandoned evangelicalism for historic forms of Christianity is indeed "indicative of the lack of hospitality" to tradition that exists among born-again Protestants. Still, Williams insists that this move is not necessary. To embrace "the norms of the ancient Christian Tradition" is to "do justice [to] the full treasury of the evangelical heritage."[17] Consequently, Williams appears to be prepared to stop at a point on the spectrum of tradition short of where Howard ended. In other words, evangelicalism for Williams is not enough, but its recovery is possible if, in the words of Mark A. Noll, born-again Protestants "let ancient Christian traditions provide norms for the more recent tradition."[18]

The trouble with Williams's proposal, as intelligent as it is, is whether the faith that results, once older Christian traditions have been received, is actually evangelical. Here the issue is not Howard's case of an evangelical turning Roman Catholic. An interest in historic Christianity could and, of course, has led to

Rome. It has also led to Canterbury, Geneva, Edinburgh, Wittenberg, and Dort. Therefore, a pressing question is whether it is possible to pour tradition into a vessel such as modern American evangelicalism, which is designed to hold only liquids that are traditionless. To borrow an image from Hughes Oliphant Old's book on Presbyterian worship, asking evangelicals to recover tradition is like coaxing a thirteen-year-old who steadily drinks Mountain Dew to taste wine. The facial reaction will not likely indicate pleasure.[19]

Here it may be useful to remember an important reason for recent evangelicalism's distaste for tradition. Williams rightly looks at developments in the early nineteenth century, when Bible-onlyism turned low-church Protestants into the captains of their faith. But he does not extend his analysis into the twentieth century, when nondenominational fundamentalists concocted the recipe for evangelicalism: combine two cups of inerrancy, one cup of conversion, and a pinch of doctrinal affirmations; form into a patchwork of parachurch agencies, religious celebrities, and churches; season with peppy music professionally performed; and bake every generation. In effect, Williams, along with many other writers on American Christianity, assumes that an evangelical tradition exists.

What *Deconstructing Evangelicalism* has attempted to demonstrate, however, is that the very notion of an evangelical tradition is a construction of mid-twentieth-century born-again Protestants who objected to the fundamentalist label but were still at odds with mainline denominations. Although the faith they created borrowed fragments from historic Protestantism, its design was to affirm a lowest common denominator set of convictions and practices. By doing so, the neo-evangelical leaders hoped to assemble a movement that would function as the real, or at least a rival, American Protestantism. As it turned out, the faith that emerged from these designs thrived in a strange combination of settings—the popular music business, parachurch organizations, and university religious studies seminars. This was hardly the stuff from which to make a tradition. Perhaps more important, this form of Christianity was not the kind that tradition could shape. Like creation after Genesis 1:1, it was formless and void. To be sure, this was a great concoction for evangelical entrepreneurs to peddle in a nation in which most

cultural goods end up being packaged and exchanged as com-
modities. Nevertheless, this evangelical brew was not an elixir
that could transport its imbibers into the past to appreciate
historic Christianity's virtues.

This indictment could well sound reactionary, but interestingly, Williams supplies the very definition of tradition that may
help readers find the argument here plausible. Actually, it is
not his own definition but one Williams took from philosopher
Alasdair MacIntyre. For this moral philosopher, whose work has
consistently revealed the shortcomings of the cultural developments on which evangelicalism has thrived, tradition is basically an argument. That is, it is an argument "extended through
time in which certain fundamental agreements are defined and
redefined." The process whereby tradition as argument is re-
fined includes two sets of conversations, one "with critics and
enemies external to the tradition" and one involving those who
identify with the tradition, insiders, who engage in "interpretive debates" about its boundaries.[20] For Williams's purposes,
MacIntyre's understanding of tradition allows an understanding
of Christianity in which its adherents are in a constant conversation with previous generations of saints as well as Scripture.
This extended argument through the ages prevents tradition from
calcifying into "intractable authoritarianism" or degenerating
into "sectarianism and fragmentation."[21]

Curiously, Williams does not apply MacIntyre's notion of
tradition to evangelicalism itself. If tried, such an application
would reveal how hostile evangelicalism, in its contemporary
meaning, is toward tradition. If a student of American Christianity wanted to identify the extended argument that has defined
evangelical Protestantism, where would he or she look? One
approach might be to trace evangelicalism back to the First
Great Awakening, with Jonathan Edwards and George Whitefield functioning as the primary interlocutors. But the variety
of evangelicalism that emerged after World War II, as much as
its leaders may have looked to America's Great Awakenings for
inspiration, was hardly a footnote on those eighteenth-century
revivalists. Of course, Edwards may have been responsible for
a MacIntyre-like tradition in the form of the New Divinity. Historians have shown how that tradition ran out of gas in the mid
to late nineteenth century.[22]

Another way to see whether twentieth-century evangelicalism amounted to anything like a tradition is to examine recent discussions among those who identify themselves as evangelicals. Is it possible to find an extended argument among born-again Protestant pastors and writers, beginning with Harold John Ockenga and Carl F. H. Henry and extending to John G. Stackhouse Jr., Thomas Howard (pre-Rome), and D. H. Williams, to pick authors readily at hand? The answer is fairly obvious. Evangelical writers today rarely interact with those neo-evangelical figures who originated the contemporary usage of the designation *evangelical*.[23] For those who think this line of investigation is overly unfair to a group of Protestants not known for their theological acumen, the arenas in which born-again Protestants have been successful, such as parachurch empires and contemporary religious music, show no more signs of a tradition under development than does evangelical theology. The "ministries" to which born-again Protestants have such easy access on the radio or Internet are brilliant examples of entrepreneurial and organizational genius, but they are also arenas in which celebrities thrive, thus creating genuine obstacles to the formation of a tradition. How does one hand down the celebrity of a Billy Graham or a James Dobson, for example? At the same time, the music that born-again Protestants enjoy in the privacy of their cars and homes and to which they sway on Sunday mornings is as dependent on the structures of celebrity as the parachurch. Even Contemporary Christian Music has little to commend itself as a form of tradition. For instance, when was the last time dc Talk actually took a line or phrase from one of George Beverly Shea's greatest hits and developed it into a new song with clear reference to what came before? Of course, this is not to say that contemporary artists avoid singing or playing old gospel songs in a contemporary way. But such new renditions of old songs, as the example of either folk or classical music demonstrates, is not the stuff from which to construct a musical tradition.

Mark A. Noll inherently recognized the traditionless character of evangelicalism in his book *The Scandal of the Evangelical Mind* (1994). Although he fits more in the Williams school of adding from other Christian traditions to born-again Protestantism's activism and zeal, his prescription for creating an evangelical mind revealed how few resources of an explicitly evangelical provenance were at the movement's disposal. Noll spends several pages showing how the Protestant Reformers offered a host of reasons for cultivating a Christian mind. This work included Calvinists in Geneva, Lutherans in Germany, and Puritans in England. He also goes on to discuss the Roman Catholic tradition of intellectual life. American evangelicals, in contrast, generally approached the life of the mind along lines drawn by Manichaeans, gnostics, and docetists. In the end, Noll concludes that "the scandal of the evangelical mind seems to be that no mind arises from evangelicalism." Indeed, evangelical Protestants who are intellectually inclined would only find "intellectual depth . . . in ideas developed by confessional or mainline Protestants, Roman Catholics, or perhaps even Eastern Orthodox."[24] A further indication of evangelicalism's traditionlessness, then, is the movement's intellectual shallowness. In other words, for an evangelical mind to exist it needs to drink from Roman Catholic, Reformed, Lutheran, Anglican, or Eastern Orthodox streams. In which case, the question that hovers over Williams's book also haunts Noll's: Is evangelicalism still evangelicalism once it aligns with any of the historic expressions of Christianity whose arguments extend across the millennia?

The point, then, is that evangelicalism is not a tradition. As much as academics and religious leaders have invested the term with some significance, it cannot carry the weight of a human endeavor that qualifies as a tradition. In its post–World War II significance, evangelicalism has been a movement or, in Jon R. Stone's words, "a coalition." According to Stone, born-again Protestantism's "changing constituency" has often "gathered into coalitions of interests and common causes," but these have usually been "short-lived." As a result, Stone adds, "the members of evangelicalism's various and competing coalitions have often changed over time."[25] The moral of this story is that movements and coalitions are generally good at mobilizing masses of people around certain goals or values, and in this sense, evangelicalism has been a remarkable success. It has functioned as a term that points to a broad coalition of Americans. For academics, the breadth of evangelicalism has allowed them to make arguments that carry greater weight thanks to the number of born-again Protestants they study. For ordinary believers and religious leaders, the size of evangelicalism has offered a way to act in concert for specific political ends. But as a shaper of a tradition, evangelicalism has been an utter failure. Its breadth has come with the price of shallowness, while its mass appeal has generated slogans more than careful reflection. Evangelicalism has a reassuring ring to it, sort of like affirming mom, hot dogs, and apple pie. At its best, it is a sentiment. At its worst, it is a solvent of tradition because religious traditions are too narrow for evangelical purposes; they are too dogmatic and therefore too confining. In other words, Christian traditions, unlike evangelicalism, rely on structures of succession and accountability that run counter to popular sovereignty. For this reason, to add the weight of tradition to evangelicalism, as Williams and others propose, is to add a burden that would inevitably crush born-again Protestantism.

The Worst Thing That Ever Happened?

If evangelicalism were merely a construction of 1940s progressive fundamentalists, later tapped by academics and political strategists, what would happen if Americans decided to give up the label? Suppose that a new government agency that regulated religious language called for a moratorium on the use of the word *evangelical* by scholars, religious leaders, and believers alike. What damage would be done to either the United States or Christianity? In a worst case scenario, what would be the harm of admitting that evangelicalism does not actually exist and that it is an abstraction created to bring together a variety of different Protestants for certain religious and social ends? The damage done to institutions such as *Christianity Today*, Fuller Seminary, and the National Association of Evangelicals might be great. But these bastions of the post–World War II neo-evangelical movement have long since come to terms with the limitations of the original 1940s project. Popular evangelical voices such as Chuck Swindoll, Charles Stanley, and James Dobson might also feel a sudden pinch if the evangelical label were not available to them. Still, Swindoll and Stanley are ministers in specific denominations (Evangelical Free Church and Southern Baptist Convention, respectively), and their radio broadcasts could well find listeners without an evangelical benediction. In addition, Dobson's membership in the Church of the Nazarene would not necessarily restrict his advice to parents and spouses any more than Dr. Laura Schlesinger's Jewish identity hurts her appeal to radio listeners across the United States. So aside from these "evangelical" outlets, would it be so bad to refer to Protestants in the United States by their church membership, from Baptist and Methodist to Lutheran and even the Willow Creek Association?

For most Americans whom public opinion surveys identify as evangelical, the damage done by the moratorium proposed here would be negligible. This is a point that reinforces the notion that evangelicalism as a religious identity is at best vague and at worst hollow. For most Christians in the United States, their week-in, week-out spiritual lives are grounded in a local congregation of believers with ministers and church leaders who try to feed the local flock with the truths of God's Word as best they can. These congregations are sites of real, though flawed, Christian ministry, where members gather together every week in the presence of God to offer praise and petitions and to receive the good news of the gospel through preaching and the celebration of the sacraments. These churches are also places where diaconal assistance is provided, the advice and warnings of discipline are rendered, and fellowship among the saints is available. Churches sponsor potluck suppers in all their glory and ignominy. Parachurch ministries do not render such services because they cannot. The worst that could happen to these believers is that they would not have a collective sense of being part of something big, like an evangelical movement. But removing that sense could be a blessing if it encouraged believers to recognize all the ways in which the local church (and sometimes the parent denomination) ministers to them and provides the real stuff of a Christian identity.

An additional advantage of abandoning evangelicalism as a religious label might be a better recognition of the fullness of Christian teaching. Post–World War II evangelicalism has thrived on a minimalist account of the Christian faith—a seven-point doctrinal affirmation in the case of the National Association of Evangelicals, a lot of excitement over the nature of biblical inerrancy, a stress on a personal relationship with Jesus usually begun by a dramatic conversion experience, or the pious rush that comes from listening to one's favorite Christian recording artist. This sort of religious minimalism is appropriate to the construction of a coalition or a movement. What are some of the basic teachings or practices that Christians share in common, and can these function as a basis for collective endeavor?

Ironically, the evangelical movement's search for a "mere" Christianity runs directly counter to one of born-again Protestantism's favorite verses in the Bible. The text that has inspired evangelistic crusades, radio broadcasts, Jesus Rock, and foreign missions, Christ's Great Commission in Matthew 28:18–20, actually contains more than a command to spread the good news. In addition to saying, "Go therefore and make disciples of all nations," Christ adds, teach "them to observe all that I have commanded you." A minimalist reading of the word *all* in that commission would at least require teaching everything Christ taught in the four Gospels. A maximalist rendering would involve the entire contents of the Bible, since the Word incarnate is the author of the Word inscripturated. Either way, the Great Commission requires more than the search for minimal affirmations and warm sentiments that drove the construction of twentieth-century evangelicalism. Indeed, the Great Commission has all the makings for the kind of tradition building that historic Christian communions have attempted and that born-again Protestantism has congenitally avoided.

A Post-Evangelical World?

In 1980, Carl F. H. Henry contributed to the *Christian Century* series "How My Mind Has Changed." It was an interesting window into the mind of one of the neo-evangelical movement's most articulate and vigorous leaders. Despite evangelicalism's growing prominence in American politics, Henry was profoundly discouraged by the movement's prospects. Evangelicals possessed impressive numbers (forty million) and resources, but in the words of Henry, evangelicals "lack . . . a comprehensive and coordinated strategy that welds intellectual, evangelistic and ethical resources into effective cooperation."[26] The article also gave Henry a chance to reflect on what might have been. "During the 1960s," he recalled, "I somewhat romanced the possibility that a vast evangelical alliance might arise in the United States to coordinate effectively a national impact in evangelism, education, publication and sociopolitical action." But the game was over. Henry identified Billy Graham as one problem. The evangelist had the chance "to rally and garner an umbrella alliance" but chose instead to seek as broad a coalition for his crusades as possible, one that extended beyond evangelicalism's real boundaries. Another problem was the failure of evangelicals to found a national university. Finally, evangelical subgroups pursued narrow agendas that caused further splintering. Henry's assessment of what might have been concluded on a sour note:

> Numerous crosscurrents now vex almost every effort at comprehensive evangelical liaison. At present no single leader or agency has the respect, magnetism or platform to summon all divergent elements to conference. Evangelical differences increasingly pose an identity crisis.[27]

This was 1980—thirteen years before David Wells wrote *No Place for Truth*, fourteen years before Mark A. Noll wrote *The Scandal of the Evangelical Mind*, and a full twenty years before Iain Murray came out with *Evangelicalism Divided*.

In fact, Henry's mind had not changed. He still believed that the evangelical project was desirable, but he knew thirty-eight years after the founding of the National Association of Evangelicals that the endeavor was no longer feasible. What Henry did not consider was whether the evangelical coalition had ever been a possibility. Was it actually conceivable that the word *evangelical* could hold together disparate Protestant beliefs and practices and mold them into some kind of unified whole? Even more basic was whether such an evangelical identity was desirable. The idea to make evangelicalism the conservative version of Protestantism was an interesting attempt to create an alternative religious voice that would counter mainline Protestantism and Roman Catholicism and would beat fundamentalism at the public relations game. But this evangelical movement was simply duplicating work already being done, not to shape a nation but to shepherd God's flock. Before evangelicalism, Christians had churches to hear the Word preached, to receive the sacraments, and to hear sound counsel and correction. Without evangelicalism, Protestant Christianity may not be as unified (when has it ever been?), but it will go on. And without the burden of forming a nationally influential coalition, American Protestants in all their Heinz 57 varieties, from Presbyterian to Calvary Chapel, may even be healthier.

Afterword

Readers perturbed by *Deconstructing Evangelicalism* may resort to noting the apparent inconsistency between the arguments in this work and those of another book I wrote, *That Old-Time Religion in Modern America: Evangelical Protestantism in the Twentieth Century* (2002). In *Deconstructing Evangelicalism*, I have argued—perhaps readers' distress will be proportionate to the argument's success—that evangelicalism does not exist, that it is in fact a construction of 1940's fundamentalists that late-twentieth-century academics found especially useful for interpreting American religion. But in *That Old-Time Religion*, I assumed more than argued that evangelicalism does in fact exist and that its reality is sufficient enough that the movement can be charted over the course of the twentieth century. Of course, not every reader of this book will have read the former. For that reason, the temptation exists to let this apparent discrepancy pass and wait to see if reviewers notice. At the same time, the small mind of this author is regularly spooked by intellectual inconsistency. So some explanation is in order, or at least an attempt at one.

A first response is, "Don't blame me. They made me do it." When I wrote *That Old-Time Religion*, I did so to fill a niche in an American history series that needed a book on twentieth-century Protestantism. With the growth and popularity of literature on evangelicalism since 1980, the decision to publish a book on those Protestants outside or ambivalent about the mainline denominations was reasonable. What is more, one of the significant lessons taught by these studies of evangelicalism is that there is life outside the mainline churches. Indeed, since the 1920s, and even before when Holiness and Pentecostal congregations broke away from the larger Methodist denominations, the ecumenically driven history of the largest and oldest Protestant denominations has become obviously inadequate to account for the variety of American Protestantism.

The communions that took the lead in forming the Federal Council of Churches (1908), reconstituted in 1950 as the National Council of Churches, have not been sufficiently inclusive to embrace other Protestant groups, many of whom had been in fellowship with the mainline churches. Some of those outside the mainline would say that the mainstream denominations became so inclusive that they could not include those who believed in basic tenets of Christianity. Doctrines and practices of a particular Protestant tradition required churches to be exclusive. The historiography of evangelicalism, what Jon Butler called "born-again history,"[1] has from one perspective been an effort to account for the diversity of American Protestantism not contained by the mainline denominations and their ecumenical organizations. The literature on these believers is wide and ever widening. To write a survey of twentieth-century evangelicalism that synthesized this literature, then, was at least work that someone had to do, and it was responsible work for at least two reasons: First, many Protestants in the United States practice their faith outside mainline Protestant churches; and second, a body of scholarship has emerged that explores these believers. Evangelicalism as a form of Protestantism that is discontent if not at odds with the ecumenical faith developed between 1870 and 1950 among the leaders of the oldest Protestant denominations does indeed exist. *That Old-Time Religion* may be read as one effort to make sense of that phenomenon and to synthesize the scholarly literature that interprets it.

Another point in favor of evangelicalism's existence is the reality and ongoing influence of a form of Protestant faith, what has been referred to in these pages as pietism, that has shaped many of the leaders, organizations, and movements often lumped in the evangelical category. Pietism and its Anglo-American equivalent, revivalism, is a large presence in American Christianity. Its stress on the subjective character of faith, usually associated with the born-again experience, and its skepticism about formal expressions of Christianity, such as creed, ordination, and liturgy, grew wildly in the spiritual greenhouse of the United States' religious free market. To the extent that the neo-evangelical leaders of the 1940s drew upon pietist notions of Christianity and that many Protestants at the beginning of the twenty-first century continue to conceive of the Christian religion in individualistic and experiential ways, evangelicalism does exist, one could say, with a vengeance, for the type of Protestantism that scholars and believers most associate with the term *evangelical* is one that is characterized by the classic marks of pietism and revivalism. In this sense, if by evangelicalism someone means simply a low-church faith that relies on small groups and parachurch agencies, then the word has some descriptive value. My questioning of evangelicalism has not included doubts about the reality of informal and experiential forms of Protestantism. Someone who questioned the existence of low-church, revivalist-driven Protestantism in the United States might legitimately be classified as certifiable.

The question this book raises is whether, since the middle decades of the twentieth century, evangelicalism has been an adequate label for either what the neo-evangelicals had in mind or for explaining the kind of religious diversity religion scholars study and interpret. On the first score, this book's answer to the issue of neo-evangelicalism's success is both positive and negative. Through tenacity, organizational know-how, devout intentions, and the unexpected benefit of Billy Graham's celebrity, neo-evangelical leaders were able to construct a new definition of *evangelicalism* that identified it with the less militant but equally conservative form of Protestantism that rallied fundamentalists during the 1920s and 1930s. Neo-evangelicals, then, were responsible for establishing the definition of evangelicalism that has dominated discussions of American Protestantism since 1950.

At the same time, however, as *Deconstructing Evangelicalism* attempts to show, this new conception of evangelicalism was insufficient to sustain an identifiable constituency of low-church pietistic Protestants who considered themselves conservative in comparison with the mainline churches. By 1980, the lowest common denominator theology, the competition among parachurch agencies, and the pop-culture-inspired devotion of the pietist Protestants who had formed a coalition during the 1950s revealed significant weaknesses. Without the formal mechanisms of church polity, creed, and liturgy, evangelicalism in the 1950s could not function as the conservator of either historic Christianity or traditional Protestantism. In case readers have missed it, this is the point at which *Deconstructing Evangelicalism* shifted from description to prescription, arguing that traditional Christianity may indeed be better off without the cutting and pasting of theology and practice that low-church Protestantism has performed. It should likely be added that this is also the place where *Deconstructing Evangelicalism* moves significantly beyond the prescriptions offered by the likes of Mark Noll, David Wells, and Iain Murray. As "wounded lovers" (Noll's phrase) of evangelicalism,[2] these authors leavened descriptions of evangelicalism's woes with suggestions for improvement, thus hoping to save the evangelical project. Instead of a hurt admirer of evangelicalism, I consider myself a victim in recovery because my own convictions about the importance of the institutional church and her ministry through proclamation and sacrament are at odds in significant ways with the antiformal devotion and parachurch creativity of the pietist Protestantism that has shaped what people regard as evangelicalism.

Still, neo-evangelicals were amazingly successful, not simply at forming a religious coalition. They also supplied a definition of conservative Protestantism that scholars of American Christianity, many of whom grew up with connections to the evangelical movement, would use to add greater precision to the scholarly analysis of American Christianity after mainline Protestantism could no longer provide the center for the study of religion in the United States. What *Deconstructing Evangelicalism* has attempted to do is reveal some of the connections between the creation of a mid-twentieth-century evangelical identity and its usefulness to academics conducting research during a time when universities were absorbed by the politics of identity. This scholarship concerning evangelicalism had clear value and offered many important insights into the history of American

Christianity. It was not, to use the memorable word from the 2003 Academy Award speech of documentary filmmaker Michael Moore, *fictitious*. At the same time, this work on American evangelicalism obscured other important features of Christianity in the United States, such as those that used to be captured by the study of denominations. By examining evangelicalism as more or less the Protestant alternative to the mainline or ecumenical denominations, students of American religion over the last twenty-five years have ignored, in a manner similar to pietist Protestants, the significance of churchly expressions of Christianity, the kind that leads Methodists, Baptists, Pentecostals, and Lutherans to form different communions.

Deconstructing Evangelicalism, therefore, is an argument with the way the study of American Protestantism has been conducted for a generation. It is also a reminder that there is more to Christianity than the prefabricated items offered by low-church Protestantism. Consequently, this book may be read as an argument against the writing of books such as *That Old-Time Religion*. Perhaps my only defense is that had I not faced the challenge of writing the history of twentieth-century evangelicalism, I would not have seen its problems as a variety of Christianity or as a tool of scholarly analysis. If possible, readers should consider both books part of a larger work in progress, which means that card-carrying evangelical readers may be encouraged to hope that God isn't finished with me yet.

Notes

Preface

1. Leo P. Ribuffo, "Afterword: Cultural Shouting Matches and the Academic Study of American Religious History," in *Religious Advocacy and American History*, ed. Bruce Kuklick and D. G. Hart (Grand Rapids: Eerdmans, 1997), 223.

2. See D. G. Hart, *The Lost Soul of American Protestantism* (Lanham, Md.: Rowman & Littlefield, 2002); and idem, *Recovering Mother Kirk: The Case for Liturgy in the Reformed Tradition* (Grand Rapids: Baker, 2003).

Introduction

1. David F. Wells, *No Place for Truth: Or Whatever Happened to Evangelical Theology?* (Grand Rapids: Eerdmans, 1993), 133.

2. Mark A. Noll, *The Scandal of the Evangelical Mind* (Grand Rapids: Eerdmans, 1994), 1.

3. See also Kent R. Hughes and John H. Armstrong, *The Coming Evangelical Crisis: Current Challenges to the Authority of Scripture and the Gospel* (Chicago: Moody, 1996); Bruce L. Shelley, *The Consumer Church: Can Evangelicals Win the World without Losing Their Souls?* (Downers Grove, Ill.: InterVarsity, 1992); and John Seel, *The Evangelical Forfeit: Can We Recover?* (Grand Rapids: Hourglass Books, 1993).

4. On the Marsden-Dayton debate, see George M. Marsden, "Demythologizing Evangelicalism: A Review of Donald W. Dayton's Discovering an Evangelical Heritage" (with reply), *Christian Scholar's Review* 7 (1977): 203–11; Donald W. Dayton, "'The Search for the Historical Evangelicalism': George Marsden's History of Fuller Seminary as a Test Case," *Christian Scholar's Review* 23 (1993): 12–33; and George M. Marsden, "Response to Don Dayton," *Christian Scholar's Review* 23 (1993): 34–40.

5. Douglas A. Sweeney, "The Essential Evangelicalism Dialectic: The Historiography of the Early Neo-Evangelical Movement and the Observer-Participant Dilemma," *Church History* 60 (1991): 70–84, quotation from 82–83. Sweeney's

essay not only cites the relevant writings by Dayton and Marsden but also documents a remarkable variety of sources related to questions about evangelical identity. See also Douglas A. Sweeney, "Historiographical Dialectics: On Marsden, Dayton, and the Inner Logic of Evangelical History," *Christian Scholar's Review* 23 (1993): 48–52; and Joel A. Carpenter, "The Scope of American Evangelicalism: Some Comments on the Dayton-Marsden Exchange," *Christian Scholar's Review* 23 (1993): 53–61.

6. These statistics come from a page on the Institute for the Study of American Evangelicals (Wheaton College) web site titled "Defining Evangelicalism"; www.wheaton.edu/isae.

7. See, for instance, Colleen Carroll, *The New Faithful: Why Young Adults Are Embracing Christian Orthodoxy* (Chicago: Loyola Press, 2002); and Lauren Winner, *Girl Meets God: On the Path to a Spiritual Life* (Chapel Hill, N.C.: Algonquin Books, 2002).

8. Martin E. Marty, "The Years of the Evangelicals," *Christian Century* 106, no. 5 (15 February 1989): 171–74.

9. See "The Church and Industry," in *American Christianity: An Historical Interpretation with Representative Documents*, vol. 2, ed. H. Shelton Smith et al. (New York: Charles Scribner's Sons, 1963), 394–97.

10. On the so-called two-party paradigm of twentieth-century American Protestantism, see Jean Miller Schmidt, *Souls or the Social Order: The Two-Party System in American Protestantism* (Brooklyn: Carlson Publishing, 1991); and Douglas Jacobsen and William Vance Trollinger Jr., eds., *Re-Forming the Center: American Protestantism, 1900 to the Present* (Grand Rapids: Eerdmans, 1998).

11. J. Wilbur Chapman, "The Church in Evangelistic Work," in *Federal Council of Churches of Christ in America: Report of the First Meeting of the Federal Council*, ed. Elias B. Sanford (New York: Revell, 1909), 391–403.

12. Ozora S. Davis, "The Church and the Immigrant," in *Federal Council of Churches*, 254.

13. William Crosswell Doane, "Family Life," in *Federal Council of Churches*, 313.

14. "Minutes of the Federal Council," in *Federal Council of Churches*, 10–11.

15. James Stalker, "Evangelicalism," in *A Dictionary of the Bible*, ed. James Hastings et al. (New York: Charles Scribner's Sons, 1898), 602, 606.

16. Samuel McCrea Cavert, *The American Churches in the Ecumenical Movement* (New York: Association Press, 1968), 19 n. 8.

17. John A. Hutchison, *We Are Not Divided: A Critical and Historical Study of the Federal Council of the Churches of Christ in America* (New York: Round Table Press, 1941), 5, 297.

18. Benjamin Warfield, "In Behalf of Evangelical Religion," *Presbyterian* 90 (23 September 1920): 20.

19. Shailer Mathews, *The Faith of Modernism* (New York: Macmillan, 1924), 35.

20. Harold John Ockenga, "Can Fundamentalism Win America?" *Christian Life and Times* 2 (June 1947): 15.

21. Jon R. Stone, *On the Boundaries of Evangelicalism: The Postwar Evangelical Coalition* (New York: St. Martin's Press, 1997), 93.

22. Carl F. H. Henry, "Evangelicals and Fundamentals," *Christianity Today,* 16 September 1957, 21.

23. Edward J. Carnell, "Post-Fundamentalist Faith," *Christian Century,* 26 August 1959, 971.

24. The series included Richard V. Pierard, *The Unequal Yoke: Evangelical Christianity and Political Conservatism* (Philadelphia: Lippincott, 1970); Tom Skinner, *How Black Is the Gospel?* (Philadelphia: Lippincott, 1970); Vernon C. Grounds, *Revolution and the Christian Faith* (Philadelphia: Lippincott, 1971); Edwin M. Yamauchi, *The Stones and the Scriptures* (Philadelphia: Lippincott, 1972); David O. Moberg, *The Great Reversal: Evangelism versus Social Concern* (Philadelphia: Lippincott, 1972); and Raymond F. Surburg, *How Dependable Is the Bible?* (Philadelphia: Lippincott, 1972).

25. Cullen Murphy, "Protestantism and the Evangelicals," *Wilson Quarterly* 5 (autumn 1981): 105–6.

26. For amplification of this point, see D. G. Hart, *The Lost Soul of American Protestantism* (Lanham, Md.: Rowman & Littlefield, 2002).

27. See Stone, *On the Boundaries,* 6–7.

28. Lewis B. Smedes, "Evangelicalism—A Fantasy," *Reformed Journal* 30 (February 1980): 3.

29. Nathan O. Hatch, "Response to Carl F. H. Henry," in *Evangelical Affirmations,* ed. Kenneth S. Kantzer and Carl F. H. Henry (Grand Rapids: Academie Books, 1990), 97–98.

30. Richard John Neuhaus, "How I Became the Catholic I Was," *First Things* (April 2002): 14–20.

Chapter 1

1. Ernest R. Sandeen and Frederick Hale, *American Religion and Philosophy: A Guide to Information Sources* (Detroit: Gale Research Company, 1978).

2. Joel A. Carpenter and Edith L. Blumhofer, *Twentieth-Century Evangelicalism: A Guide to the Sources* (New York: Garland Publishing, 1990). Norris Magnuson, *American Evangelicalism: An Annotated Bibliography* (West Cornwall, Conn.: Locust Hill Press, 1990).

3. Norris Magnuson, *American Evangelicalism II: First Bibliographical Supplement, 1990–1996* (West Cornwall, Conn.: Locust Hill Press, 1996).

4. Carl Degler, "Remaking American History," *Journal of American History* 67 (1980): 13.

5. Martin E. Marty, "The Editor's Bookshelf: American Religious History," *Journal of Religion* 62 (1982): 99, 102.

6. Jon Butler, "Born-Again America? A Critique of the New 'Evangelical Thesis' in Recent American Historiography" (paper presented to the American Society of Church History, Washington, D.C., 29 December 1992), 2.

7. Ibid., 22.

8. James Turner, foreword to D. G. Hart, ed., *Reckoning with the Past: Historical Essays on American Evangelicalism from the Institute for the Study of American Evangelicals* (Grand Rapids: Baker, 1995), 9.

9. Henry F. May, "The Recovery of American Religious History," *American Historical Review* 70 (October 1964): 79–92, reprinted in Henry F. May, *Ideas,*

Faiths and Feelings: Essays on American Intellectual and Religious History (New York: Oxford University Press, 1982), from which citations below are taken.
10. Ibid., 66.
11. Ibid., 77, 65.
12. Ibid., 77.
13. See Jon Butler, *Awash in a Sea of Faith: Christianizing the American People* (Cambridge: Harvard University Press, 1990).
14. Winthrop S. Hudson, *American Protestantism* (Chicago: University of Chicago Press, 1961), 29.
15. Ibid., 97.
16. See Charles A. Briggs, *American Presbyterianism: Its Origin and Early History* (New York: Charles Scribner, 1895).
17. Winthrop S. Hudson, *Religion in America* (New York: Charles Scribner's Sons, 1965), 178–80.
18. Ibid., 384–85.
19. Sidney E. Mead, *The Lively Experiment: The Shaping of Christianity in America* (New York: Harper & Row, 1963), 121–27, 183–85.
20. Timothy L. Smith, *Revivalism and Social Reform: American Protestantism on the Eve of the Civil War* (1957; reprint, Baltimore: Johns Hopkins University Press, 1980).
21. Ibid., 249–61.
22. William G. McLoughlin Jr., *Modern Revivalism: Charles Grandison Finney to Billy Graham* (New York: Ronald Press, 1959), v.
23. Ibid., 524.
24. William G. McLoughlin Jr., ed., *The American Evangelicals, 1800–1900* (1968; reprint, Gloucester, Mass.: Peter Smith, 1976), 1.
25. H. K. Carroll, *The Religious Forces of the United States*, American Church History Series, vol. 1 (New York: Christian Literature Co., 1893), xlv.
26. See Nathan O. Hatch and Mark A. Noll, eds., *The Bible in American Culture: Essays in Cultural History* (New York: Oxford University Press, 1982).
27. George M. Marsden, "Introduction: The Evangelical Denomination," in *Evangelicalism and Modern America*, ed. George M. Marsden (Grand Rapids: Eerdmans, 1984), ix–x.
28. Ibid., x–xi.
29. Ibid., xi.
30. Ibid., xiv.
31. Mark A. Noll, *Between Faith and Criticism: Evangelicals, Scholarship, and the Bible in America* (San Francisco: Harper & Row, 1986), 2.
32. Ibid., 3.
33. Ibid., 5.
34. George M. Marsden, *Reforming Fundamentalism: Fuller Seminary and the New Evangelicalism* (Grand Rapids: Eerdmans, 1987), 2.
35. Ibid., 9.
36. Ibid., 10.
37. William R. Sutton, *Journeymen for Jesus: Evangelical Artisans Confront Capitalism in Jacksonian Baltimore* (University Park, Pa.: Pennsylvania State University Press, 1998); Christine Leigh Heyrman, *Southern Cross: The Beginnings of the Bible Belt* (Chapel Hill, N.C.: University of North Carolina Press,

1997). Sutton defines evangelicalism this way: "Nineteenth-century evangelicals across the board shared traditional Protestant understandings of original sin, need for atonement, justification by faith (realized in a personal experience of the saving grace of Christ), authority of Scripture, and the vital importance of church communities.

Individually, evangelical consciousness revolved around ideals of religious significance: divine affirmation, personal character building, some sense of communal responsibilities, intolerance toward any behavior deemed sinful, and an awareness of God's authority in all walks of life" (x). For Heyrman, evangelicalism is marked by the nature of the conversion experience: "While differing over which theological beliefs most closely conformed to biblical teachings, and how best to organize their churches, all spoke the language of Canaan. Rather than a distinctive form of speech, the phrase was a metaphor evoking the new awareness into which believers were initiated by undergoing repentance and rebirth" (4).

38. Richard J. Carwardine, *Evangelicals and Politics in Antebellum America* (New Haven: Yale University Press, 1993), 3–4.

39. Ibid., 319–23.

40. Randall Balmer, *Encyclopedia of Evangelicalism* (Louisville: Westminster John Knox, 2002), 31–32, 430.

41. Ibid., 403–4.

42. Bruce Shelley, *Evangelicalism in America* (Grand Rapids: Eerdmans, 1967), chap. 3.

43. See William G. McLoughlin, "Is There a Third Force in Christendom?" in *Religion in America*, ed. William G. McLoughlin and Robert N. Bellah (Boston: Beacon Press, 1968), 47ff.

44. Paul K. Conkin, *The Uneasy Center: Reformed Christianity in Antebellum America* (Chapel Hill, N.C.: University of North Carolina Press, 1995), 65.

45. Ibid., xiii.

46. Ibid., 297.

47. David W. Lotz, "A Changing Historiography: From Church History to Religious History," in *Altered Landscapes: Christianity in America, 1935–1985*, ed. David W. Lotz (Grand Rapids: Eerdmans, 1989), 312–29.

48. See D. G. Hart, "The Failure of American Religious History," *Journal of the Historical Society* 1 (2000): 1–32.

Chapter 2

1. Will Herberg, *Protestant, Catholic, Jew: An Essay in American Religious Sociology* (Garden City, N.Y.: Doubleday, 1955), 15.

2. Ibid., 134.

3. Ibid., 61.

4. Rodney Stark and Charles Y. Glock, *American Piety: The Nature of Religious Commitment* (Berkeley: University of California Press, 1968), 30.

5. Andrew M. Greeley, *The Denominational Society: A Sociological Approach to Religion in America* (Glenview, Ill.: Scott, Foresman, and Co., 1972), 183.

6. Ibid., 104–5.

7. Ibid., 176–77.

8. Ibid., 165.

9. David F. Wells and John D. Woodbridge, eds., *The Evangelicals: What They Believe, Who They Are, and Where They Are Changing* (Nashville: Abingdon, 1975).

10. James Davison Hunter, *American Evangelicalism: Conservative Religion and the Quandary of Modernity* (New Brunswick, N.J.: Rutgers University Press, 1983), 49.

11. Ibid.

12. Hunter, *American Evangelicalism*, 7.

13. Ibid., 53, emphasis added.

14. Ibid., 60.

15. For a lengthier discussion of the *Christianity Today*–Gallup Poll, see chapter 3.

16. Hunter, *American Evangelicalism*, 14.

17. Ibid., 75.

18. Ibid., 85.

19. Ibid., 94.

20. Ibid., 99, 101.

21. James Davison Hunter, *Evangelicalism: The Coming Generation* (Chicago: University of Chicago Press, 1987), 15.

22. Ibid., ix–x.

23. Ibid., 73.

24. Ibid., 46.

25. Ibid., 151.

26. Ibid., 186.

27. Ibid., 210.

28. Ibid., 223.

29. Hunter, *American Evangelicalism*, 118.

30. Hunter, *Evangelicalism*, 126, 129.

31. John C. Green, James L. Guth, Corwin E. Smidt, and Lyman A. Kellstedt, *Religion and the Culture Wars: Dispatches from the Front* (Lanham, Md.: Rowman & Littlefield, 1996), xv.

32. Lyman A. Kellstedt, John C. Green, James L. Guth, and Corwin E. Smidt, "Grasping the Essentials: The Social Embodiment of Religion and Political Behavior," in *Religion and the Culture Wars*, 179–82.

33. Lyman A. Kellstedt, John C. Green, Corwin E. Smidt, and James L. Guth, "The Puzzle of Evangelical Protestantism: Core, Periphery, and Political Behavior," in *Religion and the Culture Wars*, 248–49, 260.

34. Kellstedt et al., "Grasping the Essentials," 187.

35. John C. Green, James L. Guth, Lyman A. Kellstedt, and Corwin E. Smidt, "Evangelical Realignment: The Political Power of the Christian Right," *Christian Century*, 5–12 July 1995, 676.

36. James L. Guth, John C. Green, Lyman A. Kellstedt, and Corwin E. Smidt, "God's Own Party: Evangelicals and Republicans in the '92 Election," *Christian Century*, 17 February 1993, 174.

37. John C. Green, James L. Guth, Lyman A. Kellstedt, and Corwin E. Smidt, "A Defeat, Not a Debacle," *Christian Century*, 23–30 December 1998, 1238.

38. Lyman A. Kellstedt, John C. Green, James L. Guth, and Corwin E. Smidt, "It's the Culture, Stupid! 1992 and Our Political Future," *First Things* 42 (April 1994): 32.

39. John Green, Lyman Kellstedt, James Guth, and Corwin Smidt, "Who Elected Clinton: A Collision of Values," *First Things* 75 (August/September 1997): 40.

40. James L. Guth, Lyman A. Kellstedt, John C. Green, and Corwin E. Smidt, "America Fifty/Fifty," *First Things* 116 (October 2001): 22.

41. Guth, et al., "God's Own Party," 176.

42. Christian Smith, *American Evangelicalism: Embattled and Thriving* (Chicago: University of Chicago Press, 1998), 20.

43. Ibid., 22–23.

44. Ibid., 25.

45. Ibid., 118–19, italics in original.

46. Ibid., 125–43.

47. Ibid., 143.

48. Ibid., 181.

49. Christian Smith, *Christian America? What Evangelicals Really Want* (Berkeley: University of California Press, 2000), 4.

50. Ibid., 194.

51. Smith, *American Evangelicalism*, 218.

52. Smith, *Christian America?* 50.

53. James M. Penning and Corwin E. Smidt, *Evangelicalism: The Next Generation* (Grand Rapids: Baker, 2002), 165.

54. Ibid., 174.

55. Mark A. Noll, *The Scandal of the Evangelical Mind* (Grand Rapids: Eerdmans, 1994), 226.

Chapter 3

1. Robert S. Lynd and Helen Merrell Lynd, *Middletown: A Study in American Culture* (New York: Harcourt, Brace & Company, 1929), 316, 318–19.

2. Ibid., 323–24.

3. Ibid., 331, 316–19.

4. Theodore Caplow, Howard M. Bahr, and Bruce A. Chadwick, *All Faithful People: Change and Continuity in Middletown's Religion* (Minneapolis: University of Minnesota Press, 1983), 334.

5. "Gallup Poll Ranks Status of 5 Protestant Groups," *Christianity Today,* 18 August 1967, 51.

6. Dean M. Kelley, *Why Conservative Churches Are Growing: A Study in the Sociology of Religion* (1972; reprint, Macon, Ga.: Mercer University Press, 1986).

7. Quoted in Diane Winston, "A Measure of Faith: George Gallup Jr.," *Christian Ethics Today,* December 2002, online issue.

8. "We Poll the Pollster: An Interview with George Gallup Jr.," *Christianity Today,* 21 December 1979, 1665.

9. "The *Christianity Today*–Gallup Poll: An Overview," *Christianity Today,* 21 December 1979, 1666.

10. Ibid., 1667.

11. Ibid., 1668.
12. "Who and Where Are the Evangelicals?" *Christianity Today*, 21 December 1979, 1671.
13. "We Poll the Pollster," 1664.
14. "*Christianity Today*–Gallup Poll," 1667.
15. Ibid.
16. Ibid., 1668.
17. Ibid., 1669.
18. "Who and Where Are the Evangelicals?" 1673.
19. "*Christianity Today*–Gallup Poll," 1668.
20. George Gallup Jr. and David Poling, *The Search for America's Faith* (Nashville: Abingdon, 1980), 133.
21. Ibid., 134.
22. George Gallup Jr. and Jim Castelli, *The People's Religion: American Faith in the 1990s* (New York: Macmillan, 1989), 60–66.
23. Ibid., 92.
24. Ibid.
25. Ibid., 168, 171.
26. Ibid., 199.
27. Ibid., 212–13.
28. Ibid., 217.
29. Timothy K. Jones, "Tracking America's Soul" (an interview with George Gallup Jr.), *Christianity Today*, 17 November 1989, 22.
30. Ibid., 23.
31. Ibid., 24.
32. George Gallup Jr. and D. Michael Lindsay, *Surveying the Religious Landscape: Trends in U.S. Beliefs* (Harrisburg, Pa.: Morehouse Publishing, 1999), 65, 67.
33. Ibid., 18.
34. Ibid., 4.
35. Tim Stafford, "The Third Coming of George Barna," *Christianity Today*, 5 August 2002, 35.
36. George Barna and William Paul McKay, *Vital Signs: Emerging Social Trends and the Future of American Christianity* (Westchester, Ill.: Crossway, 1984), 3, 5.
37. Ibid., 3–5.
38. George Barna, *The Barna Report, 1992–1993: America Renews Its Search for God* (Ventura, Calif.: Regal, 1992), 78.
39. George Barna, *Virtual America: What Every Church Leader Needs to Know about Ministering in an Age of Spiritual and Technological Revolution* (Ventura, Calif.: Regal, 1994), 141.
40. Ibid., 107.
41. Ibid., 149.
42. Stafford, "The Third Coming," 34.
43. Ibid., 35.
44. Kelley, *Why Conservative Churches Are Growing*, chap. 5.
45. "God Is Alive," *Maclean's*, 12 April 1993, 32.

46. Ginsberg quoted in Susan Herbst, *Numbered Voices: How Opinion Polling Has Shaped American Politics* (Chicago: University of Chicago Press, 1993), 15.
47. Ibid., 166.
48. "God Is Alive," 37.

Chapter 4

1. David Van Biema, "In the Name of the Father," *Time*, 13 May 1996, 69.
2. Ibid., 74.
3. Mark A. Noll, *American Evangelical Christianity: An Introduction* (Malden, Mass.: Blackwell, 2001), 53.
4. George M. Marsden, *Understanding Fundamentalism and Evangelicalism* (Grand Rapids: Eerdmans, 1991), 6.
5. On the origins of the NAE, see Joel A. Carpenter, *Revive Us Again: The Reawakening of American Fundamentalism* (New York: Oxford University Press, 1997), chap. 8; and James DeForest Murch, *Cooperation without Compromise: A History of the National Association of Evangelicals* (Grand Rapids: Eerdmans, 1956).
6. Harold John Ockenga, "The Unvoiced Multitudes," in *A New Evangelical Coalition: Early Documents of the National Association of Evangelicals*, ed. Joel A. Carpenter (New York: Garland Publishing, 1988), 19.
7. Carpenter, *Revive Us Again*, 129–31.
8. Ockenga, "Unvoiced Multitudes," 19.
9. Carpenter, *Revive Us Again*, 148–49.
10. See Virginia Brereton, *Training God's Army: The American Bible School, 1880–1940* (Bloomington, Ind.: Indiana University Press, 1990); and William Vance Trollinger Jr., *God's Empire: William Bell Riley and Midwestern Fundamentalism* (Madison, Wis.: Wisconsin University Press, 1990).
11. Carpenter, *Revive Us Again*, chap. 1.
12. Ibid., chap. 3.
13. For an interpretation that stresses born-again Protestantism's roots in pietism, see D. G. Hart, *The Lost Soul of American Protestantism* (Lanham, Md.: Rowman & Littlefield, 2002), chaps. 1–2.
14. Mark A. Noll, *America's God: From Jonathan Edwards to Abraham Lincoln* (New York: Oxford University Press, 2002), part 1, fleshes out the ramifications of religious disestablishment in the United States particularly well.
15. Bruce Shelley, *Evangelicalism in America* (Grand Rapids: Eerdmans, 1967), 124.
16. Carpenter, *Revive Us Again*, 161.
17. Ibid., 162.
18. Torrey Johnson and Robert Cook, *Reaching Youth for Christ* (Chicago: Moody, 1944), 37.
19. Ibid., chap. 9.
20. Ibid., 167, 169–70.
21. Marsden, *Understanding Fundamentalism and Evangelicalism*, 81.
22. John Naisbitt and Patricia Aburdene, *Megatrends 2000: Ten New Directions for the 1990s* (New York: William Morrow, 1990), 278.

23. Robert Wuthnow, *The Restructuring of American Religion* (Princeton, N.J.: Princeton University Press, 1988), 100–101.

24. Ibid., 112–13.

25. Ibid., 125.

26. Steve Bruce, *God Is Dead: Secularization in the West* (Malden, Mass.: Blackwell, 2002), 44.

27. Ibid., 227.

28. Ibid., 94.

29. Ibid., 93.

Chapter 5

1. Joel A. Carpenter, *Revive Us Again: The Reawakening of American Fundamentalism* (New York: Oxford University Press, 1997), 207.

2. *Bulletin of the Evangelical Theological Society* 1, no. 1 (winter 1958): inside cover.

3. Harold Lindsell, *The Battle for the Bible* (Grand Rapids: Zondervan, 1976), 319–20.

4. On the cultural importance of the Bible, see Paul C. Gutjahr, *An American Bible: A History of the Good Book in the United States, 1777–1880* (Stanford, Calif.: Stanford University Press, 1999); and Peter J. Thuesen, *In Discordance with the Scriptures: American Protestant Battles over Translating the Bible* (New York: Oxford University Press, 1999).

5. Richard Hofstadter, *Anti-Intellectualism in American Life* (New York: Vintage Books, 1962), 15. For his assessment of fundamentalists, see chap. 5.

6. See Carpenter, *Revive Us Again*, 187–90.

7. Ibid., 190–91.

8. George M. Marsden, *Reforming Fundamentalism: Fuller Seminary and the New Evangelicalism* (Grand Rapids: Eerdmans, 1987), 56.

9. Ibid., 62–63.

10. On the origins of the ASA, see Ronald Numbers, *The Creationists* (New York: Knopf, 1992), chap. 9.

11. Quoted in ibid., 159.

12. This quotation came from the ASA web site.

13. For some background on the CFH, see D. G. Hart, "History in Search of Meaning: The Conference on Faith and History," in *History and the Christian Historian*, ed. Ronald A. Wells (Grand Rapids: Eerdmans, 1998), 68–87.

14. "Proposed Constitution," *Fides et Historia* 1 (fall 1968): 5.

15. Ibid., 5–6.

16. Mark A. Noll, *Between Faith and Criticism: Evangelicals, Scholarship, and the Bible in America* (San Francisco: Harper & Row, 1987), 60–61.

17. Ibid., 112.

18. Ibid., 115.

19. Mark A. Noll, *The Scandal of the Evangelical Mind* (Grand Rapids: Eerdmans, 1994), 19.

20. Carl F. H. Henry, "American Evangelicals and Theological Dialogue," *Christianity Today*, 15 January 1965, 29.

21. Ibid.

22. George E. Ladd, *The New Testament and Criticism* (Grand Rapids: Eerdmans, 1967), 11–12.

23. Fuller Seminary statement quoted in Lindsell, *Battle for the Bible*, 107.

24. Edward J. Carnell, *The Case for Orthodox Theology* (Philadelphia: Westminster, 1959), 110.

25. See Marsden, *Reforming Fundamentalism*, 207.

26. Ibid., 208.

27. For the intrigue at Fuller over inerrancy, see the fascinating account in ibid., 205–18.

28. Quoted in ibid., 218.

29. The revised Fuller statement is quoted in Lindsell, *Battle for the Bible*, 116.

30. Ibid., 25.

31. Harold Lindsell, *The Bible in the Balance* (Grand Rapids: Zondervan), 306.

32. The following paragraphs are based on D. G. Hart, "Evangelicals, Biblical Scholarship, and the Politics of the Modern American Academy," in *Evangelicals and Science in Historical Perspective*, ed. David N. Livingstone, D. G. Hart, and Mark A. Noll (New York: Oxford University Press, 1999), 306–9.

33. Lindsell, *Bible in the Balance*, 367–68.

34. Robert M. Price, "Inerrant the Wind: The Troubled House of North American Evangelicals," *Evangelical Quarterly* 55 (1983): 130.

35. This series included Norman L. Geisler, ed., *Inerrancy* (Grand Rapids: Zondervan, 1979); Norman L. Geisler, ed., *Biblical Errancy: An Analysis of Its Philosophical Roots* (Grand Rapids: Zondervan, 1981); Gordon Lewis and Bruce Demarest, eds., *Challenges to Inerrancy* (Chicago: Moody, 1984); John Hannah, ed., *Inerrancy and the Church* (Chicago: Moody, 1984); and Earl Radmacher and Robert Preus, eds., *Hermeneutics, Inerrancy, and the Bible* (Grand Rapids: Academie Books, 1984). Another book that should be included as an ICBI project that was not formally part of this series is James Montgomery Boice, ed., *The Foundations of Biblical Authority* (Grand Rapids: Zondervan, 1978), a book that includes essays by the leadership of the International Council.

36. Jack B. Rogers and Donald K. McKim, *The Authority and Interpretation of the Bible* (San Francisco: Harper & Row, 1979), 347. For their critique of Old Princeton, see especially chaps. 5–6.

37. Robert K. Johnston, *Evangelicals at an Impasse* (Atlanta: John Knox, 1979); William J. Abraham, *Divine Revelation and the Limits of Historical Criticism* (New York: Oxford University Press, 1982); and idem, *The Coming Great Revival* (New York: Oxford University Press, 1984).

38. John D. Woodbridge, *Biblical Authority: A Critique of the Rogers/McKim Proposal* (Grand Rapids: Zondervan).

39. George M. Marsden, *Fundamentalism and American Culture: The Shaping of Twentieth-Century Evangelicalism, 1870–1925* (New York: Oxford University Press, 1980), especially chaps. 12–14, 24.

40. John D. Woodbridge, however, did firmly believe that Marsden had taken sides. See John D. Woodbridge, "Recent Interpretations of Biblical Authority, Part 4: Is Biblical Inerrancy a Fundamentalist Doctrine?" *Bibliotheca Sacra* 142 (1985): 292–305.

41. George M. Marsden, "Everyone One's Own Interpreter? The Bible, Science, and Authority in Mid-Nineteenth-Century America"; Timothy P. Weber, "The Two-Edged Sword: The Fundamentalist Use of the Bible"; and Grant Wacker, "The Demise of Biblical Civilization," in *The Bible in America: Essays in Cultural History,* ed. Nathan O. Hatch and Mark A. Noll (New York: Oxford University Press, 1982), 79–100, 101–20, and 121–38, respectively.

42. Noll, *Between Faith and Criticism,* 181–85.

43. D. A. Carson and John D. Woodbridge, eds., *Scripture and Truth* (Grand Rapids: Zondervan, 1983); and D. A. Carson and John D. Woodbridge, eds., *Hermeneutics, Authority, and Canon* (Grand Rapids: Academie Books, 1986).

44. Mark A. Noll, *Between Faith and Criticism,* 2d ed. (Grand Rapids: Baker, 1991), 202.

45. Marsden, *Reforming Fundamentalism,* 291.

46. Nathan O. Hatch, *The Democratization of American Christianity* (New Haven: Yale University Press, 1989) remains among the most compelling accounts of Bible-onlyism's appeal.

47. W. G. T. Shedd, *Calvinism: Pure and Mixed* (1893; reprint, Carlisle, Pa.: Banner of Truth, 1999), 145–46.

48. Alan Wolfe, "The Opening of the Evangelical Mind," *Atlantic Monthly* 286 (October 2000): 74, 76.

49. Noll, *Scandal of the American Mind,* 243–44.

50. Ibid., 253.

Chapter 6

1. Larry Nager, "Graham Draws Big Names," *Cincinnati Enquirer,* 30 June 2002.

2. "CMNow Nuggets, Names, and News," 23 October 2002, at ChurchMusic Now.com.

3. Michael S. Hamilton, "The Triumph of Praise Songs," *Christianity Today,* 12 July 1999, 30.

4. George M. Marsden, *Reforming Fundamentalism: Fuller Seminary and the New Evangelicalism* (Grand Rapids: Eerdmans, 1987), 61–63.

5. Joel A. Carpenter, *Revive Us Again: The Reawakening of American Fundamentalism* (New York: Oxford University Press, 1997), 165.

6. Ibid.

7. Ibid., 220.

8. Ibid., 127.

9. Ibid., 128.

10. Ibid., 135–39. See also Philip Goff, "'We Have Heard the Joyful Sound': Charles E. Fuller's Radio Broadcast and the Rise of Modern Evangelicalism," *Religion & American Culture* 9 (1999): 67–95.

11. Carpenter, *Revive Us Again,* 138.

12. Ibid., 137.

13. Randall Balmer, *Encyclopedia of Evangelicalism* (Louisville: Westminster John Knox, 2002), 112.

14. John Hall, "In Music and Ministry, Kaiser Wants to Pass It On," *Baptist Standard*, 7 January 2002, at www.baptiststandard.com/2002/1_7/pages/ kaiser.html.

15. Randall Balmer, "Hymns on MTV," *Christianity Today*, 15 November 1999, 35.

16. The following several paragraphs are based on material from D. G. Hart, *That Old-Time Religion in Modern America: Evangelical Protestantism in the Twentieth Century* (Chicago: Ivan R. Dee, 2002), 190–200.

17. "Larry Norman: Crossrhythms Interview 1993"; http://members.iinet.net.au/ ¯wpe/larry/intvw93.html.

18. Hamilton, "Triumph of Praise Songs," 32.

19. Donald P. Hustad, foreword to Barry Liesch, *The New Worship: Straight Talk on Music and the Church* (Grand Rapids: Baker, 1996), 10.

20. George Barna, *Virtual America: What Every Church Leader Needs to Know about Ministering in an Age of Spiritual and Technological Revolution* (Ventura, Calif.: Regal, 1994), 102–3.

21. Ibid., 105 n. 2.

22. Charles Trueheart, "The Next Church," *Atlantic Monthly* (August 1996): 37.

23. Ibid., 42.

24. Ibid., 58.

25. Hamilton, "Triumph of Praise Songs," 32.

26. Verla Gilmore, "Community Is Their Middle Name," *Christianity Today*, 13 November 2000, 50.

27. Tim Stafford, "A Regular Purpose-Driven Guy," *Christianity Today*, 18 November 2002, 44–45.

28. Rick Warren, *The Purpose-Driven Church: Growth without Compromising Your Message and Mission* (Grand Rapids: Zondervan, 1995); and idem, *The Purpose-Driven Life: What On Earth Am I Here For?* (Grand Rapids: Zondervan, 2002).

29. Ibid., 280–81.

30. Ibid., 279–81, 285.

31. See, for instance, Lester Ruth, "Lex Agendi, Lex Orandi: Toward an Understanding of Seeker Services as a New Kind of Liturgy," *Worship* 70 (1996): 385–405; and Gordon W. Lathrop, "New Pentecost or Joseph's Britches? Reflections on the History and Meaning of the Worship Ordo in the Megachurches," *Worship* 72 (1998): 521–38.

32. Lynne and Bill Hybels, *Rediscovering Church: The Story and Vision of Willow Creek Community Church* (Grand Rapids: Zondervan, 1995), 98–99.

33. Chuck Fromm, "Hybels on Worship" (interview with Bill Hybels), *Worship Leader* (September/October 1996): 28.

34. Hybels, *Rediscovering Church*, 174.

35. Michael G. Maudlin and Edward Gilbreath, "Selling Out the House of God?" (interview with Bill Hybels), *Christianity Today*, 18 July 1994, 23.

36. Donald E. Miller, *Reinventing American Protestantism: Christianity in the New Millennium* (Berkeley: University of California Press, 1997), 11.

37. Kimon Howland Sargeant, *Seeker Churches: Promoting Traditional Religion in a Nontraditional Way* (New Brunswick, N.J.: Rutgers University Press, 2000), 189.

38. Michael S. Hamilton, "Willow Creek's Place in History," *Christianity Today*, 13 November 2000, 62–63.

39. James Davison Hunter, *Culture Wars: The Struggle to Define America* (New York: Basic Books, 1991), 44.

40. H. L. Mencken, "Doctor Seraphicus et Ecstaticus," *Baltimore Evening Sun*, 14 March 1916.

Conclusion

1. Ronald Wells, "With Jews in the Hot Tub," *Reformed Journal* 31 (January 1981): 4–5.

2. See David Brooks, "One Nation, Slightly Divisible," *Atlantic Monthly*, December 2001, 53–65.

3. John G. Stackhouse Jr., *Evangelical Landscapes: Facing Critical Issues of the Day* (Grand Rapids: Baker, 2002), 19–20.

4. Ibid., 22.

5. Thomas Howard, *Evangelical Is Not Enough* (Nashville: Thomas Nelson, 1984), 2–3.

6. Ibid., 152–53.

7. Thomas Howard, *Evangelical Is Not Enough*, 2d ed. (San Francisco: Ignatius, 1985).

8. Stackhouse, *Evangelical Landscapes*, 20.

9. D. H. Williams, *Retrieving the Tradition and Renewing Evangelicalism* (Grand Rapids: Eerdmans, 1999), 1.

10. Ibid., 9–10.

11. Ibid., 20.

12. Ibid., 22.

13. Ibid., 25.

14. Ibid., 35.

15. Ibid., 39.

16. Ibid., 31.

17. Ibid., 31, 39.

18. Mark A. Noll, "Scandal? A Forum on the Evangelical Mind," *Christianity Today*, 14 August 1999, 22.

19. See Hughes Oliphant Old, *Worship That Is Reformed according to Scripture* (Atlanta: John Knox, 1984), 177.

20. Alasdair MacIntyre, *Whose Justice? Which Rationality?* (Notre Dame, Ind.: University of Notre Dame Press, 1988), 12.

21. Williams, *Retrieving the Tradition*, 38.

22. See, for instance, Joseph A. Conforti, *Jonathan Edwards, Religious Tradition, and American Culture* (Chapel Hill, N.C.: University of North Carolina Press, 1995).

23. One exception might be the conservatives in the Southern Baptist Convention, some of whom have appealed to parts of neo-evangelicalism. See Barry

Hankins, *Uneasy in Babylon: Southern Baptist Conservatives and American Culture* (Tuscaloosa, Ala.: University of Alabama Press, 2002).

24. Mark A. Noll, *The Scandal of the Evangelical Mind* (Grand Rapids: Eerdmans, 1994), 35–56, quotation from 239.

25. Jon R. Stone, *On the Boundaries of American Evangelicalism: The Postwar Coalition* (New York: St. Martin's Press, 1997), 7.

26. Carl F. H. Henry, "American Evangelicals in a Turning Time," *Christian Century,* 5 November 1980, 1060.

27. Ibid., 1061.

Afterword

1. Jon Butler, "Born-Again America? A Critique of the New 'Evangelical Thesis' in Recent American Historiography" (paper presented to the American Society of Church History, Washington, D.C., 29 December 1992), 2.

2. Mark A. Noll, *The Scandal of the Evangelical Mind* (Grand Rapids: Eerdmans, 1994), ix.

Index